RUSSIA'S PLACE IN THE WORLD

RUSSIA'S PLACE IN THE WORLD

THE STRUGGLE FOR SURVIVAL

ANDREJ KREUTZ

Algora Publishing
New York

Library of Congress Cataloging-in-Publication Data —

Names: Kreutz, Andrej, author.
Title: Russia's place in the world : the struggle for survival / Andrej
    Kreutz.
Description: New York : Algora Publishing, 2016. | Includes bibliographical
    references and index.
Identifiers: LCCN 2015041441 (print) | LCCN 2015042896 (ebook) | ISBN
    9781628941449 (soft cover : alkaline paper) | ISBN 9781628941456 (hard
    cover : alkaline paper) | ISBN 9781628941463 (pdf)
Subjects: LCSH: Russia (Federation)—Foreign relations. | Soviet
    Union—Foreign relations. | Russia—Foreign relations. |
    Survival—Political aspects—Russia (Federation) | Great powers. |
    International relations—Philosophy.
Classification: LCC DK510.764 .K73 2016 (print) | LCC DK510.764 (ebook) | DDC
    327.47—dc23
LC record available at http://lccn.loc.gov/2015041441

Printed in the United States

Table of Contents

Table of Contents

INTRODUCTION

I was born in Cracow, Poland, three and a half years before the outbreak of World War II. What I associate with this event are mere snatches of memories, overwhelming panic and the unsuccessful flight of my family, the causes of which were at the time above my understanding. I remember much more from the years of German occupation and the fears and deprivation that occupation caused. The coming of the Soviet Army to Cracow in January 1945 remains in my mind as a great breakthrough, the end of a long nightmare and the beginning of a new, much more normal, life and education. I started to attend Polish school, where in addition to Polish and many other subjects I was taught French and Russian. Though many Poles were not happy with the Soviet (Russian) influence in their country after the war, it was nevertheless an enormous contrast to the years of war and German extermination, and there were many chances for revival and further development.

I started to learn Russian in 1949. I seriously wanted to understand the language, history and culture of this great, and at that time powerful, neighbor of Poland. However, I soon became critical about many aspects of the imposed regime, which included limitations of political and social freedoms, overseas travel and control of the cultural life of the nation. This control was much milder in Poland and more relaxed than in the Soviet Union, and in many ways it was in fact a splendid period in the history of Polish culture, including the cinema, literature, and a flourishing religious life — though there were still enough reasons to be discontent. As I never joined the Communist Party (or any political organization), and was often too outspoken, I began to be seen with suspicion. Because of that, when I was working as an assistant professor at the Nicolaus Copernicus University in Torun I was not allowed to travel with the university delegation to Kiev and Moscow. A few years after that, I lost my academic employment, and in 1968 I left Poland for Israel, which was at that time the only country open to me. Living for more than five years in the Middle East and for a few months in Western Europe I met with many emigrants from the Soviet Union and other Eastern European countries in a similar situation to mine. I practiced my Russian with them, and I heard many good and bad things from them about their countries of origin. However, neither then nor during the first two decades of my new life and academic work in Canada were Eastern Europe and Eurasia the main focus of my studies and intellectual interests. At that time I mostly concentrated on the Palestinian–Israeli conflict, the Middle Eastern region and the political role of religions.

The decline and final disintegration of the Soviet Union and the ensuing destruction of Yugoslavia and the often brutishly imposed transition to global capitalism of the former state-socialist countries of Eastern European shifted the main focus of my interest and personal involvement back to Europe. All these events were for me not only quite shocking, but even more important, they led to the end of the world in which I was brought up and had lived for so many years. The collapse of the previously existing balance of power also brought to an end the bipolar world system, and the future shape of international relations became an open question.

Between 1996–2005, teaching as a visiting professor at various Polish universities, I was also able to visit and spend some time in European countries including Russia, Belarus, France, and Germany where for a short time I taught at the University of Nuremberg. I thus had a chance to see the then ongoing transformations in Europe, and I started to think about the possible future of the Old Continent and the emerging international system. For both of these issues the future role of Russia and its place in the global system have been and still remain of crucial importance.

In addition to this there were two main reasons why, in spite of my advanced age and numerous health issues, I decided to work on this subject and write this monograph.

The first was the fact that, to my great astonishment, I found that in spite of its obvious importance in the post-Soviet period, the present and future place of Russia in the world had attracted very little informed discussion and was, perhaps, rather avoided by scholars and experts in Russian studies. Though it had never been my special field before, I intended to fill the existing gap and at least to give my own view on this subject, which should not be left without careful analysis and critical discussion.

The second and, since the fall of 2013, even more important reason was my deep concern and fear of a new and unnecessary major war in Europe and Asia, with its likely destructive outcomes and consequences. Even if it were to be mainly initiated and led by the Americans against a new, much weaker "enemy," it would be fought on the European and Asian territories and at the cost of the local populations, with all their cultures and material achievements.[1] It might even bring to an end the traditional European civilization, which had already suffered both World Wars and is now in a noticeable crisis.

In his excellent academic study of the Ukrainian crisis Professor Richard Sakwa recollects that, "On hearing of the outbreak of World War I, Pope Benedict XV declared that it represented 'the suicide of Europe.'"[2] More than 100 years later we can hear the threat of a "new suicide," this time probably a terminal one. Though some of its causes might be disputed, its results could be much more tragic than any other war in the Old Continent's long history. I deeply believe that the now influential War Party in the West needs to be stopped and that the triumphant hegemonic power should let the other nations follow their own ways to development, at their own pace and in accordance with their own traditions and interests.

Though I have consulted numerous sources in various languages, all the research was done by myself and the opinions expressed in this monograph are mine. I would like to express my thanks and deep gratitude to a number of people who enabled me to complete this work with their generous financial, personal, and technical support. My work was only possible because of a grant from the Canadian Northcliffe Foundation in Toronto, and the research support facilitated by the University of Calgary Library, particularly Danny Pakhulia and Lana Wong. I need to also express my special gratitude to Evan, who more than once retyped the manuscript and kept my spirits up in "times of trouble."

Finally, last but not least I am most grateful to Algora Publishing in New York for its decision to publish my manuscript and for all the support, patience and encouragement of its editors, particularly Ms. Andrea Sengstacken. They were most kind and were not discouraged by my numerous delays and mistakes, which can only be partly excused by the fact that English is my fourth language and that I learned it relatively late in my turbulent life. In addition, I am from the pre-computer generation and my practical skill with this gadget is far from perfect.

At a time of increased political passions and propaganda campaigns, my goals were to provide some well-researched information and to call for a better understanding of all the involved parties and their often conflicting views and interests.

---

1 Among the many voices of warning and concern, see *Policy Brief* by the European Leadership Network, "Preparing for the Worst: Are Russian and NATO Military Exercises Making War in Europe More Likely?" August 12, 2015.

2 Richard Sakwa, *Frontline Ukraine. Crisis in Borderland*, I.B. Taurus, 2015, p. 227.

Chapter 1. Historical Background of Russia: Pre-Soviet and Soviet Heritage

When discussing the foreign policy of any major country and its place in the international system, one needs to take into account its historical background and the impact that has on the country's future development and its perception of other nations. Because of the special and rather unusual features of both Russia's geopolitics and history, this seems even more necessary. Unfortunately, in practice it is often not like that, and as American scholar Marshall T. Poe noted, "Most people, particularly those pundits who take it upon themselves to inform the public about such things, have no real conception of the basic rhythms of Russian history."[1] Why did Russia evolve in a way so different from other European and Asian nations? What are the deep-rooted causes of both its present foreign and domestic dilemmas and its hidden strengths? Why is Russia's historical background so important for the present and future of the nation and perhaps even the rest of the world?

Writing about Russia's origins and past, I intend neither to provide a detailed summary of its lengthy history nor to present its new philosophical interpretation. The main focus of my work is post-Soviet Russia, and I am dealing only with those aspects of the Russian past that I think to be relevant to the better understanding of the present. At the same time, I am rather skeptical of any effort to find a main key to socio-political and economic developments, especially in the case of Russia which has been submitted to numerous changes and transformations that were impossible to predict.

---

1 Marshall T. Poe, *The Russian Moment in World History* (Princeton: Princeton University Press, 2003) p XI.

The American scholar's view that "Russia was founded in a part of the world where there were no earlier civilizations and in which contemporaneous civilizations were very distant"[1] might perhaps be applicable to the far northern parts of the country but certainly not to its south, which for many centuries had been penetrated by the ancient Greeks and since the early medieval period became a close neighbor to the Byzantine empire.

Byzantium originated with this name from the Greek colony of Megara, founded around 660 BC. Since the 4th century AD it was the new capital of the Roman Empire. The city, known also by the name of its Roman second co-founder, Constantinople, had an excellent harbor and occupied a strategic position between the Black and Mediterranean Seas, linking the continents of Europe and Asia. After the final division of the Roman Empire into East and West in AD 395, the Greek elements slowly overtook the Latin language and culture, but the Byzantines still preserved many Roman institutions and traditions, and until the end of the 12th century AD they were in all aspects far more advanced and civilized than medieval Europe.

Kievan Rus — often transliterated as Kievan Rus — was positioned along the trade route between Scandinavia and Constantinople. Known since the 9th century, it soon became involved in close, though not always peaceful, relations with the Byzantine Empire. Starting from the agreement of "peace and love" signed after the Russian attack on Constantinople in 860,[2] several treaties were concluded between Kievan Rus and the Byzantine Empire. The most comprehensive of them was concluded in 911, but it was preceded by a preliminary agreement in 907 and followed by the treaties of 944/945 and 971 between Prince Sviatoslav of Kievan Rus and the Byzantine Emperor John Tzimiskes.[3]

At the end of the 10th century, relations between Kievan Rus and Byzantium culminated in the official conversion of the Rus people to the Eastern Orthodox form of Christianity.[4] However, a part of the Russian population had already been converted to Christianity earlier,[5] and Greek

---

1 *Op. cit.*, p. 12

2 *Povest Vremennykh Let*, part 2, Moscow, 1950 Biblioteka Literatury Drevney Rusi, vol. 1, 1997.

3 *Pamyatniki Russkogo Prava*, vol. 1, A.A. Zimin, Moscow 1952. See also Vibikov, M.V., "Rus Bizentiynskoy Diplomatii, Dogovory Rusi c Grekami, XV," *Drevnyaya Rus Voprosy Medievistiki*, 2005, Nil. The same article is available on the internet http://www.drevnyaya.ru/vyp/stat/sl191.pdf

4 John Meyendorff, *Byzantium and the Rise of Russia*, St. Vladimir's Seminary Press, Crestwood, New York, 1989.

5 At the signing of the 944 treaty with the Byzantine Empire, some of the Rus representatives were already of the Christian religion and, according to the oldest Russian Primary Chronicle, a sizable part of the population of Kiev was Christian in the mid-10th century, although the ruling princes continued to follow pagan customs.

colonies had been founded in Crimea and in some parts of the present Eastern Ukraine since the 6th century BC.[1]

In addition to the Greek and Christian cultures, Kievan Rus was also submitted to the influence and relationship with some others, including the Jewish one, when in the 8th century the ruling elite of its neighbor (and sometime hegemon) the Khazar Khaganate converted to Judaism.[2] The Khazars, who were a semi-nomadic Turkic people, settled by the lower Volga River and created a powerful state dominating the vast area from the Volga-Don steppes to the eastern Crimea and the northern Caucasus. It was able to control the western marches of the Silk Road and played an important role as a crossroads between China, the Middle East, and Kievan Rus.[3] It is widely suggested that it had for some time dominated Kievan Rus and that there must have also been a number of political and economic problems between the two nations. As an outcome of that, in the period 965–969, the Kievan Rus Prince Sviatoslav I conquered the Khazar capital of Alit and destroyed their state.[4] Although the fact of the influence of the Khazars on the Kievan Rus is generally accepted, we do not have very much information about the end of the Khazars as an independent state, and their role both in Eastern Europe and among the Jewish community is still hotly disputed.[5]

From the beginning of its history, the Russian civilization has been a pluralistic and multicultural one. Relations with Byzantium and Khazaria had not been exceptions. Extended political and commercial ties with central Asian and Middle Eastern states existed as early as in the 9th century. This is an interesting fact to be kept in mind if one is to understand today's geopolitical relations between Moscow and its eastern and southern partners. In discussing the Russian lands' relations with the West and Europe, it is impossible to forget the fact that Kievan Rus as a state and embryonic nation was established with the active participation and probably the leading role of the Scandinavian Vikings from which originated the first Russian imperial dynasty, the Rurikids.

However, Professor Marshall T. Poe is certainly right in indicating that some other causes of Russia's late start and long-lasting relative backwardness were these:

---

1 Their center was the Bosphoren Kingdom located in Eastern Crimea and the Taman Peninsula on the shores of the present-day Strait of Kerch.

2 Thomas Noonan, "European Russia c. 500–1050," in Timothy Reuter, Rosamond McKitterick, *The New Cambridge Medieval History*, Vol. 3, 900–1024, Cambridge University Press, 1999, p. 493.

3 *Op. cit.* See also Thomas Noonan, "The Khazar Qaganate and its impact on the early Rus state: the Translatio Imperii from Itil to Kiev" in Khazanov, Anatoly M., Wink, Andre. *Nomads in the Sedentary World*, Carson II IIAS Asian Studies series, Routledge, 2001, pp. 76–102.

4 *Op. cit.*

5 Shlomo Sand, *The Invention of the Jewish People*, London, Verso, 2009, pp. 240-249.

1. Although the lands and people of future Russia were open and had many relations with other nations and cultural centers, it had not benefited from the developed material infrastructure and political and socio-economic institutions which some Western European nations inherited from the ancient Roman Empire and which some other Central European and northern nations, such as Poland and the Scandinavian countries, were later able to acquire after their acceptance of the Western form of Christianity and the following political and socio-economic integration with the West.

2. It is also true that the extremely harsh climate of most of the Russian lands made both their economic and social–civilizational development far more difficult than for many other parts of Europe and Asia. As I will discuss later, the climate provided the country a certain protection against the threat of foreign conquests and invasions; at the same time it has always been one of the main obstacles to its internal integration and general development.

The Mongolian conquest and domination of Russian lands from 1240 to 1480, the role of which is neglected or played down by some American scholars, in fact had a great impact on the situation in the country and all directions of its future development.

Kievan Rus was finally torn apart by the Mongol invasions between 1237–1240, and the southern part of the country, including Kiev itself, were either completely destroyed or subjugated. According to Polish tradition, Kiev was a flourishing commercial and cultural urban center before the Mongolian conquest, which attracted traders and visitors from the East and West, and until the Mongolian invasion Kievan Rus was never seen as peripheral or backward.[1]

There were two major causes of the decline of Kievan Rus and its final collapse to Mongolian domination:

3. The first of them was the nature of the political system, which led to the division of the country among various princes who, despite being members of the same Rurikid family and often even brothers or very close kin, fought each other in fratricide wars. Similar feudal fragmentation was common in the other European countries. However, in Kievan Rus the situation was aggravated by the fact that the power was transferred not from father to son but to the (at that time) oldest member of the ruling dynasty, which entailed even more rivalry and quarrels within the royal family. Junior members

---

[1] Writing at the beginning of the 13th century, the first Polish Chronicler Gall Anonymus explained the reason for his work by the fact that he wanted to inform the rest of the world about a "country of Poles, which is little known to others, with the exception of those who travel to Rus for trade."

of the dynasty started their careers as rulers of minor provinces, then progressed to more important principalities, and finally competed for the throne of Kiev.[1] As a result of that, the security and well-being of the nation were often neglected. In addition to such political problems, Kievan Rus was weakened by the collapse of its commercial and diplomatic ties with the Byzantine Empire after the conquest and destruction of Constantinople by the 4th Crusade in 1204. Among the negative outcomes of this was Kiev's loss of an important political and cultural ally and the declining economic importance of the Black Sea and the ancient trade route between the Varangues (Scandinavians) and the Greeks.[2]

4. Another negative result, though it was not immediately noticed, was a new dislike of and alienation from the West which the Orthodox peoples blamed for the conquest of Byzantium. That was also the real reason for the broken relations and the schism between the Eastern Orthodox and Western Catholic Churches, with all the future social and political implications. The impoverished southern Rus later on became easy prey of Lithuanian and Polish conquerors; one outcome of that was the division of the East Slavic Orthodox people into three separate nations — modern day Russia, Ukraine and Belarus.[3] Another result was the fact that the political and socio-economic center of Rus moved to the north where some city-states, such as Novgorod, Pskov and some other East Slavic principalities sought to take on Kiev's leadership role and its cultural and political legacy. Since the end of the 13th century one of them, the Grand Duchy of Moscow, accepted the Tatars' overlordship and paid them tribute, while at the same time its princes built up their own power and received support from the Orthodox Church, the head of which (the Metropolite) moved from Kiev to Moscow. Being submissive to the Mongols, the Muscovite princes became the main intermediaries between the Mongol (Tartar) rulers and the other Russian principalities. In order to reward them, the Tatars rarely raided Moscow-controlled lands, a fact that attracted an influx of people and wealth. The Grand Duchy of Moscow thus

---

1 Janet Martin, *Medieval Rus: 980–1557*, Cambridge University Press, 2008.
2 Edwin S. Hunt and James Murray, *A History of Business in Medieval Europe: 1200–1550*, Cambridge University Press, 1999.
3 Boris A. Rybakov, *Early Centuries of Russian History*, Progress Publishers, 1965, p. 41. See also Karl Marx, *Secret Diplomatic History of the Eighteenth Century*, London: 1899, p. 75. The feudal division of the country among the descendants of the Rurikid princes, before the Mongolian conquest, did not have to lead to that. This kind of situation was typical for the feudal period and existed also in Poland, France and various other European countries.

drew people and capital to the northern part of Kievan Rus and was able to establish trade links to the Baltic Sea, Siberia and the Caspian Sea. However, the submissive relations with the Mongols had some negative impacts on Moscow and future Russian development. Because of Ukrainian nationalism, which has always been supported by the West, and the present Ukraine crisis, the issue might be seen as highly controversial. However, I think that without the impact of the Mongolian conquest and the destruction of the eastern and southern parts of the country, Russia might have developed in a different way and followed a path that would have been closer, though by no means identical, to the general European pattern.

Kievan Rus and/or it successor state might have continued to be a successor of the Byzantine civilization, but it would not have acquired so many Mongolian and semi-Asiatic features and institutions, including a highly centralized political system whose traditions, including the harsh penal system, would exert a powerful influence on the future development of Russian society.

The re-unification of the Russian lands under Moscow's leadership and the subsequent creation of the Russian Empire was probably also one of the ensuing consequences of the Mongolian conquest and the subsequent long occupation. However, Professor Poe's rejection of Moscow's claim to be the successor to Kievan Rus, and his sarcastic comment that Moscow succeeded not Kiev but "Sarai, which was the seat of the Kipchak Khanate (or "Golden Horde" as it was called in Russian sources) on the lower Volga River,"[1] is too farfetched and devoid of a proper historical perspective. His intention is to present the Muscovite princes' reunification of the Russian lands as a kind of imperial conquest and to undermine all national traditions and legitimacy of the reborn Russian statehood. This might correspond to some American politicians' desire to divide the present Russian Federation into a number of smaller statelets, but it does not correspond to the historical realities. In fact the Great Princes of Moscow bided their time and for a long period wanted to preserve good relations with the Mongolian overlords. This kind of cautious and compromising policy enabled them to enlarge their territory and to provide more security to their subjects. At the same time they followed a great national project, the legitimacy of which was based on the ethnic and religious traditions of the great majority of the Russian population and their own descent from the old Kievan Rurikid royal family. They welcomed the title "collectors of the Russian soil," and as some American historians

---

1 Marshal T. Poe, *The Russian Moment in World History*, Princeton University Press, 2003, p. 30.

admit, "The Russian people, wherever they might be living, had come to look upon the Moscow princes as national leaders, as champions of the cause of national independence, and as harbingers of national unity."[1] The existence of the time gap between the destruction of Kiev and the rise of Moscow has been nothing unusual in the history of the other nations. In the first part of the 14th century, after more than 200 years, the Kingdom of Poland was reunified and rebuilt and there are several more similar examples in the history of China and some other places, where the ethnic and cultural basis was preserved and it nourished the will to recreate national unity.

According to a Russian historian, Karl Marx "justly placed Kievan Rus alongside the largest state of medieval Europe, the Empire of Charlemagne."[2] He was probably right because Kievan Rus was not only a very large and populous country, but had already achieved a high level of economic and cultural development by the standards of the era. In the first part of the 11th century, German chronicler and bishop of Merseburg Thietmer described Kiev as "a large city where there were more than 400 churches, eight market squares and an extraordinary accumulation of people."[3] In addition because of their conversion to the Eastern Orthodox form of Christianity, which did not impose the Latin language on their religious life and cultural expression, East Slavs developed their own original literature and arts.[4] Even after the Mongolian conquest and the destruction of a large part of the country, the general level of development remained sufficient to nourish, at least at the social elite level, the quest for unity and the will to regain the country's former glory. Comparing Kievan Rus and the Empire of Charlemagne, it is necessary to remember that although both of them were later fragmented into smaller entities, Kievan Rus was never legally divided into two or more separate states, as was the case of the Carolingian Empire, which the Verdun Treaty of 843 divided between three of Charlemagne's grandsons: Lothar I, Louis the German, and Charles the Bold.

As a result of the existing and linguistic divisions, the Treaty of Verdun initiated the establishment of France and Germany and resulted in the unsettled (until the 19th century) political status of some other territories, such as Lotharingia and Italy.

The situation in Kievan Rus developed differently. Though the country became fragmented and various parts were given to different members of

---

1 Melvin C. Wren and Taylor Stults, *The Course of Russian History*, Fifth Edition, Waveland Press Inc., 1994, p. 74.
2 Boris Rybakov, *Early Centuries of Russian History*, Moscow: Progress Publishers, 1965, p. 7.
3 Warner, David A. (translator): *Ottoman Germany. The Chronicles of Thietmar of Merseburg*, Manchester, 2001, English translation.
4 Simon Franklin, *Writing, Society and Culture in Early Rus*, Cambridge University Press, 2002, p. 64.

the Rurikid family, they did not receive them as independent statelets but rather as a kind of endowment to secure their income and social prestige. According to the last will of Kievan Great Prince Yaroslav the Wise, issued in 1054: "The rule of the Kievan state should descend to all his five sons as a group, the oldest son standing as leader and protector of the rest."[1]

Although the political practice quickly began to deviate from the legal theory, according to reputed American historians the Kievan experience produced certain socio-political attitudes to which the Russian people would cling throughout their history, including a deep attachment to the Russian land "as a land meriting the love and respect of the people, quite apart from the administration of the prince who ruled over it."[2]

In addition to all those historical traditions and moral convictions and the undoubtedly cunning policy of its rulers, Moscow's geopolitical location was to its greatest advantage. It was located in the very center of the country with little need to fear foreign aggression and at the junction of trade routes, both of land and water.[3]

The unification of the former Kievan Rus under Moscow's leadership did not result only from the fact that its princes held the "yarlick," the title from the Khan of the Golden Horde, making them the Khan's tax collectors in Rus (which might also have increased their authority and power over the other princes of the divided nation). As is the case of most similar major political developments, it was rather the outcome of a number of causes, and the temporary Mongolian support for Moscow's princes stressed by Professor Poe was just one of the factors which, although helpful, was certainly not the most important one.

Under the existing circumstances it was probably the only possible way towards Russian unity and independence. Even liberated from the Tartars, but fragmented among a number of entities and devoid of a strong central power, the country would have become easy prey for its more powerful or better organized and more developed neighbors.[4]

The rise and the development of Moscow had resulted from, or at least had been facilitated by, a number of factors. In addition to those which have already been discussed, one was the role of the Russian Orthodox Church in the country and its influence on the majority of the people. At that time it was

1 Melvin C. Wren, Taylor Stults, *The Course of Russian History*, Waveland Press, Inc., 1994, p. 25.

2 *Op. cit.*, p. 36

3 *Op. cit.*, p. 63.

4 At the end of the 14th century the Grand Duke of Lithuania Witold conquered the Russian principality of Smolensk and thus became next door neighbor to the princes of Tver, Moscow and Riazan. At that time only those principalities and the northern cities of Novgorod and Pskov remained in native Russian hands and the Lithuanian and Polish rulers intended to conquer them in the future.

a powerful and wealthy religious organization which enjoyed tolerance and even some respect from the Tartars. Its churches, monasteries and various charitable and other institutions were spread all over the country's territory, thus providing a feeling of unity and identity for the population. After Great Prince Alexander Nevsky's death in 1263, the Church became the only native cohesive force in the territory, aside from those imposed by the Mongolian conquerors.[1] That the Church later canonized Alexander Nevsky, and that the Princes of Moscow might have claimed to be his descendants, were facts of some political value. However, even more important were the political developments. Since the rule of Alexander Nevsky's grandson Ivan Kalita, the Moscow principality started to acquire such power and importance that the Church leaders began to perceive its rulers as the best possible partners and protectors. Due to the destruction and depopulation of the south of Rus, at the end of the 13th century, its spiritual head, the Metropolitan of Kiev moved to Vladimir, the new capital of Rus Great Principality on the Klyazma River in the north of the country. His successor, Metropolitan Peter had formed a friendship with the Great Prince of Moscow Ivan Kalita and in 1326 the seat of metropoly was finally moved to Moscow, which thus became a center of the very influential, all Russian, organization.

When the power of the Tatars declined, the princes of Moscow started an alliance with the Orthodox Church and a slow gathering of the Eastern Slavic lands under their leadership. Subsequently they created the early modern Russian state. One of them, Ivan III tripled the territory of his state and in 1476, by refusing to pay the customary tribute to the Grand Khan Ahmet, terminated the domination of the Golden Horde over Rus. Because of his marriage to Zoe Paleologus, the niece of Constantine XI, the last Byzantine Emperor, he started to be considered as a successor of the Byzantine Emperors and at the same time opened the country to some relations with Europe. During his time the Italian masters renovated the Kremlin. Since his rule, the nations to the west, including Poland, became the main partners and protagonists of Russia.

Professor Poe is right that in its boundaries and all geopolitical situations the new Muscovite Russia differed greatly from its Kievan predecessor. Not only was its center located far more to the north, but at least in its first century large parts of former Kievan Rus south and west, including Kiev itself, had not been included, and not until the end of the 17th century or even later was Moscow able to get a hold on them. For about 300 years all present-day Ukraine and Belarus were parts of the Polish–Ukrainian Commonwealth, which was, at that time, one of the great European powers.

1 Melvin C. Wren, Taylor Stults, *The Course of Russian History*, Fifth Edition, Prospect Height, Illinois: Waveland, 1994, p. 35.

During the ensuing end of the Rurikid Dynasty's "Time of Troubles" in Russia (1598–1613), its armed forces occupied Moscow and plundered even the golden tsarist crowns. Although the popular uprising, initiated by the Orthodox clergy, led to the regaining of independence and the election of the new Romanov Dynasty, Russia became weakened and exposed to external and internal threats. At the same time the neo-Russian state with its capital in Moscow, preserved a strong continuity with the old Kievan Rus tradition which was based on three most important elements:

1. The first and most important was the ethnic identity and continuity with the Kievan Rus population, because of ethnic issues. Of the population of Moscow, 80%, and 85% of the nobility, were descendant of Kievan Rus.

2. Religious and cultural, because of the presence of the Orthodox Church, which preserved the old traditions. No one can deny that during the 240 years of Mongolian control Kievan Rus absorbed some Asiatic traits, but it was still able to maintain its own ethnic and cultural identity. However, it is possible that, as already mentioned, the political and legal system became harsher and more authoritarian than before Mongol rule.

3. The Rurikid dynasty. The same dynasty that had ruled during the Kievan Rus period, with the active support of the Orthodox Church.

The prominent German historian Edward Winter argued that Moscow had left Europe when it fell under the Mongol-Tartar yoke in the first part of the 13th century, but once again became a full partner in the European association of nations in the second part of the 15th century. At that time, it had regained its independence and the Grand Duke Ivan III's marriage to the niece of the last Byzantine Emperor Constantine XI, Zoe Paleologus, signified Moscow's acceptance as a European power.[1] However, I believe that Professor Winter was too optimistic in his judgement. Russia's route to Europe and the Western community was going to be much longer and, as I think, does not need to be completed. Russia has always had different cultural traditions from the rest of Europe and Europe, itself has lost its previous dominant political and cultural importance.

However, in the 17th century and probably until World War II, Europe was the most dynamic civilization and "the world's geopolitical center of gravity."[2] Byzantium, whose religion and culture Russia inherited and which during Kievan Rus time was the most advanced country of Europe, had disappeared a long time ago, and as Professor Poe indicates emerging from its

1 Edward Winter, *Russland und des Papsttum*, Vol. 1, Academie-Verlag, Berlin, 1960, p. 179.
2 Luis Simon, "A Post European World? American-Russian Relations in Perspective," http://eurostrategy.org, April 20, 2014.

own "Time of Troubles," Russia had to face " a new kind of human civilization in Europe, one more powerful and dangerous than any to have appeared in world history."[1] Early modern Europe of the 16–17th centuries, and the ensuing modern Europe of the 19th and 20th centuries, greatly differed, both in its power and civilization, from its medieval predecessor, which was in many ways much closer to Kievan Rus than the early modern and modern Europe to Russia. The Western-oriented direction of policy and a need for internal mobilization and transformations thus became necessities, and in spite of all possible defeats and obstacles needed to be continued. Because of its new geopolitical situation and the enormous increase of Western power, the new Rus with its capital in Moscow, had to make its relations with early modern Europe its top priority.

Until the 20th century the US had not been involved in Eurasian affairs, and in spite of the different political systems in both countries, its relations with the Russian Empire were overall friendly or at least not antagonistic.[2] The Russian relations with the European powers had been far more complex and involved, both the inter-state relations and the need for domestic reforms.

Though the diplomatic opening to the West, which at that time meant Western Europe and the Polish–Lithuanian Commonwealth, started shortly after the end of the "Time of Troubles" in 1613 and the following peace treaty with Sweden in 1617 and Poland in 1618, its political outcomes were neither smooth nor uninterrupted.

The first two tsars of the Romanov dynasty, Michael and Alexis, hired hundreds of foreigners to teach Russians Western skills, to reorganize the army, establish industries and stimulate the economy. However, the task of modernizing the huge country was too difficult to be achieved by a weak and still semi-medieval state apparatus and without any developed middle class in the country.

Developments in foreign affairs had also run into problems. Although Tsar Alexis had learnt both Latin and Polish and originally intended to improve relations with Warsaw, it soon proved to be impossible because of the major Ukrainian crisis started by the Zaporozhian Cossacks uprising against Polish rule in 1648. As Cossacks could not expect to preserve their independence from the Polish–Lithuanian Commonwealth with their own forces, they turned to Moscow, and using both their common ethnic background and the Eastern Orthodox religion arguments, asked the Russian leaders for protection. By the Pereyaslav Treaty of 1654 the General Cossack Council recognized the Tsar of Russia as its sovereign, providing

---

1 Marshall T. Poe, *The Russian Moment in World History*, Princeton University Press, 2003, p. 39.
2 During the American civil war the Russian Empire offered its support for the Union and in 1867 the Americans were able to acquire Alaska from Russia.

that its rights and autonomy would be respected. The inevitable outcome of that was a long war with Poland until a truce was signed at Andrusovo in 1667 and the following divisions of Ukraine between Russia and Poland. As the Ukrainian issue had not been resolved it became a source of further tensions in the future. At the same time because of the semi-medieval state apparatus Russia proved unable to absorb the knowledge and services needed and imported from the West. At the beginning of the 17th century it led to the modernization reforms of Tsar Peter the Great (1672–1725). It is commonly accepted that by the end of his rule the country, to which he gave the name of the Russian Empire, had become a great power. However, even after that, neither its international status nor cultural identity became finally settled and determined. Russia's relations with the West have still remained an open question and a major challenge to the nation.

The recognition of Russia as a great power, because of its military strength and material resources, did not preclude the fact that the country was still classified as semi-barbarian (as opposed to civilized) and the Russian leaders were aware of that. A prominent advisor to Peter the Great, who was later to become Vice-Chancellor of Russia, Peter Shafirov noted that the European powers now sought out Russia as an ally "despite the fact that a decade ago, in the states of Europe people thought and wrote of the nation and state of Russia in the same way as they did of Indian, Persian and other nations [that had] no intercourse with Europe apart from a little trade."[1] According to him, "the great part of our neighbors view very unfavorably the good position in which it has pleased God to place us," and "they would be delighted should an occasion present itself to imprison us once more in our earlier obscurity and that if they seek our alliance it is rather through fear and hate than through feelings of friendship."[2] Russia had accumulated the necessary material resources and had already proven itself in battle against Sweden, which was at the time seen as a great power. However, for cultural and geopolitical reasons all these achievements were still unable to bring her a much coveted "club membership". For the Western European nations, Russia still remained an unsolved problem, and in the words of Winston Churchill, "a riddle wrapped in a mystery, inside an enigma".

Peter the Great was in fact a very absolute ruler, but with frequent use of harsh methods he had changed many of the country's institutions and greatly advanced its internal development and international status. His major achievements included reorganization on the Western pattern of a central state apparatus and army, using which he finally won the Northern War with Sweden and with the Peace in Nystadt, signed on August 3, 1721,

---

1 Iver Neumann, "When did Russia Become a Great Power?" citation.allacademic. com
2 *Op. cit.*

achieved access to the Baltic, his main foreign policy goal. Until then Russia, in spite of being a very large country was in fact completely landlocked, and because of that suffered numerous economic and political difficulties. Getting the outlet to the Baltic provided Russia access to sea trade and a much-desired window to Europe. Because of these considerations Peter decided to move the Russian capital from Moscow to the newly built Baltic coast city, which was named after him, St. Petersburg.

Following his efforts to strengthen his country's international position he established regular diplomatic representations with most European countries and founded or encouraged the development by private entrepreneurs of numerous factories and commercial institutions. The success of his political efforts was in fact astounding, but from the historical perspective one needs to keep in mind that it was possible only because in his time the West which he had to face meant only a divided Europe and not, as now, the quasi-global American Empire which dominates not only all Western Europe but even some parts of the former Russian Empire, including the Baltic states. Peter the Great was in a much better situation and enjoyed incomparably easier geopolitical conditions than the 21st century Russian leaders.

Peter the Great's domestic modernization reforms were successful overall, but they were mainly focused on practical issues. More Western ideas and high culture did not get to Russia before Catherine the Great's time (1762–1796) and in the 19th century. Even then they were studied and up to a point accepted just by some elites (state officials and intellectuals) and had rather little impact on most of the country's population. Partly because of that, but probably more because of its geopolitical differences with the rest of Europe, in spite of its widely recognized political and military importance, neither Russia's international status nor its social identity became finally settled and determined. As I am going to discuss this more again later, it was a very large nation extending deep in Asia with a very harsh climate but with many natural resources coveted by the West. It was in a way heir to the Byzantine religion and culture but had also absorbed some Asiatic influences. Its political and cultural accommodation to Europe might have required a long time and was neither simple nor easy. However, since the 17th century Russia played a major role in European history especially in the defeat of Napoleon and Nazi Germany. Although its contribution to high European culture and science had been time-delayed, it later also became magnificent. It would be difficult to imagine today's European culture without Russian classical music, ballet, and literature and poetry — to just remind us of such composers as Nikolai Rimsky Korsakov, Alexander Glazunov, Sergei Rachmaninoff, Peter Tchaikovsky, Shostakovich and Prokoviev, and writers such as Pushkin, Tolstoy, Dostoevsky, Pasternak, and Solzhenitsyn. In the

19th and 20th centuries many Russian scholars and scientists such as Pavlov, Mendeleev and many others were among the best and most respected in their fields. Some of their achievements in the field of technology and space exploration inspired the Soviet space program and in 1961 the first human flight into space by Yuri Gagarin. After the collapse of the Soviet Union and the ensuing general crisis and disintegration of the country, many of those leading scholars and experts were forced by the different situation to emigrate mainly to the US or Europe in order to find the means to live on and to continue their work. Their knowledge and experience thus became useful for other nations.

Although the international system and its institutions as we now know them, are relatively late historical developments, the issue of the place and role of Russia among the nations has been disputed for centuries. Because of its Euro-Asian location, acquiring its continental size in the 17th century, its rather unusual history and its brilliant but complex culture, Russia in fact substantially differs from other European nations. Due to its long historical development, rich cultural background and the fact that Russian inhabitants, including its numerous ethnic minorities are living in their ancestral homelands and by and large are preserving their own historical identities, it also differs greatly from the US and similar settler nations, which have been built by the Europeans on the new continents discovered by them.

Largely because of that, Russia's relations with the West were always prone to be full of conflicts and misunderstandings, which were apparently difficult to avoid. In addition, there were probably three major reasons for their long-standing alienation.

1. The first, and from a historical point the oldest, was isolation from Europe and Western development of the Russian lands. The Russian nation and its culture originated in a remote place and in addition during the Mongolian rule were even more isolated from European developments. The real and full reintegration into the European fold has never been later completed.

2. The second reason is religion. Russia was a Christian but an Eastern Orthodox nation, and in contrast to Germany and Poland, received its religion not from Rome but from Byzantium. Relations between the two major branches of Christianity, Eastern and Western, sharply deteriorated from the 11th century and even more so after the conquest by Crusaders of Byzantium in 1204. The political and cultural implications of this were long-lasting and had a major impact on the development of their nations and their mutual relations.

3. The third and probably the most important reason were Russia's geopolitics and what was related to it, the political and socio-economic situation in the country. It had always been a huge country with, in relation to its size, a sparse population and a very harsh climate. Being located on the East European lowlands, it was exposed to numerous invasions from the East and the West, and yet, as already mentioned, in spite of all these adversities, Russia was the only non-Western pre-modern empire able to resist the Western conquest or other forms of domination. According to Poe, Russia accomplished this "remarkable feat because of ... a highly effective, durable and resourceful political system — autocracy"[1] which allowed the Russian ruling class to pursue an alternative path to early modernity.[2] Though the American scholar seems to exaggerate the point, the fact remains that both the Russian way of development and their social and political institutions differed from Western ones. This contributed to making their relation with the Western powers more complex and often tense and antagonistic. As a result, Western European perceptions of the country, which in the early modern period was called Muscovy, were predominantly negative.

The country had not been a part of the West as it was established in the medieval and early modern period, and expanded after that to some other parts of Europe such as Poland and to the newly discovered parts of the world.[3] At the same time it was still a Christian country and in spite of its relative backwardness compared to Western nations, had a centralized and efficient political system, enabling it to mobilize a substantial military power if needed. For those two reasons it was difficult to treat Russia in the same way as the Western explorers treated indigenous populations in America, Africa, India and Australia. In addition, because of its geography and extreme climate, for the most part it was not practical to think about its conquest and direct subjugation in the same way as many other non-Western peoples of the era.

By creative adoption of some of the Western technologies and institutions and combining them with its own cultural tradition, Russia was able to create its own alternative way of development (*Sonderweg*) and to survive the early modern period (16th to mid-19th centuries) as a sovereign nation and original civilization. At that time no other pre-modern empire including

---

1 Poe, *Op. cit.*, p. 70
2 Ibid.
3 Martin Malia, *The Soviet Tragedy. A History of Socialism in Russia, 1917–1991* (New York, The Free Press, 1994) pp. 53-71

even the historically much older and well established Chinese empire proved able to do that.

Writing about this historical success Professor Poe put stress mainly on the use by Moscow of semi-totalitarian methods such as a strict border control, regulation of land and labor and at some periods even their full nationalization (state ownership and control). These means and the advanced techniques and technologies, imported from the West, were supposed to explain the whole process. I do not think this is a completely sufficient explanation.

All the factors discussed by Professor Poe had been easily noticeable and certainly played their role in Russian history. However, it is necessary to remember that the same or similar means had been also used by the other pre-modern empires without yielding the same results.

In geopolitical terms Russia had some advantages such as a huge territory, harsh climate and a very limited, or close to, or at some period non-existent access by the seas. At the same time compared with the other pre-modern empires it had also a number of liabilities including first of all its relative proximity to the Western powers and some of its real or alleged defensive assets such as a harsh climate and lack of access to the seas and oceans, which greatly limited its chances of participation in global trade and development. The harsh climate made any efforts towards social modernization slower and more difficult.

As I have already indicated, Russia had never been a part of the West, as the latter was established in Western Europe in the medieval and early modern period and expanded after that to some other parts of Europe such as Poland and the newly discovered parts of the world, especially America and Australia. However, it was still a Christian country with a long historical tradition and might have been perceived as an heir of Byzantium, which had some common beliefs and moral and cultural values with the West. The differences between the Christian East and West have always been worldlier than spiritual or cultural and their mutual relations were dependent largely on accidental circumstances and the shifting balance of secular power. There had never been such a cultural gap between Kievan Rus or the early modern Russia and the West, as used to be in the case in most of the other pre-modern empires and also because of that it was difficult to treat Russians in the same way as the Western explorers treated indigenous peoples in America, Africa, India or Australia. There have always been many more civilian and military experts from Europe who were willing to work for Russia than in the case of other non-Western nations. Since the mid-17th century or even earlier they were willing and able to train the Russian army and administration and to establish these factories and business centers. In addition to the centralized and efficient political system of the country and its geopolitical advantages, its religion and cultural tradition made it difficult for the early modern West to think about conquest or direct subjugation in the same way as for many non-Western peoples of the period. As an outcome of that Russia was for a long time left in a somewhat grey area and lacking determined legal and political status. It was neither fully accepted and integrated nor rejected and put under this or that form of Western control as was the case even in China and various other states and statelets of Asia. Its usage of some of the Western models and technologies but essentially its self-generated own alternative way of development and growing power contributed to even more dislike and fear in Europe. A respected German scholar and diplomat, Adam Olearius, who had visited Russia several times between 1634–1643, and whose work which was published in 1647, had influenced the European opinion in the 17th century, wrote on the Russians that: "If a man considers the nature and manner of [their] life he will be forced to avow there cannot be anything more barbarous than that people."[1] About a century earlier, an Elizabethan poet and the secretary of the English Embassy in Moscow (1568–69), George Tuberville, was apparently more benevolent and compared the Russians with England's most hated and despised neighbors, the Irish. According to him, "[The] Wild Irish are as civil as Ruses in their kind; hard choices, which is best of both, both bloody, rude and blind."[2] The title of an account of English travelers to Russia in the 16th century: *Rude and Barbarous Kingdom, Russia in the Accounts of the Sixteenth Century English Voyagers*, speaks for itself, and various German publicists and Polish politicians, who, at that time, had to directly face the growing power of Moscow presented a no less alarming picture of the country.[3]

The opening of Russia to the West, which has increased since the 17th century, and even some successful interventions in European politics did not do much to change its reputation and did not dissipate the persisting prejudices. Quite often, the impact was rather the opposite, causing fear and more mistrust of its great Eastern neighbor.

The victory in the Northern War with Sweden and the Nystad Treaty in 1721 marked the final recognition of Russia as a European power, which was going to play a leading role in the continent during the first decades of the 19th century, including the Napoleonic Wars and the Congress of Vienna in 1815. As one possible result of that, French scholar and clergyman Chappe

---

1 Francesca Wilson, *Muscovy Russia Through Foreign Eyes 1553–1900* (New York: Praeger Publisher, 1970) p. 71

2 "A people passing rude, to vices vile inclined." As reprinted in Anthony Cross, *Russia Under Western Eyes 1517–1825* (London: Elek Books, 1971) p. 7

3 Philip Longworth, "Muscovy and the Antemurale Christianitatis," Guya Svakfed *The Place of Russia in Europe*, (Budapest, 1999) p. 83

D'Autroche, who travelled throughout Russia in 1760, noted, "in France people expected her to overrun our little Europe, like Scythians and Huns. Hamburg and Lubeck trembled at her name. Poland and Germany considered Russia as one of the most formidable powers in Europe."[1] According to the French visitor, Western fears of Russia were unfounded.[2] Both the country and its army were socially too backward and devoid of proper training and equipment to be able to present any real threat to the more developed European powers. The case of Poland and its forthcoming partition was a special one because, as D'Autroche wrote, "the sovereign was there without authority, and the state without defense, it was open to every invader."[3] Nevertheless, such a fear still persisted for centuries and contributed to the perception of Russia as a problem. The most influential description of the country in the 19th century in Europe was from the Marquis de Custine's: *La Russie en 1839* (Paris 1843), and was entirely hostile and negative. This attitude was predominant in Europe until the Russian Revolution in 1917. Relations with St. Petersburg were seen as a political necessity, often running against domestic public opinion.

The Russian *Sonderweg* (special path) of development, which had often been criticized by foreign observers, resulted from the objective geopolitical and historical circumstances and the interests of Russian elites; but it did not mean that as such it would be prone to be a failure. Under the conditions of a harsh climate, a weak economic basis and unfavorable political circumstances, the new nation nevertheless proved to be stubborn and resilient. It was able to create its own original culture and for a long time kept its political institutions and identity. However, throughout those centuries, its power waxed and waned, and on more than one occasion its very survival as a nation was uncertain. Being located in the Eurasian lowland and devoid of any natural boundaries, the country has been invaded many times and probably suffered more than any other nation because of these human and material destructions, the most important of which resulted from World War II, during which Russia had more than 20 million military and civilian casualties. In fact "as a bearer of modernity, albeit not the best form, the Russian path represented a vast improvement over pre-modern life" in the country[4] and following this path, the Russian state achieved some of its most glorious military and civilian successes, including the victory over Napoleon's army, the establishment of St. Petersburg and the golden era of Russian high culture in the second part of the 19th century.

---

1 Wilson, *Op. cit.* p 142
2 *Op. cit.* p 143
3 *Op. cit.* p 139
4 Poe, *Op. cit.*, p. 90

One of the greatest achievements of early modernity in Russia in the 16th–17th centuries was the creation of the early modern state with a bureaucratic organization, a standing and relatively well-trained gun power army and a state-run financial system. The Polish–Lithuanian Commonwealth, which had been much more integrated with the Western civilization was nevertheless unable to achieve that and paid for this by its own extinction. With the help of its own path to early modernity the Russian Empire was able to survive and play an important role in European politics until World War I and the 1917 revolution. At that time, both its political system and socio-economic model proved to be outdated and too fragile to stand up against the powerful challenges of the 20th century. Isolated by its geopolitical Eurasian background and its immense territory, Russia until the 18th century was in fact not even part of the European world economy and culture, but a separate system with special economic and socio-cultural features.[1] The post-Petrine period and especially the reforms introduced after the Crimean War in the second part of the 19th and early 20th century opened the country for the fast economic and industrial developments based on Western capital and technology and cheap local labor. However, alongside this positive, the development caused increased social tensions and discontent of the factory's workers and peasants and the emergence of a new social group, typical for Eastern Europe, the Russian intelligentsia, which was largely socially alienated and quite vocal in its social and political criticism. Although it was ideologically divided, large parts turned against the existing system and all Russian tradition. The intelligentsia did not have much direct influence on the economy and political power, but in Russia and some other Eastern European countries such as Poland, it still enjoyed, social prestige and influence unknown in the West. When the First World War exposed the fragility and weaknesses of the regime, the way became open to dramatic shocks and transformation.

However, I believe that in spite of all social and political challenges existing there, on the eve of World War I the Tsarist regime was still not necessarily doomed to collapse. Russians are rather conservative people and the regime supported by the Orthodox Church and national tradition also has to its account some positive achievements, such as the liberation of the millions of landowners' serfs in 1857 and a number of other administrative and judicial reforms. During the last two decades before the outbreak of

---

1 J.H Elliot, *Europe Divided [1559–1598]* (London: Collins, 1968) p. 47. According to his probably exaggerated opinion: "the serf society of Moscovy, ... remained a world of its own, threatening to its neighbors because of its growing military power, but still economically unrelated to the European world." A similar point stressing the special Russian Eurasian background was later elaborated by *Georgy Derlugyen*: "Was Russia Ever a Colonial Empire?" *International Affairs* (Moscow) March 1991, p. 83-89

war the country was going through quick industrial and general economic growth. Its socio-political outcomes and prospects for the nation might have been disputed, but according to some scholars, "Pre-revolutionary Russia needed only a few decades more of peace to be transformed into a society no longer conspicuously backward as compared with the West, and no longer endowed with dangerous tensions. Russia was well on the way towards entering the family of nations enjoying the advantages of civilization."[1]

Unfortunately, these few decades of peace were not in the offing. In spite of the warning from the former Russian Minister of the Interior, Pyotr Durnovo, who had clearly predicted the coming disaster[2] and the reluctance of many other military and civilian officials in August 1914, the Russian government decided to join France and Britain in their war against Germany and the Austro-Hungarian Empire, which became World War I.

Although the more detailed analysis of this subject is not the topic of my monograph, one of its features seems still to be worthy of our attention.

The Russian leaders of the period considered their country to be a great power and the Russian Empire was certainly coveted as an ally by France and Britain. However, at the same time Russia was still far less developed and in more than one aspect more backward than the advanced Western nations. Just as in the Crimean War in 1853–1856 with France and Britain supporting the Ottoman Empire, such a military confrontation was unlikely to bring victory for Russia.

The ensuing military defeat caused inevitable political backlash, which in the situation then existing facilitated social revolution and the destruction of the Tsarist Empire. However, as Professor Poe rightly indicates, "the Russian Moment in World History" did not come to an end and the new leaders in more than one way followed the path of their imperial predecessors.[3]

The collapse of the Soviet Union (run by the "new leaders"), which replaced the Tsarist Empire, seems more difficult to explain, and some of its causes might remain controversial. The Soviet Union was victorious in its great war with Hitler's Germany and it also achieved numerous successes in social, industrial, scientific and cultural development. In spite of its lack of democratic institutions and its often repressive rule over its subjects, it was still much more powerful and obviously more modern than the Romanov Empire. Even in the early 1980s, the collapse of the Soviet system and disappearance of the USSR had seemed unpredictable or even impossible.

1 N.S. Timasheff, *The Great Retreat: The growth and decline of Communism in Russia*, New York: E.P. Dutton and Company, 1946. See also Jacob Walker, *The Rise of democracy in pre-revolutionary Russia: political and social institutions under the last three Czars*, New York: Praeger, 1962.

2 "Pyotr Durnovo Memorandum. February 1914," www.novaonline.nvcc.edu

3 Marshall T. Poe, *The Russian Moment in World History*, Princeton University Press, 2003, pp. 76-85.

President Putin was probably right that "the collapse of the Soviet Union was the major geopolitical disaster of the century."[1]

In this speech Vladimir Putin discussed Russian domestic issues almost exclusively; he did not analyze the causes of the Soviet collapse nor its implications for Russian foreign policy and the international system as a whole. However, the fact that he talked about "the major geopolitical disaster of the century" might have indicated that he still kept both of these issues in mind and this suspicion contributed to the anger and criticism of many Western commentators[2] who conflated Putin's remarks about the internal consequences of collapse with the desire to perpetuate empires.

Although during the last ten years before its demise the USSR had experienced various problems and some apparent decline, the bipolar world system seemed fairly stable at that time, and its collapse was not anticipated. The USSR was neither militarily defeated nor did it face a large scale popular uprising against its social system and statehood as such. With the possible exception of a few peripheral republics such as Latvia, Lithuania and Georgia, most of the population supported the existing political situation, or at least were loyal to the country and the Soviet system. The dissidents, though intensively supported from the West, represented only a small group of intellectuals who lived mainly in Moscow and Leningrad. They might have been used in the political struggle by some other domestic and international forces, but their own social influence was limited. The collapse of the second superpower was caused by infighting among the Soviet elites and their notorious corruption, which was skilfully used and stimulated by foreign powers and their political and economic envoys to the country.[3]

A more detailed analysis of these developments is beyond the scope of my work, and in any case it is almost impossible to be accomplished right now. However, everyone should have noticed its impact and results.

The collapse of the USSR caused enormous economic, social and political hardship for millions of the post-Soviet peoples, and in geopolitical terms put Russia back into a similar situation to that which existed during the first part of the 17th century. The country lost one sixth of its territory, half

---

1 Vladimir Putin, "Address to the Federal Assembly of the Russian Federation," http://eng.kremlin.ru/transcripts/7863, April 25, 2005.
2 For the recent review of some of those critical voices see: „Did Vladimir Putin call the breakup of the USSR 'the greatest geopolitical tragedy of the 20th century?'" *Tampa Bay Times*, http://www.politifact.com/punditfact/statements/2014/mar/06/john-bolton/did-vladimir-putin-call-breakup-ussr-greatest-geop/, February 14, 2015.
3 Stephen Cohen, *Failed Crusade: America and The Tragedy of Post-Communist Russia* / New York: WW Norton, 2000, Stephen Cohen, *Soviet Fates and Lost Alternatives* / New York: Columbia University Press, 2011 pp. 112 – 140, David M. Kotz with Fred Weir, *Revolution from above The demise of the Soviet system* / London and New York: Routledge, 1997.

---

its economy and more than half of its population. The losses included many strategically important locations, and because of the NATO enlargement that followed, Russia found itself in a precarious situation.[1] Since the former Warsaw Pact countries joined NATO, the Conventional Armed Treaty in Europe negotiated in 1990, lost its previous meaning, and the European security system turned against Russia. In the following decade in 2002 US President George W. Bush's administration abrogated the ABM Treaty, which for 30 years had provided both Moscow and Washington with certain guarantees of security and mutual survival. No less important and painful for the Russian and other post Soviet peoples were the costs of the ideological and economic transformations in the 1990s.[2] However, in spite of all its historic achievements, the Soviet Union probably had too weak a socio-political basis to be able to continue its successful development or even to secure its own political survival.

In Russia, and probably in most Eastern European countries as well, the basic preconditions for a successful socialist transformation were missing — at least by the criteria which the majority of Marxists at that time considered to be explicitly or implicitly entailed by Marx's theory.[3]

It is true that the writings of Max and Engels were "silent on the practicalities of socialist construction and did not provide a road map to socialism."[4] However, at the beginning of the 20th century this issue was widely discussed by the socialist leaders and theoreticians both in Europe and in Russia.[5] Most of them such as the political leaders of the Second International and its main theoretician Karl Kautsky in Europe and Georgi

---

1 As a prominent American Relations scholar and leading neorealist Kenneth Waltz noted, "rather than learning from history, the United States repeats past errors by expanding NATO eastwards and extending its influence over what used to be the provinces of the vanquished. Despite much talked about 'globalization' of international politics, American political leaders to a dismaying extent, think of East or West rather than of their interaction". / K. Waltz, "Globalization and American Power," *The National Interest*, Spring 2000, p. 55.

2 "We have not given enough thought to how painful the Soviet collapse was," www.wilsoncenter.org July 2, 2013. Interview with Pilar Bonet, Chief correspondent in Moscow of *El Pais*, upon the completion of her Wilson Center Policy Scholarship, "The Long Agony of the Russian Empire and its Legacy", by Mary Elizabeth Malinson. See also James W. Carden, "Why Russians Still Don't Hate Communism," *The National Interest*, 10, 23-2013.

3 According to Silviu Brucan, Czechoslovakia was "the only Eastern [European] country that was ripe for socialism according to Marx's paradigm," Silviu Brucan, "Europe in the Global Strategic Game," in Bjorn Hettne, *Europe Dimension of Peace* (London: Zed Books Ltd, 1988 p. 17.

4 Poe, p.8 0.

5 For more analysis of the various Marxist perspectives on the Bolsheviks' revolution see my article: Andrej Kreutz, "The Rise and Fall of Soviet and Eastern European Communism. An Historical Perspective," Studies in Political Economy (Ottawa, Canada) Vol. 38 (Summer 1992) pp. 109–138.

Plekhanov in Russia believed in the objective laws of history according to which the full capitalist development would be a necessary precondition for a chance to successfully establish the socialist society. Lenin and his followers the Bolsheviks did not share the conviction.

In fact they deviated from the then common understanding of the Marxist philosophy of history and social development. The prominent Italian Marxist thinker Antonio Gramsci called Russia's October 1917 revolution "a revolution against Karl Marx's 'Capital',"[1] and the father of Russian Marxism, G. Plekhanov, criticized himself for "propagandizing of Marxism too early in backward, semi-Asiatic Russia."[2] He had also predicted that a premature attempt to establish the socialist system in "an isolated and backward country could only result in the sort of 'patriarchal despotism' practiced by the Incas."[3]

Plekhanov and his colleagues might have exaggerated in their criticism, but for any analyst it might have then been obvious that the implementation of the socialist ideas in Russia would be extremely difficult and that both the means which might have been used and the received results would deviate from Marx's vision and expectation.

Consequently, the Bolshevik Soviet system established by the Bolsheviks' revolution was a "mixed one," with significant socialist elements, but with non-socialist elements as well.[4] It replaced the relatively backward Tsarist Empire, with a kind of "state socialism" where the people were passive recipients, not active participants, in the political and economic life of the nation.[5] The enactment of the social rights of the population for work and retirement, to free medical services and education at all levels, made the Soviet system very different from modern and even more post-modern global capitalism. At the same time, as almost all valuable property was under state control even members of the Soviet party elite ruling the country, who were effectively state managers, could neither acquire their own wealth nor pass their socio-political higher status to their offspring. As time passed and the original revolutionary vanguard became replaced by the less idealistic and more down-to-earth people, many Soviet elite members thus became discontent, especially if travelling abroad where they were able to compare

---

1 Antonio Gramsei, "Lo Revoluzione contre il Capitale," Avanti 24, December 1917.

2 Samuel Baron, "Plekhanov: Russian Comparativist." In John H. Kautsky ed., Karl Kautsky and the Social Science of Classical Marxism, E. J. Brill, Leiden, The Netherlands, 1989.

3 As quoted by Michael Ellman, *Socialist Planning*, Cambridge: Cambridge University Press, 1989, p. 350.

4 Kotz with Weir, *Revolution from Above*, p. 26.

5 *Op. cit.* p. 30.

themselves to their Western counterparts.[1] In addition, as the distribution of money income was overall much more egalitarian in the Soviet system than in Western-type capitalist nations, the elite members always had a reason to be discontented.[2] One of the paradoxes of the Soviet kind of socialism was the fact that a large part of its powerful, and in many ways privileged, ruling elites had no material economic incentives to protect and defend the system itself. Until the 1970s, those people had no choice but to accept its terms if they wished to work within it.[3] However, the situation was soon going to change.

Alongside its ability for rapid growth of output and industrialization, the Soviet economy had experienced many problems, often stemming from its too rigid central planning and lack of a broad-based democratic and consumer input. Until the mid-1970s, it was still able to engender growth and technological and social advances, but later started to markedly deteriorate. Gorbachev, who was then the communist party's first secretary, had to admit that "Historical experience has shown that socialist society is not insured against the emergence and accumulation of stagnant tendencies and even against major socio-political crisis."[4] The reforms he wanted to introduce in order to save the Soviet state and system proved to be either poorly conceived or poorly implemented by the reluctant or corrupt bureaucracy. At the same time under his leadership, Russia and all the Soviet Union experienced political freedom and openness as never before. Both the intensified economic difficulties and rapid democratization provided the hostile forces to socialism a unique chance to put an end to the Soviet experiment. While a large part of the Soviet elites and intellectuals, including those in Russia proper, had not seen sufficient social and economic incentives to preserve the Soviet system and the Soviet state itself, the majority of the population, who had always been kept out of political involvement and who, at that time, had neither the much-needed political knowledge nor experience, remained passive or were attracted by the demagogues including Boris Yeltsin and his Democratic Russia. in the March 1991 referendum, held in Russia and eight other republics (the populations of which included 93% of all citizens of the Soviet Union), the 76.4% turnout voted to preserve the Soviet Union. Nevertheless,[5] on December 8, at a hunting lodge in the Belovezha Forest near Minsk, Yeltsin (as president of the Russian Republic) and the

---

1 The first president of Ukraine Leonid Kravchuk admitted that he had stopped being communist when travelling to Italy, as the director of the missiles factory discovered that his Italian counterpart was many times better paid than him.
2 Kotz and Weir, p. 28 and 244.
3 *Op. cit.* p.33.
4 Mikhail Gorbachev, *Perestroika*, 1988, pp.27, 32, 37.
5 Stephen F. Cohen, *Soviet fates and lost alternatives from Stalinism to the New Cold War* (New York: Columbia University Press, 2009, pp. 90-91.

presidents of Ukraine and Belorussia signed an agreement abolishing the Soviet Union. The second superpower ceased to exist, peacefully, on December 31, 1991. The Soviet chapter of Russian history came to an end. However, the demise of the Soviet Union was not only due to internal domestic reasons such as economic stagnation, the ensuing socioeconomic crisis and part of the ruling elites' desire to acquire their own property and bring to an end the socialist experiment. Although these and some other domestic causes could have been perceived as the direct reasons for the demise, there were also some major international forces and factors, which facilitated their final success.

Since 1947, the Cold War with the American superpower and its allies had taken a toll on the Soviet Union, which had been far less developed and had lost well over 20 million people during World War II. The cost of the arms race with the more developed nations had been hard to bear, and the negative social impact was increased by the information warfare conducted by the US and other Western media. Its political influence and impact on the Soviet bloc populations varied, depending on the ethnic groups and timing, but it should not be underestimated. During the last decade of Soviet history, some Islamic forces allied with the West including Saudi Arabia played a certain but by no means negligible role. The Soviet unsuccessful military intervention in Afghanistan and the Muslim World's negative reaction to that accelerated the collapse of the second superpower. Since September 12, 1985, Sheikh Ahmed Zaki Yamani, the Minister of Oil for Saudi Arabia announced that his country would stop protecting oil prices, and the oil production in Saudi Arabia increased fourfold, while the oil prices collapsed by approximately the same amount in real terms. As a result, Moscow lost about $20 billion per year, which was of critical importance for the country's economic and political status. According to some analysts the Saudis' oil weapons provided a final blow to the Soviets.[1]

In spite of all these problems, the Soviet Union did not collapse spontaneously.[2] In fact it was brought down by its own top leadership, which undermined the central planning of its economy and compromised the leading role and authority of the Communist party.[3] A fraction of the Soviet leadership around Gorbachev wanted to change the whole system and being in control of levels of power was effective in its actions. Those people were often hostile not only to the Soviet heritage but also to all

---

1 Andrew Nikiforuk, "What Really Killed the Soviet Union? Oil shock? Red Empire just run out of fuel, say growing number of experts," *The Tyee*, March 13, 2013. See also Tyler Cowen, "Why did the Soviet Union fall?," History/ Permalink, June 13, 2007.
2 David Lane, *The Capitalist Transformation of State Socialism. The making and breaking of state socialist society and what followed.* (London: Routledge, 2014), p. 108.
3 *Op. cit.*

Marxist and socialist ideas and admired Western capitalism.[1] They created the pre-conditions for Yeltsin and his people to come to power. Yeltsin and his team had been instrumental in the destruction of the Soviet Union.

Keeping in mind the fact that the Soviet Union had always been a much weaker protagonist in the global confrontation, its final defeat could just have been seen as a normal outcome of a political contest. more unusual was its long persistence in the struggle and its cautious but still important role in global events post-World War II. After 1945, Red Moscow expanded its zone of influence to neighboring Eastern European countries without asking for the democratic consensus of the local populations; however, its ideology and practical example of providing social rights to the great majority, and its ability to balance the Western imperial powers, probably contributed decisively to the development of the welfare state in the capitalist countries and the decolonization of the African, Asian and Latin American nations. The USSR had supported their national liberation movements, and after that it provided generous economic and political assistance to the developing nations. Thus, the United States was obliged to follow a similar policy, and the Third World nations were able to get more favorable conditions for their further development. On October 1, 1949, Chinese Chairman Mao Zedong declared that, "The Chinese people have stood up" and proclaimed the establishment of the People's Republic of China. In January 1959 Fidel Castro had successfully completed a guerrilla campaign to take control of Cuba, and in the wake of this was going to establish the first "socialist" state in the Western hemisphere.

As argued by the American scholar I previously quoted, the "Russians seem to have travelled the same road to modernity that they had travelled to early modernity, one characterized by autocracy, command economics, cultural insularity, and an emphasis on arms."[2] However, he is still willing to admit that, "statist modernization seemed to work well in the Russian context. In 1920 Russia was starving and defenseless, in 1960 Russia enjoyed a high standard of living and was a superpower. Finally, most Russians

---

1 For example Alexander Yakovlev, former Soviet ambassador in Ottawa (Canada), and later a member of the Politburo in charge of ideology, in fact the chief party ideologue during Gorbachev's time, publicly admitted that according to him, "Marxism has brought us to the abyss, to backwardness and the destruction of one's conscience. Any person on earth knows that Marxism in the first place is teaching the annihilation of both private ownership of the means of production and the national, legal and spiritual foundations of Western civilization. Marx as long as he lived remained loyal to the Communist Manifesto, this guide for the proletarians to destroy everything that had until now safeguarded private ownership." "Yakovlev on Abyss of Marxism," BBC World Broadcast, October 8, 1991. It was obvious that with leaders like that neither the social system nor the political institutions based on the social system might hope to have a chance at a future.
2 Poe, p. 82.

believed in Communism, particularly after it was Russianized in World War II."[1]

The creation of a state socialism in the less than fully developed and largely isolated nation was certainly harsh, costly and often cruel operation. And yet according to him most of those sacrifices were not in vain. As he writes, "The country was modernized, the Germans were defeated, and by the 1960s Russians were better governed, educated, fed and protected than anyone could remember. The Russian road to modernity, clothed in Communist guise, had delivered the goods for millions of Soviet citizens and their followers in the Second and Third Worlds."[2]

Although the history of the USSR (and the other nations of the last century claiming to be socialist) was full of internal and external conflicts and contradictions, they had some positive achievements that should be neither denied nor neglected. The Soviet period was a time of great achievements and Moscow enjoyed greater power than at any other time in history. What would follow, after the collapse of the Soviet Union, was a time of tremendous human suffering and national humiliation. According to a recent opinion poll there, almost two thirds of the interviewed people viewed the Soviet time in a favorable way. A resounding 69 percent of respondents over the age of 60 viewed life under the old Soviet regime in a positive light, as did nearly 50 percent of those polled between the ages of 18 and 30.[3] As time passes and the people who lived during the Soviet period die out, the social memory and the image of the Soviet past are changing. However, shortly after the Soviet demise in 1999, 75 to 85 percent of Russians regretted the breakup of the Soviet Union, and a large majority of them in 2000 considered Brezhnev's reforms of the 1970s and early 1980s, before Gorbachev, to be a golden era.[4]

Last but not least, during the Soviet period — for the first time in its long history — Russia enjoyed the sympathy and support of millions of the people on all continents. Many of them might have disliked totalitarian methods and did not believe in the Marxist ideology, but they still admired Moscow's promotion of social rights for all of its citizens and national liberation movements in the African, Asian and Latin American countries. At that time there was no lack of Russian supporters, even in North America. Perhaps in part because of that, Washington's policy toward Red Moscow had always been much more cautious and respectful than it was after the USSR collapsed. No Soviet leader was ever treated with such disrespect as

---

1 Poe, p. 84.
2 Poe, p. 85.
3 James W. Carden, *"Why Russians Still Don't Hate Communism?"* National Interest, October 23, 2013.
4 Stephen F. Cohen, *"Failed Crusade: America and the Tragedy of Post-Soviet Russia,"* New York. W.W. Norton, 2000, p.48.

the present Russian president, and during the Soviet era it was unthinkable that American-led forces might approach the historic heartland of Russia.

The demise of the Soviet Union certainly took a heavy toll on the life of the post-Soviet peoples, and one of its other important outcomes was the greatly diminished international status and power of Russia.

place in the international system. During the last two decades, all efforts in these directions have been difficult, and there are still many impediments to reaching a more promising future.

In my opinion the first and probably the most important one is the social situation in Russian itself, where the neo-liberal reform of the late 1980s and early 1990s created enormous and previously unknown socio-economic divisions among the Russian population.

As Professor Stephen Cohen, a well-known American scholar, indicated, "Since 1991, Russia's realities have included the worst peacetime industrial depression of the twentieth century," and the collapse of agriculture was worse than that caused by Stalin's collectivization of the peasantry in the early 1930s.[1]

The inevitable outcome of the events was the impoverishment of about 75 percent of the nation and more orphans than had resulted from World War II, which was enormously destructive for Russia.[2] At the same time according to the well informed Polish-Canadian businessman and politician Stan Tyminski, a man who in 1990 ran for the Polish presidency and received more than 25 percent of the popular votes, about $500 billion was taken out of Russia for the private accounts of members of ruling elites and business people supported by them.[3]

Although Prime Minister Yevgeny Primakov's reforms in 1998 and Putin's rise to become President of the country in 2000 brought some improvements to this critical situation, the level of social stratification in Russia still remains one of the highest in the world, and at least 30 percent of all the wealth of Russian households belongs to the billionaires. At the same time, according to the Federal Service for State Statistics (Rosstat), 18 million people, which is almost 13 percent of the Russian population, live below the poverty line, and the ratio of the average income of the most affluent to the least affluent has grown from 4.5:1 in 1990 to 16.5:1 in 2012.[4] The existing social problems of the working and largely impoverished population could now be aggravated because of Russia's recent severe economic slowdown, which might result in widespread discontent and lack of confidence in the future. It seems obvious that without more hope and mobilization of social

---

1 Stephen F. Cohen, *Failed Crusade America and the Tragedy of Post-Communist Russia*, New York: W W Norton Company, 2000, p.28.

2 Ibid.

3 Personal information. According to Tyminski in the case of Poland the figure amounts to $67 billion for the same period. As Poland is a much smaller nation, it still caused substantial damage to the country. For the similar figures on Russia, see Michael Hudson, "The New Cold War's Ukraine Gambit," www.nakedcapitalism.com, May 16, 2014.

4 "Report on Growing Wealth Inequity," *Rossiyskaya Gazeta*, October 15, 2012. See also D. Treisman "Inequity: The Russian Experience", *Current History*, October 2012, pp. 264 – 268.

energy by the majority, the country will not be able to move forward and stand up to its external threats.

According to a number of experts and public opinion polls, most Russians still do not consider the 1990s privatization of major branches of industry and all economic institutions to have been legitimate, and if they were able to they would call for their renationalization.[1] Although Putin defends privatization and the market economy, even during the last presidential election the majority opinion had not changed, and the capitalist system in the country cannot enjoy the same level of acceptance and legitimacy as in the US or even Western Europe.[2]

Another important new cause of internal social tension is the political aspirations of the Russian bourgeoisie (upper middle class or creative class) which was recreated during the last 25 years and now seems to be much stronger and more self-confident than 20 or even 10 years ago. These people who are no longer afraid of a return to Communist rule, and are relatively secure in their advantageous socio-economic situation, do not need as much state protection as before, and are demanding more political influence and direct access to power. An additional source of their discontent might be the fact that the super-wealthy billionaires, who often have well-established political connections, own relatively more wealth than the millionaires and some other wealthy (but still not super-wealthy) people. Although the protests and demands of the working and impoverished population and Moscow and St. Petersburg's creative classes are different in nature and often not compatible, all of them are nevertheless critical, or even outwardly hostile, towards the present political regime and might represent a threat to the stability of the country and its respectability in the globalized world.

The Russian liberal so-called "non-systemic" and pro-Western opposition has an importance that by far exceeds its relatively modest

---

1 As Professor Stephen Cohen stressed, "the Russian capitalist system" rests on stolen state property. Every poll done of the Russian people shows they want the state to take back the property from the oligarchs, including middle class people. According to him, "the nation doesn't accept the privatization of property that occurred in the 1990s" and "the reason that the people who control the financial oligarchy in Russia don't want free elections is they know that if they had free elections in parliament, the people would vote for candidates pledging to confiscate their properties [which they stole]." Stephen Cohen, "Hidden History Behind Russia Election Demonstrations" at http://www.democracynow.org/2011/12/30/election_fraud_galvanizes_russian_opposition_communist

2 However, the outbreak of the social revolution in Russia now seems very unlikely, not only, and not even primarily, because of the power of state control, but because of the lack of credible ideology and organization which is needed to lead the way for it. The Communist Party of the Russian Federation has always been too shy and timid for that. About its early periods and Zyuganov's reluctance to fight for the presidency of the country in 1996, see Simes, *After the Collapse*, pp. 167 – 175.

popular support. The Russian internal situation is largely still unclear and in some ways far from normal. While in almost all other countries, the intellectuals (intelligentsia) and the business people are integrated with and support their national states, the situation in Russia is rather different. The non-systemic opposition might not be very popular among the common people, but their representatives are strategically located, well funded and quite outspoken. They have access to the media and receive constant Western protection and support. Largely because of their efforts it is now almost impossible to improve Russia's international image, and it is difficult to imagine the country regaining an effective soft power. Because of the substantial means at their disposal, those people seem to represent a major challenge not only to the present political leadership but also to the existing Russian state as such, whose nature and direction of development they seem to question.

Alongside the creation of an effective economy and social safety net for the population, the Russian political class needs to work out a clear cut concept of the national interests of the country, and to create some kind of political consensus around them as is typical for Western and even a number of non-Western nations.

The lack of such consensus could be very dangerous for the future of the country. At present, according to the Russian scholar Valeriy Tiskhov, the divisions within the elites of Russia, rather than external threats, represent the main risk for the nation. "In spite of the last 10 years' general socio-economic improvements, the political and ideological disagreements and tensions among the elites have become more severe and articulated."[1] He considers this "self-destructive trend" in Russia very dangerous because, as he argues, "while there is no fundamental consensus among the leading and most active top 5% of the people, such a society is going to lose its identity and coherence. It did not become a real society, but its metaphor which can be easily manipulated by the self-serving interested political forces and even their minor disagreement might cause a major general crisis."[2]

The political divisions within the Russian political and economic elites and the intensity and bitterness of their conflicts at present have no analogy in any other country. Their origins lie in the events of the 1990s, which brought to an end both the relatively egalitarian socio-economic system of state socialism and the existence of the Soviet Union as a global power

---

1 Valeriy Tiskhov, "Mezhnatsionalnoe Soglasie: Usilenie Vnutri Nas," *Vestnik Kavkaza*, December 5, 2013. See also Paul Gobel, "Domestic Divisions Not External Aggression, Threaten Russia Now, Tishkov Says", Stanton, Dec. 6, 2013.
2 Tishkov, *Op. cit.*

center independent from the West, and in fact a superpower. The outcomes of that included:

1. The rapid decline of Russia as a sovereign state both in international and domestic affairs. During the last decade of the 20th century, Russia in fact became a semi-colony of the West. Its economic resources were mercilessly looted and its previous military might was almost completely annihilated.

2. The rapid privatization of most of the national wealth and economy, going into the hands of a relatively quite small group of people, who were either well connected to the new political leadership or were able to get from the West sufficient funds to pay the artificially low, greatly manipulated prices for Soviet industries and natural resources. The new Russian bourgeois elite (the oligarchs) was thus established and quickly acquired control of the media and a strong influence in politics.

3. However, the greatly weakened Russian state apparatus, though now devoid of its previous power, did not disappear, and even during Yeltsin's presidency the Russian business elites did not achieve the power and legitimacy of their American and other Western counterparts.

Vladimir Putin, who became acting president on December 3, 1999, when Yeltsin resigned, and who won the subsequent 2000 presidential election, brought some major changes. Most of his efforts have been focused on strengthening the Russian state at both the domestic and international level. That included both the re-imposition of some state control on the national economy and on the oligarchs, and a persistent effort to rebuild the political independence and international status of the country. Although he was unable to achieve all his ambitious goals during the 2000–2013 period, the Russian state became stronger internally and the social situation of the working majority has markedly improved.

Russia has also re-emerged as a substantial power, one which is able to "play a more convincing and authoritative role in international affairs."[1] Consequently, as Professor David Lane indicates, the political elites in Russia "work in the context of a hybrid economic system."[2] Differing from the US and most of its allies, in Russia "the state has an independent

---

1 Richard Sakwa, "Can Putinism solve its contradictions?" *Opendemocracy.net*, December 27, 2013. As Chief Geopolitical analyst of Stratfor Robert Kaplan admits, Putin is "someone who has taken Russia from the point of chaos and made it a credible regional power" {Putin's Geopolitical Logic", *The Glover Cottage Portal*, August 12, 2012.

2 David Lane, "Divisions Within the Russian Political Elites", *Valdai Club*, August 4, 2013.

economic property base as well as a stronger coordinating role over business."[1] Although Russia has not become a state capitalist formation like China, and Putin has persistently rejected the quest for renationalization of the national wealth and means of production (an idea which is still popular among the Russian people), there is still a "potential for conflict between the state and corporations if the state intervenes to direct their resources to politically-inspired though legitimate (and socially well-justified) goals, or when it redefines relationships with foreign corporate interests."[2]

The hybrid economic system existing in Russia is probably the main reason for the political divisions within the Russian political elites. The division lies between the statist bloc supporting Putin and the broadly understood pro-liberal opposition. Part of the opposition which was traditionally led by Dmitry Medvedev, and in a less official way by the former finance minister Alexei Kudrin, is willing to cooperate with Putin, and is included, up to a point, in the present state system. Another part of it, the so-called "non-systemic opposition", rejects any form of cooperation and even the basic legitimacy of the "powers that be." One such person, the "arch liberal" Anatoly Chubais, who in the 1990s was one of the main architects of the rapid and severe privatization of Russian state assets and the establishment of the capitalist system in the country, coined, even in relation to Putin's Russia, the idea that the country was a "fascist state," a view that was taken up by many Western journalists including Edward Lucas (*The Economist*) and Luke Harding (*The Guardian*).

One example of this massive Western media campaign in 2011–2012 was an attempt to delegitimize the election process in Russia by largely exaggerating the scale and extent of fraud in the parliamentary elections and falsely denying the legitimacy of Putin's presidential election. The non-systemic liberal opposition attacked Putin and his political bloc's independent foreign policy; they want Moscow to integrate into the US-led international system.[3] In the domestic field, the economic liberals demanded a new round of privatization, the opening of the country to foreign firms, and a move to an American-type corporate economy.

However, neither Putin's statist bloc nor the liberal opposition can be seen as homogeneous. Among Putin's supporters, some would be ready to

---

1 *Op. cit.*
2 *Op. cit.*
3 For instance according to a professor at the National Research University in Moscow, Evgeny Gontmakher, Russia should "actively integrate into the world, not only economic but also political and military spaces, conventionally called the West, receiving at least small guarantees of the maintenance of internal stability," "Reconstruction of The Real Putin's Doctrine," *Vedomosti*, October 19, 2012. Gontmakher is still seen as a moderate person among the Russian Liberals.

join the West if Washington and Brussels were willing to respect Russian national interests; some others would rather prefer an alliance with China and other BRICS nations, with the vision of a multipolar world in the future.

There are also some noticeable personal and political differences within the liberal opposition.[1] It is also necessary to remember that both Putin's bloc and the liberal opposition represent the Russian economic and political elite which emerged because of the demise of state socialism and which support the capitalist system in the country. Alongside them there exists the still strong communist party of the Russian Federation, whose candidates polled 1.7 million votes in the federal elections of 2012 and remains the second most influential political party in Russia. The communists criticize pro-capitalist transformations in the country and consider Putin's foreign policy as often too soft and submissive to Western demands and interests.

Although the majority of not only Russians but also the people in most of the post-socialist countries have negative feelings towards the privatization of the national economy and the new very non-egalitarian social stratification thus caused, in practice all Russian elites support the basic capitalist transformation which brought them wealth and power. Even the communist party's leader Gennady Zyuganov considers the renationalization of the economy impossible without a new and bloody civil war which might destroy the nation.[2]

However, the Russian political elites are still essentially divided on two major issues:
- The state –business class relations and the division of wealth; the social welfare state model or American-type capitalist system.
- Russia's place and role in the international system.

Though both issues are mutually related, the second one is at present most widely discussed and is probably the most visible bone of contention among the divided upper crust of Russian society. As President Putin indicated, "For the first time in 200–300 years, Russia is challenged by the possibility of losing its great power status and becoming a country of minor importance."[3] According to him and the "Sovereignists" supporting him, this is a great threat, and "to prevent it we need to concentrate all the intellectual,

---

1 One of the examples of that has been severe attack on Alexei Navalny by the leader of Russian Liberal Yabloko Party, Sergei Mitrokhin, "Navalny Oligarchic Project," *Interfax*, December 16, 2013.
2 See for instance the transcript of one of his early statements "The Zyuganov Two Step," *Online Newshour*, May 24, 1996. See also Dimitri Simes, *After the Collapse: Russia Seeks its Place as a Great Power*, Simon &Schuster, 1999, p.167 and passim.
3 Vladimir Putin, "Russia on the Threshold of Century", *Nezavisimaya Gazeta*, December 30, 1999.

physical and moral resources of the nation. Everything depends on our ability to realize the danger, to unite and to be ready to work hard."[1]

However, the influential part of the Russian middle class has a different opinion. According to those people, Russia should willingly resign from its great power status, reject its imperial heritage and follow the US and/or the EU leadership in order to get Western recognition and support to stabilize its market economy and to solve its current social problems.[2] These "Atlantic Integrationists" include not only the non-systemic opposition but also some people who are an important part of the present political system and whose influence on Russian foreign policy could not be neglected. In March 2011, in spite of Putin's criticism (he was then premier of the country and thus not in direct control of foreign policy of the nation), Russia did not veto the U.N. Security Council 1973 Resolution which enabled NATO to start bombarding Libya, leading to the collapse of Gadafi's regime and his cruel assassination. Several times before, the same influence was noticeable in Russian policy towards Iran, Syria and some other nations disliked by the West. The stubborn support for President Assad's regime in Syria that Moscow Sovereignists now demonstrate is an apparent reaction to those developments in Libya.

Richard Sakwa, a respected British scholar, admits the Atlantic integrationists did not want to perceive "the hegemonic character of the present international order, the systemic inadequacies of the neo-liberal economy, and the structural demands placed upon Russia by its geopolitical location and history. Liberals are typically only too happy to throw all this on the bonfire of the arbitrariness of the regime."[3]

At the same time the Eurasian Sovereignists opposing them might often exaggerate Moscow's strength, its ability to go it alone and its alliance with China or some other non-Western nations. However, as Vladimir Putin himself admitted, "Russia should scare its neighbors less, but should work to rid itself of its imperial image which prevents even Europe from cooperating with us."[4] Russia needs more foreign investments and technological cooperation, and the ongoing Western information war against the country has already done enormous harm to it. Better relations with the US and its allies would be very helpful and highly valuable.

---

1 *Op. cit.*
2 For the expression of this liberal attitude see Fyodor Lukyanov, "Foreign Policy Breaking Away from National Interests," *RIA Novosti*, December 26, 2013, and to a lesser extent and in a more nuanced way Sergei Karaganov, "A Lop-Sided Power", *http://eng.globalaffairs.ru*, December 26, 2013.
3 Richard Sakwa, *Op. cit.*
4 "Conversation with Vladimir Putin," http://government.ru/eng/docs/1709/videohtml15.12.2011

However, in the first decade of the 21st century, all Putin's and Medvedev's efforts to achieve a real reconciliation with and acceptance from the West did not bring the expected results. As professor Andrei Tsygankov correctly indicates, "The psychological and ideological traits of national leaders do not fully explain this divide. The larger course of the divide between Russia and the West is a disagreement between national elites over the emerging world order."[1] Western nations continue to consider themselves as the leading part of the world, and they want the others to accept their leadership and the priority of their interests. The Russian Sovereignists do not want to submit to these demands, though the Russian Atlantic Integrationists are more inclined to do that. The bitter struggle among them, which is still far from being solved, might decide not only the foreign policy strategy of the country but also its civilizational choice for the future.[2]

Internal debate and political divisions within the Russian political and even the economic elites are largely focused on Russia's international relations and foreign policy. This has been caused by three main factors:

1. As noted above, at present all Russian elites with the possible exception of the Communists and some other much smaller radical left-wing groups support the pro-capitalist transformations in the country, or at least consider them to be irreversible.

2. As I will discuss, Russia has always been in a particularly vulnerable and sensitive geopolitical and even geo-civilizational situation, which, since the late 1980s, has further deteriorated. By the end of the 20th century, the very survival of Russia as a state and nation could have been a matter of serious doubt. Even now, according to a number of analysts, Putin's 2013 foreign policy achievements have apparently remained just tactical and cannot change the general situation and weakening of the country. As I discuss later, during the last two years (2014–2015) the new "Cold War" with the West has taken a heavy toll on Russia's economy and the international image of the country. Though I consider Putin's policy to be essentially defensive, some of his steps might have been used by the West to further increase the anti-Russian campaign and international tension. However, according to the former Carnegie Endowment President Jessica Mathews: "no other politician can play so well as Putin with such a weak hand."[3]

---

1 Andrei Tsygankov, "Great Divide with West", *Moscow Times*, September 9, 2013.
2 Tatiana A. Shakleina, "Russia Between West and East", http://www. allacademic.com/ise/ise06/indo pp. Click_kg_2.
3 Dmitri Trenin, "Putin's Syria Gambit Aims at Something Bigger Syria. What is Russia up in the Middle East?" www.tabletmag.com

3. In Russia, which is a historical nation with a long tradition of past development, the issues of its place in the world and its international status can find a strong appeal and interest among the whole population, and not only among the socio-political elites. And because of that the situation there is quite a difference from that in North America and even some European nations, where such issues are usually left for the consideration of the elites and groups of experts.

One of the most negative outcomes of Russia's domestic problems is the fact that, with the possible exception of its traditional zone of influence, the country does not have any convincing soft power in the eyes of the world community.[1] If the Russian Empire claimed to be the protector of the Slavs and Eastern Orthodoxy as well as the transmitter of European civilization to the vast expanses of Eurasia, and the Soviet Union was, at least until the mid-1960s, seen by many as the champion of socialism and the leader of an ideological alternative to the Western world,[2] during the last 20 years or more, the Russian Federation's foreign policy has been devoid of any deep theoretical, framework and ideological premises.[3] In the era of mass media and the Internet, the bare appeal to pragmatically understood self-interest, the understanding of which could often be dubious and questionable, cannot be sufficient to win international recognition and support. The most powerful empire in history, the United States, achieved its position largely because of its enormous reserve of skillfully operated soft power, and similar efforts could be observed in the cases of a number of other great states of the era such as, for instance Britain, France and China.[4] As one of former Russian President Dmitry Medvedev's advisors, Igor Yurgens, admitted, "Russia has not formulated a unique value-based ideology similar to the Western ideology of democracy and post-industrial development. Nor has it demonstrated a success story comparable to that of other BRICS countries,"[5] one of which, China, has become the world factory. Partly due to that, and partly because of typical early post-Soviet neglect and privatization, if not an outward theft, of social (public) properties, Moscow started looking for

1 T. Gomart, "Dva Orientira dlya Rossii," *Rossiya V Globalnoi Politike*, 8/2010/Nz6, November / December, p. 121. See also A. Kramarenko, "Ideologiya Vneshnei Politiki Sovremennoi Rossii," *Mezhdunarodnaya Zhizn* 8-3/2009.

2 J. Panfilova, "Problemy Osmysleniya Mesta Rossii Mire," *Kosmopolis* 3/19/2007/2008 p. 41-42.

3 Igor Jurgen's, "Political Analyst sets out to develop soft power," *Rossiyskey Gazeta*, September 16, 2011.

4 J. S.Nye, Jr. *The paradox of American power. Why the world's only superpower can't do it alone*, Oxford University Press 2002 p. 69-76.

5 Jurgen's, *Op. cit.*

ways to influence the world media much later than the Americans or even some other non-Western nations.

One of the most blatant examples of the failure here was the case of major mass media presentation of the Russian–Georgian war in August 2008. As a former French diplomat and a member of the board of the prestigious International Institute for Strategic Studies (IISS) in London (Britain) admitted: "Everything that has been said by Georgia, the BBC and other hangers-on, was in fact a lie. It took a year for us, diplomats, the media, and everyone who wanted to know the truth, to turn the situation around."[1] Probably even more harmful for Moscow was the Western media's description of the last parliamentary and presidential election in Russia as a total fraud and sham, and the persistent characterization of President Vladimir Putin as a "ruthless dictator" who dismantled Russia's democratic and free market reforms in order to become a "totalitarian leader."[2] However, according to two respected and more unbiased American scholars on Russia, Professor Nicolai Petro, University of Rhode Island, who served as the US State Department's special assistant for policy on the Soviet Union under George H. Bush, and Gordon M. Hahn, Senior Associate of the Center for Strategic and International Studies (CSIS), Washington DC, the reality was rather different. As Professor Petro indicated: "The national exit polls by the Foundation for Public Opinion and VTsiom, as reported by the Christian Science Monitor and CBS News, were very close to the final results [in the parliamentary elections]. Such close correspondence is typically seen as evidence for the credibility of the overall vote tally, just as the discrepancy between the two was taken as evidence of fraud in Ukraine in 2011."[3] According to the more critical Dr. Hahn, "outright illegal fraud was limited to 2–3%, perhaps up to 5%, if you include all the quasi-peer pressure in the number."[4] Dr. Hahn himself did not want to do that because, as he noted, "peer pressure is a fact of life; there is no natural law which would say that

---

1 Russia and France. "A new Quality of relations – International roundtable," *International Affairs*, 57/2011/vol. p. 43

2 In fact almost all major newspapers such as the Moscow Times and Vedomosti and privately owned media in Moscow and St. Petersburg are openly extremely hostile to Putin and to existing regime see for instance the article by S. Korn, "New radio liberty to carry its old mission," *Moscow Times*, October 16, 2012 and the article by the editor of the paper M. Bohm, "Why the Foreign Ministry Should Keep Quiet," *Moscow Times*, November 2, 2012. Ironically Freedom House, located in Washington D.C., describes the Russian Federation as a "non-free country" the same as or even worse than China or Saudi Arabia.

3 "Russia profile weekly expert panel: From Arab Spring to Russian Winter," 12/16/2011.

4 Johnson's List, December 23, 2011 and the Gordon M. Hahn article: "The Thaw at the Polls. Tandem Liberalization Policy Rock the Vote", *Russia: Other Points of View*, December 8, 2011.

people must vote according to their true intention all the time, disregarding the opinions of their reference group."[1]

Elections in Russia, just like those in other countries at more or less the same socio-economic level of development, are often far from perfect, and in 1996 the Yeltsin presidential election seem to be rigged. The question remains, why did the recent parliamentary elections cause such an uproar and outburst of popular discontent and international condemnation, which had never been seen before, when those elections were probably relatively clean and when the ruling party, United Russia, counted 15% fewer votes than it did years earlier?

In 2012, although Vladimir Putin won the presidential elections with about 60% of the popular votes, the Western campaign against his election still continued, using for its purposes the demonstrations of the defeated Russian pro-liberal opposition.[2] Although the US professor Stephen K. Wegren argues, "No one questioned whether Putin actually won the presidential election,"[3] the reactions of the American establishment and its allies implied something rather different. The official recognition of Putin's election was long delayed and even after that the Russian leader has been constantly attacked and demonized.

The biased or in any case exaggerated propaganda, which was supported in Russia itself by part of the pro-Western opposition in the country, was in fact quite effective.[4] The campaign to discredit the Sochi Olympic Games in February 2014, which Barack Obama and other Western leaders including Canadian Prime Minister Stephen Harper, and the French and German presidents François Hollande and Joachim Gauck, did not attend in order to demonstrate an unofficial protest over real or alleged Russian human rights concerns, in particular the law against "gay propaganda" that Moscow enacted in 2012, was only a further part of the continuing information war against the country and its vital interests.[5]

---

1 Ibid.

2 Nicolai Petro, "How to not lose Russia," *Asia Times*, March 12, 2012.

3 Stephen K. Wegren ed., *Return to Putin's Russia. Past Imperfect, Future Uncertain.* Rowman Littlefield Publishers, Inc., 2013, p2. According to the official data in 2012 Putin polled 63.36% of votes. However, in Moscow which was the stronghold of the opposition only 46.9%. Even if in some districts Putin's supporters secured a number of fraudulent votes and Chechnya and Dagestan, which experienced strife of civil war proportions, the result of the poll could have been compromised, his overwhelming victory cannot be questioned. David Lane, *The Capitalist Transformation of State Socialism, The making and breaking of state socialist society and what's followed.* London: Routledge, 2014, p. 296.

4 According to Gallup poll on September 18, 2013. 50% of the Americans consider Russia unfriendly or an enemy of American interests and 54% of them had an unfavourable opinion of Putin, Gallup Politics, January 12, 2014.

5 Moscow expected the Sochi Olympic Games to improve Russia's international image and to increase country's soft power.

In Russia there has now been some reaction against it. Patriarch Kirill, head of the Russian Orthodox Church, noted that "physical battles have been replaced by information wars. A battle for minds is in progress from which we must not retreat,"[1] and some experts are calling for Russia to "stop shying away from defending itself in the foreign press."[2]

However, in spite of some tactical achievements, Moscow is still on the defensive in foreign policy matters. It still does not have the strength or opportunity to formulate an international agenda; it can only participate in discussing such an agenda.[3] The reason for that is not that the Russian leaders do not understand the current international agenda; they simply do not have enough power at their disposal to be more proactive and effective, and any of their efforts in this direction are immediately counteracted. At present only Americans, and in the Middle East Israel, can do that, and even they are not always successful.

The third major source of present difficulties is the fact that the geopolitical situation of Russia, which has always been a challenge, is now getting even worse.[4] As one leading US expert, Thomas Graham, indicates, "in contrast to the past, Russia is no longer the dynamic core of Eurasia... it is surrounded beyond the former Soviet space by states and regions of greater energy. Chinese power, radical Islamic fervor, and European prosperity are penetrating into Russia's historical space or acting as powerful poles of attraction for former Soviet states including regions of Russia proper."[5] This reversal of the former balance of power which started during the Gorbachev era has already lasted for a generation, and a return to the traditional pattern does not seem either certain or imminent.

Although in my opinion neither China in the East nor the Islamic world in the South can now create any major threat to Russian state security, the situation seems to be different in the West where, during the last two decades, two main pillars of Western power, the EU and NATO, "have moved their borders steadily eastward."[6] In practice, both these organization have excluded Russia from their membership, and as even some American scholars admit, "No state would welcome the extension of an historically hostile military alliance up to its borders no matter how often the alliance

1 "Patriarch Kirill Comes out for Russian History", RIA Novosti, October 2, 2012.
2 "Russia Should Stop Shying Away from Defending Itself in the Foreign Press", interview by A. Pankin of W. Dunkerley, *Komsomolskaya Pravda*, October 22, 2012.
3 "Russia and France: A New Quality of Relations, "International Roundtable", *International Affairs*, 57/2011 No.1, p.43.
4 George Friedman, "The Geopolitics of Russia: Permanent struggle," *Stratford* 10/15/2008.
5 Thomas Graham, "Managing Russian Unsettled Borders", *Nezavisimaya Gazeta*, April 18, 2011.
6 *Op. cit.*

said its intentions were peaceable."[1] In addition NATO is led by the US, which is not a Eurasian but a global power whose strategic goals of global domination are evidently contradictory to Russian national interests.

Since all the former Warsaw Pact countries have joined NATO, the conventional armed forces treaty in Europe negotiated in 1990 has lost its previous meaning, and the European security system has been turned against Russia. As a prominent American international relations scholar and leading neo-realist, Kenneth Waltz, observed, "rather than learning from history, the United States repeats past errors by expanding NATO eastwards and extending its influence over what used to be the provinces of the vanquished. Despite much talk about the 'globalization' of international politics, American political leaders, to a dismaying extent, think of East or West rather than of their interaction."[2]

On June 12, 2002, US President George W. Bush's administration abrogated the ABM treaty, which for 30 years had provided both Moscow and Washington with certain guarantees of security and mutual survival. Even though some American experts and politicians criticized this decision as harmful to international peace, or at least premature and unnecessary,[3] it was nevertheless a logical consequence of the shift in the balance of power, and it was an expression of America's quest for global dominance, which became a goal of the leaders of the United States. Keeping in mind NATO expansion in Eastern Europe, which still plans to include Georgia and Ukraine, the deployment of anti-ballistic missiles in Poland, Romania and some other European countries, which was approved by the NATO summit in Chicago on May 20–21, 2012, and the relentless propaganda and psychological warfare against Moscow which accelerated during and after the 2011/2012 Russian parliamentary and presidential elections, one might start to believe that despite the disappearance of the Soviet Union and the enormous social political transformations in Russia itself[4], the Cold War against the country has not come to an end.[5]

Even according to the report prepared by the American Carnegie Endowment Center for International Peace in Moscow, though Moscow recognizes an immediate threat coming from the political and religious

1 A. Shleifer, D. Treisman, "Why Moscow Says No: A Question of Russian Interest, Not Psychology," *Foreign Affairs*, January – February 2011 p.128.

2 Kenneth Waltz, "Globalization and American power," *National Interest*, spring 2000 p.55

3 David Krieger, "Farewell to the ABM treaty by David Krieger" *Nuclear Power Foundation*, June 13, 2002.

4 Mark Adomanis, "7 Reasons that Russia is Not the Soviet Union", *Forbes*, December 31, 2013.

5 Stephen F. Cohen, *Soviet Fates and Lost Alternatives: From Stalinism to the new Cold War*, New York: Columbia University Press, 2011, p. 162-220.

radicalization in the Moslem world in the South, "strategically the United States is still Russia's de facto main political adversary."[1]

The US policy towards Moscow has been determined by geo-strategic and geo-economic considerations, which are overwhelmingly important for Washington, and probably no efforts by Russian leaders would have been able to achieve the kind of mutual recognition and partnership which they desired.

Even though the ideological and social systemic antagonism, which at least officially lay at the core of the Cold War, ended a long time ago, American hostility and various forms of tensions with Moscow have persisted for at least two major reasons:

1. Since the end of World War II, the US has followed and still follows the traditional British policy of preventing one single independent power center from dominating the rest of the continent much less Eurasia as a whole. As Thomas Graham admits: "The United States as a matter of policy has sought to prevent the re-emergence of a threat of Soviet dimensions in Eurasia," and the ideological identity of the potential rival has been of only secondary importance. That is why "since only Russia could form the core of such a renewed threat, US policy has sought to limit Russia's options in the former Soviet states and enhance the independence of all the former Soviet states."[2] For the same reasons Washington has provided vigorous support to a belt of mainly newly-established states across Eastern and Central Europe, from the Baltic and the Black Sea to the Adriatic, which although formally independent, have been friendly to the United States and hostile to Russia. During the last decade all those countries were admitted to NATO and the EU. The most recent example of this policy is America's vigorous opposition against the creation of the Eurasian Economic Community and the common economic space of some post-Soviet nations.[3] Washington still considers Russia a defeated country on probation and wants to

---

1 A. Malashenko, M. Lipman, D. Trenin, N. Petro, "Russia on the Move, Policy Outlook," Carnegie Endowment for International Peace, http://carnegie.ru/2012/06/01/russia-on-move/b16g
2 Graham, *Op. cit.*
3 In December 2012 the U.S. secretary of State Hilary Clinton clearly articulated this American opposition, saying that this is an attempt to re-integrate the post-Soviet countries into a new Soviet Union type Union. According to her, "It is not going to be called that {USSR}. It is going to be called Custom Union, it will be called Eurasian Union and all of that. But let's make no mistake about it. We knew what the goal is and we are trying to figure out effective ways to slow down or prevent it". "Failed reset: United States decries 'Sovietization' of former USSR states", 10. 12. ARMENIANOW.com

submit the whole post-Soviet Russian zone of influence to the old Roman rule: *divide et impera* (to divide and to rule over).

2. The second reason is the fact that Russia has always been and still remains one of the richest countries in terms of almost all natural resources, and it is still a relatively independent nation. American and multinational corporations do not have free, unlimited access to its natural resources, and whatever they had achieved during the Gorbachev–Yeltsin period was later limited or returned to Russian control.[1] In this case the Americans and their allies can count on firm support from a part of the Russian oligarchs (the comprador bourgeoisie) whose business interests are linked with the foreign companies and who have located their money in US and other Western banks and other institutions. As those people control many media outlets in Russia itself, their influence could be very beneficial for Western interests and harmful for the Russian government.

In my opinion the deepest and probably the most important causes of Russia's predicament should be traced back to the interests of the American and European financial and political elites. As American professor Andrew Levine comments, President Eisenhower's warning notwithstanding, "the erstwhile republic [the USA] became a warfare state, [and] it needed enemies."[2] After Gorbachev's capitulation at the summit meeting with the American President George H. Bush at Malta in December 1989 and the ensuing collapse of the USSR, the American power elite urgently needed to find a suitable new replacement in the form of bogus enemies in order to provide profit for its Industrial Military Complex and to preserve the existing socio-economic and political system.[3]

The alternatives which have been suggested, such as "the war against terrorism" after 2001 and the neo-colonial style interventions in the Middle East and certain other Asian and African nations, seem to have been insufficient and failed to convince the majority of Americans. Russia, the former and, as they believed, the defeated Cold War enemy, fit the bill perfectly.

In a marked contrast to all of America's previous real or attempted military interventions in Vietnam, Afghanistan, Iraq, Somalia, Syria and a number of other places, where some dissent has always been heard, when it

---

1 About Russia's economic disengagement from the U.S. see Andrei Shleifer and Daniel Treisman, op at p. 133.

2 Andrew Levine, "Cold War Obama Style," *Counterpunch*, May 16–18, 2014.

3 Because the present American Congress' corruption some American commentators have now started to write about the Military-Industrial-Congress Complex.

comes to Russia — and Putin especially — almost all the political elites and media have provided their unlimited support, which in fact exceeded even traditional support for Israel in its conflicts with the Palestinians.

According to Dmitri Trenin, "It is logical that Putin does not need trouble with the US. However, the US dimension of Russia's foreign policy is among its most challenging."[1] Although Trenin, who is the Director of the American Carnegie Fund Center in Moscow, does not want to discuss the issue in depth, and even blamed Putin for "using crude anti-Americanism against his liberal opponents, accusing them of being in the US government's pay,"[2] the reality of American relations with post-Soviet Moscow is of the greatest importance for the present development and future of Russia.

The collapse of the USSR and the critical situation in Russia itself made the US an apparent winner and, at least for a while, the dominate global power. As Charles Krauthammer noted, the post-Cold War world then became not multi-polar but, perhaps for the first time in human history, truly unipolar.[3] As he wrote: "The center of world power is the unchallenged superpower, the United States attended by its Western allies."[4] Although Krauthammer had been seen as an aggressive right-wing analyst, soon the American mainstream journalists, scholars and politicians accepted his opinion. Moscow's loss of its previous allies and the enormous socio-economic and political crisis in Russia, which threatened further disintegration of the nation, seemed to justify and confirm their decision. Consequently the successor state of the Soviet Union, the Russian Federation, started to be perceived in a way similar to Germany and Japan after World War II, as a defeated nation which could not expect to "be treated as equal."[5] Going even further, Russia started to be denied the right to run its domestic affairs without constant interference and supervision from the US and/or the EU.[6]

Applying these assumptions towards a nation with whom one is not in a state of war but with whom one is entertaining normal diplomatic relations has been highly unusual and offensive, but beyond that, this kind of policy would in my view be wrong for at least four main reasons:

---

1 Dmitri Trenin, "What will Putin do in foreign policy?", *Diplomaatia*, Tallinn, May 2012 no.105
2 *Op. cit.*
3 Charles Krauthammer, "The Unipolar Moment", *Foreign Affairs*, vol. 70, No 1, 1990/91
4 *Op. cit.*
5 Mark Katz, "Can Russia Be a Great Power?" *Moscow Times*, January 26, 2004. Similarly Anne Appelbaum on *Washington Post*, April 19, 2003.
6 The prestigious American Council of Foreign Relations argued that the US had the right to reject Russia's future elections and its leaders as illegitimate (Council of Foreign Relations, *Russia's Wrong Direction*, New York, 2006). Similarly one of the leading American experts on Russia, Celeste Wallander, wrote that the Russian political system as a whole "lack any legitimacy" (Johnson's Russian List/ JRL), December 3, 2006.

1. The collapse of the USSR and the decline of Russia were caused by internal crises and were not the outcome of any US military victory and occupation of the country, as had been the case in Germany and Japan. The Americans therefore have neither direct power nor the moral authority to claim comparable rights and privileges in the target country.

2. In spite of all its problems the Russian Federation is still a powerful nation and is second or equal to the US as a nuclear power in the world. A violent bilateral conflict might cause a war with unpredictable and painful consequences for both sides.

3. It is very doubtful that the US would be able to control and introduce its peace and order to the whole Eurasian landmass. It was apparently unable to do that either in Afghanistan or Iraq, which are incomparably smaller than the former Soviet Union. It is far more likely that after the destruction of Russia, this great semi-continent has become a center of new threats and conflicts. Both China and militant Islamism might prove to be the real winner, which would be more difficult to check.

4. At least for now, I do not see any convincing reasons for America's new Cold War against Russia. This country is perhaps still able to resist foreign invasion, but unlike the Soviet Union, it does not and cannot represent any real security threat to the overwhelming US military, economic and soft power. In addition, as has been discussed before, a substantial, though as yet not decisive, part of the Russian elites is quite pro-Western, and the Russian leaders including Putin himself have already made many substantial concessions to the West. While the US has good (and by now well-established) relations with different countries such as China and Saudi Arabia, which have completely different political systems and ideologies from the US, Washington's hostility to Moscow seems difficult to explain on an ideological basis. Few people want to remember now that Putin's ascension to the presidency in 2000 was well received by the American establishment and mainstream media, which at that time compared him favorably with his predecessor Boris Yeltsin.[1] Being brought to power by the Russian financial oligarchs who

---

[1] The prominent American scholar on Russia Martin Malia assured even Wall Street Journal readers that Yeltsin had triumphantly found a "like-minded successor" and brought his own era to "this promising finale," *Wall Street Journal*, March 15, 2008. Some American journalists were even ready to welcome Putin as "a human version of Peter the Great." Stephan F. Cohen, *Failed Crusade America and the Tragedy of Post-Communist Russia*, New York: W.W. Norton, 2000, p. 173.

wanted him to protect their interests, he was unlikely to be either anti-capitalist or anti-Western.[1] The symbol of that policy course was his immediate support of Washington after September 11, 2001, and its expression was his speech on October 5, 2001, in Germany's Bundestag.[2] He also made a number of strategic concessions to the US, then facilitating American's easy victory in Afghanistan and closing Russian military bases in Cuba and Vietnam.

A number of commentators then described his decisions as an "attempt to embrace the West" and as an abandonment of former Prime Minister Yevgeny Primakov's multi-polar concept.[3] After the collapse of the Soviet Union, not many Russian ships ventured into the Indian Ocean and South Pacific, so the Cam Ranh naval base in Vietnam was perhaps of little importance. However, the Electronic Surveillance Centre at Lourdes in Cuba was an ideal "listening post" and Russia was able to get more than 75% of its intelligence data on the US through the center. Its closure, which was criticized by both the Russian intelligence offices and the Cuban officials, was seen as a special gift presented by Putin to US President George W. Bush in order to soften his stance on the AMB Treaty and to accept Russia's admission to the World Trade organization.[4]

None of those expectations came true. On December 13, 2001, President George W. Bush announced that the US would withdraw from the Anti-Ballistic Missile Treaty in six months. Although at that time American anti-ballistic missiles could not represent a major threat to the Russian nuclear deterrent, the Bush administration's decision was the beginning of a consistent effort to achieve full spectrum nuclear dominance.

Of more pressing concern was NATO's expansion in the Russian neighborhood and in the former Soviet zone of influence. President Clinton's administration did not want to respect the promises of George H. Bush's administration that, in return for Moscow's acceptance of a reunited Germany as a NATO member, the Western military alliance would never "move one inch to the East."[5] However, after the fall of the Soviet Union

---

1 *Op. cit.* pp. 169–175.

2 "Putin Tells Budenstag: "The Cold War is Over."" *Executive Intelligence Review*, October 5, 2001. For the comments about the political importance of this speech see Dimitri Trenin, "What will Putin do in foreign policy?" *Diplomatia* May 2012

3 John Cherian, "Putin's games. Russia announced the closure of its military facilities in Cuba and Vietnam is seen as an attempt to appease the West," *Frontline India's National Magazine from the publishers of HINDU*, vol. 18, issue 23, November 10-23, 2001.

4 *Op. cit.*

5 Stephen F. Cohen, *Soviet Fates and the Lost Alternatives*, p. 172. See also Philip Zelikov, Condolezza Rice, *Germany Unified and Europe Transformed. A Study in Statecraft*, Cambridge Massachusetts: Harvard University Press, 1995, p. 183 and

and the ensuing changes in the European and global balance of power all these promises were quickly forgotten. In July 1997, the NATO Summit in Madrid invited Poland, the Czech Republic, and Hungary to start official negotiations in order to join the alliance. After the positive conclusion on December 16, 1997, on March 12, 1999, those three nations became NATO members. It was just the first step on the way to Russia's encirclement.

In spite of all Putin's pro-American concessions in 2001, in November 2002 NATO's Summit in Prague invited three former Soviet Republics: Lithuania, Latvia, and Estonia, to join the alliance. According even to pro-American Polish experts, this new enlargement "radically deteriorated the geostrategic situation of Russia,"[1] surrounding the Russian enclave in Kaliningrad and deploying NATO forces at the Russian borders very near its former capital and second most important city, St. Petersburg.[2] Following that, the West has been active in two other former Soviet republics, Georgia and Ukraine, stirring up international tensions.

During the years 2011-2013, serious tension between Moscow and Washington was focused on two major issues:

- The civil war in Syria and the notion of the Western powers' right to intervene in the domestic affairs of another nation under their adopted policy of "Responsibility to Protect" (R2P).
- The ABM deployment in Europe and probably also in the Arctic and in Asia, which disregarding even their present efficiency, might in any case undermine the existing geostrategic balance of power and change the present geopolitical situation in Europe.

However, in the spring of 2014 the Ukraine crisis evolved into the most recent and even more severe culmination of an extended process of estrangement between Russia and the West. As an American scholar observed, "Ukraine is Russia's single biggest national security issue beyond its borders,"[3] and not only the present Russian leaders but also the majority of Russians considered the Kiev coup of February 21, 2014, and the Western political takeover of this country, as a vital threat to their national interests.

For Russian leaders, Ukraine, which during Soviet times used to be the second most important Union republic after the Russian Federation, has always been and still remains perhaps the most important Russian neighbor.

Stephen F. Szabo, *The Diplomacy of German Unification*, New York: St. Martin Press, 1992, p. 62. Gorbachev strongly insisted on this Western obligation, saying to the U.S. Secretary that "Any extension of the zone of NATO is unacceptable." Baker replied "I agree" (Zelikov, Ric, p. 183).

1 "Ekspansja USA na 'rosyjska strefe wplywow," *Stosunki miedzynarodowe info* 2009-30 80.20.42

2 *Op. cit.*

3 Ian Bremmer, "A Tortured Policy Toward Russia," *New York Times*, March 26, 2014.

Among the many reasons for this are Ukraine's geopolitical location adjacent to other European nations, its better climate, and the similarity in language, culture and history of the populations of Russia and Ukraine. However, an often overlooked but most important fact is that Russia, which is a very large country, is now for the most part landlocked and lacking access to all-season ports. At present Moscow has only its enclave Kaliningrad in the north, on the Baltic Sea — and access to it is limited by Lithuania and Poland, plus Crimean Sevastopol, and Novorossiysk in the neighboring Krasnodar krai on the Black Sea. Ports of the Russian Far East, such as Vladivostok on the Pacific Ocean, are located too far from the Russian population and economic centers to be of much help. Only ports on the Black Sea, and especially Sevastopol, which is well developed and surrounded by the historical legend of victory, can provide Moscow relatively easy access to the Mediterranean Sea and a chance to play an active role in developments in the Middle Eastern and in Southern Europe and Northern Africa.

In his 1997 book the *Grand Chessboard*, Zbigniew Brzezinski argues, "Ukraine is a geopolitical pivot because its very existence as an independent [from Russia] country helps to transform Russia."[1] In his view, if "Moscow regains control over Ukraine, with its [at that time] 52 million people and major resources as well as access to the Black Sea, Russia automatically regains the wherewithal to become a powerful imperial state, spanning Europe and Asia."[2] Such a powerful Russia would be a serious obstacle to the persistence of American global hegemony and the unipolar world system, which until now all American presidential administrations have wanted to continue.

Ukraine became an independent nation in December 1991, after the end of the Soviet Union, but many economic and political links with Russia still persisted. The first Western attempt to divide the two nations was the Orange Revolution, in November 2004, after the vociferously claimed presidential election fraud in Ukraine. The election of President Viktor Yanukovych was invalidated and Viktor Yushchenko, who was at that time the opposition candidate supported by the West, was named. However, Yushchenko failed to meet popular expectations and both he and his political party proved to be no less corrupt than their predecessors. In the 2010 Ukrainian elections, he won only 5.5% of the vote and Yanukovych, who gained 52.5%, was re-elected as president of the country.

While Yushchenko was very pro-Western and wanted Ukraine to join NATO, Yanukovych, who represented the eastern and southern provinces of the country, which are largely of Eastern Orthodox religion and Russian-

---

1 Zbigniew Brzezinski, *The Grand Chessboard: American Primacy and Its Geostrategic Imperatives*, New York: Basic Books, 1997, p. 46.
2 *Op. cit.*

speaking, was more inclined to cooperate with Moscow and preserve the neutral status of Ukraine. At the same time he wanted to keep the close ties with the West, and in November 2013 he intended to sign the Association Agreement with the European Union. However, because the preconditions set by Brussels would have had a negative impact on the more industrially developed eastern and southern parts of the Ukraine and would have degraded the situation of the working people in the country, and because the economic assistance offered by the EU was at that time insufficient, he asked for a delay in the signing of the agreement. He also asked Russian President Vladimir Putin for a quick and quite substantial loan ($15 billion) and other economic help. Moscow, which was uneasy to see Ukraine's association with the EU, was ready to provide the economic assistance, but President Yanukovych's political about-turn caused discontent among the pro-Western Ukrainian oligarchs and among a large part of Western Ukrainian nationalists.

The result was "Maidan" (an ongoing gathering of protesters) in Kiev and unrest in other parts of the country. The USA and the EU strongly and openly supported the opposition to Yanukovych's actions. Political officials such as the US Deputy Secretary of State Victoria Nuland, US Senator John McCain, EU leaders and the foreign ministers of Poland, Sweden and other countries visited Kiev in order to support them against Yanukovych. Ukraine, just like almost all post-Soviet type socialist countries, was in practice a plutocracy ruled by groups of the new-rich oligarchs, and the social problems were probably even more severe than in other similar nations. Thus, the protest movement against the president, legitimately elected in 2010, was able to achieve strength and importance. Many people hoped to improve their everyday economic and social conditions, as Western and pro-Western propaganda promised they would. Victoria Nuland admitted that the Americans generously funded the movement to the tune of $5 billion,[1] and probably more help came from other countries allied with Washington.

At the same time, even though Ukraine is a country of crucial importance for Moscow, the Russian leaders, including Putin himself, seemed to be focused mainly on the Sochi Olympic Games and perhaps underestimated the seriousness of the Ukrainian developments. Putin stated that he was not even aware of the coming putsch in Kiev, and in order to appease the West, he persuaded Yanukovych to sign, on February 21, 2014, an agreement with the opposition which apparently satisfied all its demands, including forming

---

1 Regime Change in Kiev, Victoria Nuland Admits: US Has Invested $5 Billion in the Development of Ukrainian "Democratic Institutions" International Business Conference in Washington-National Press Club – December 13, 2013. Posted on February 9, 2014, www.informationclearinghouse.info/article37599. htm

a temporary "national unity" government, planning speedy presidential and parliamentary elections, and a return to the 2004 constitution, removing some of the president's powers.

Putin, who in December 2013 offered Ukraine a Russian loan of $15 billion without preconditions, and who wanted to preserve the stability of this country, was taken by surprise. As he had said at his press conference on March 4, 2014, he had not anticipated that the agreement sponsored by the EU, and one that was very favorable for the opposition, would almost immediately be violated. However, although Yanukovych had complied with all his obligations, the following night the opposition, supported by Ukrainian radical nationalists (the Right Sector or Pravy Sektor) took power by force in the capital of the country and President Yanukovych, in fear for his life, had to flee.

The details and motivations of the actors involved remained far from clear and can still be disputed as of this writing (late 2014). However, the radical opposition takeover was certainly violent and unconstitutional. It was also in accordance with US government interests in the country.

Because of Ukraine's geopolitical importance to Russia, American leaders have long wanted to prevent any kind of Kiev–Moscow rapprochement, preferring instead to alienate the two countries and make them hostile to each other. At the time when Moscow was working to create the Eurasian Economic Community, including Ukraine, this issue became even more urgent for Washington. In addition, Moscow's active role in the Middle East, particularly in Syria, and to a lesser extent in Iran, greatly irritated America and might have led them to create more problems for Russia in its close neighborhood. For Washington, it would be preferable to cut Moscow off from access to the Black Sea and thus to limit its direct naval contact with the Eastern Mediterranean countries. It is also possible that at the time when, due to its new fracking policies, the US had become the largest provider of gas and oil in the world, it was especially keen to eliminate possible competitors such as Russia and Iran.

The post revolution Ukrainian government led by Prime Minister Arseniy Yatsenyuk is the most anti-Russian and most Russo phobic in Ukrainian history. One of its first decisions was to forbid the use of the Russian language in state offices, teaching, schools, and media, even though almost half the country's citizens are native Russian speakers and a great majority of them are familiar with this language and culture. At the beginning of February, Yatsenyuk had already been recommended for the post of Prime Minister by the US Deputy Secretary of State, Victoria Nuland, in her phone call to the US Ambassador in Kiev, Geoffrey Pyatt (this call was leaked to the media on

February 6, 2014).[1] One of the consequences was that, as Professor Andrei Tsygankov has noted: "The February revolution in Ukraine, in violation of the agreement reached by Ukrainian President Victor Yanukovych and opposition, means the end of all hopes to normalize relations with the Obama administration."[2] Expressing a view common among such commentators, the American expert on the former Soviet countries and a member of political establishments admits that "the disequilibrium and instability triggered by the Ukraine crisis seems likely to endure for some time, [while] the search for a 'new normal' promises to be long, costly and highly disruptive to both individuals and international order."[3]

The present Ukrainian crisis is complex and it could have numerous causes, but the most important reason for its severity and the difficulty of finding a solution acceptable to all sides can be found in the contradictory geopolitical interests of Russia and the West. While Putin, "a defensive thinker,"[4] is aiming to protect Russia's national interests in its direct neighborhood, to secure the country's access to the warm waters of the Black Sea, and to protect the rights of the Russian speakers in eastern and southern Ukraine, Washington's goals are to contain Russia and to prevent it from strengthening its international position, to breathe new life into NATO (which is its major global military instrument), and probably also to strengthen its position in the global energy market. In its dangerous essence this local crisis might now boil down to a confrontation between American full-spectrum imperial aspirations and Putin's "last stand" to defend Russia's historical rights and traditions. For Russia the stakes are much higher. As a CIA veteran admitted: "Whether we like to think this way or not, Russia has a substantially greater strategic interest in the distribution of power in and around Ukraine than the United States."[5]

Although Russia's annexation of Crimea from Ukraine might have been seen as violating some commonly accepted international legal principles,[6] just like the separation of Kosovo from Serbia that was supported by the West (and which Moscow at the time strongly opposed), the Russian move

---

1 "Ukraine Crisis: Transcript of Leaked Nuland-Pyatt call," *BBC New Europe*, 7 February 2014.
2 Andrei Tsygankov, "Ukraine is Putin's last stand," *Moscow Times*, April 27, 2014.
3 Samuel Charap, "The Ukraine crisis and the search for a new normal," *International Institute for Strategic Studies*, www.iis.org, April 24, 2014.
4 Tsygankov, *Op. cit.*
5 Paul Pillar, "Twist of History and Interests in Ukraine," *The National Interest*, April 20, 2014.
6 The international law might be seen as ambiguous on this question of Crimea. Although it stresses the principles of sovereignty and territorial integrity of the nations, which the Americans many times violated, the UN Charter has also included "the right of nations to self-determination" (Article 2, Chapter I), and in July 2010 the UN International Court of Justice ruled that "general international law contains no prohibitions on a declaration of independence."

was a reaction to the coup in Kiev on February 21, 2014, and was considered by the Russian leaders and the majority of the Russian population as an indispensable step in assuring the security of the nation.

Russia could not have had any interest in initiating the Ukrainian crisis. The Ukrainian President Yanukovych was not a Putin puppet or even a close political ally; he represented Eastern Ukrainian oligarchs, and was willing to cooperate with both the West and Moscow (Russia was a major market for Ukrainian industries and provided Yanukovych with relatively inexpensive gas and oil. In addition, any destabilization of Ukraine could have had numerous geopolitical and socio-economic implications for the situation in Russia itself. The Western politicians, media and academics have already blamed Vladimir Putin for all possible vices, but they have never (to the best of my knowledge) been able to accuse him of a lack of realism and political acumen.

Both the origins of the Ukrainian crisis and the present critical situation in the country resulted from covert or open Western interventions.[1] Moscow, as almost always, was only able to react to them. Its reactions might have been clumsy or ineffective, but overall they have still been remarkably mild and cautious. One can only imagine the American or even the Chinese reaction to similar acts of destabilization in their geopolitically vital neighborhood.

Russia did not initiate "Maidan" and it cannot be held responsible for the violent overthrow of the elected president and the constitutional order as it existed in Ukraine in February 2014. It is quite noticeable that, as I have already mentioned, during the Olympic Games in Sochi and for some time even after that, Moscow tried to keep its distance and showed restraint in its reactions to the Ukrainian events. According to the Polish Foreign Minister Radoslaw Sikorski, it was Putin himself who on February 21, 2014, persuaded Yanukovych to sign the agreement with the opposition, which in fact seemed to satisfy all its demands and might have meant his political capitulation.

The violent coup, which took place just a few hours later, greatly surprised not only Putin but also many other observers. I think that one of the most likely causes of the development was the fact that the people who initiated the coup knew they did not stand a chance in the coming elections. They had already lost twice before in elections and now they had accepted the IMF austerity program, which could not have made them more popular, especially among the working class people of the eastern and southern

---

1 In his very hostile article about Putin and the Russian majority, Mark Ames admits: "The fact that we, the US and EU and a few billionaires, funded violent regime change groups in bed with Ukraine fascists and Russophobes has only made Putin's domestic job [to attract the Russian majority] easier." Mark Ames, "Sorry America, the Ukraine isn't all about you," http://pando.com/2014/05/14/sorry-america-the-ukraine-isnt-all-about-you/, May 14, 2014.

regions. Additional impetus probably came from the Americans, who did not want to lose the results of their $5 billion investment in the insurgent "Maidan" movement in the country and whose Industrial Military Complex needed a new Cold War with Russia.

Moscow seems to have recognized the situation created by the coup. On May 7, 2014, after his talks with the Swiss president, Putin stated that, although "in Russia's view, the blame for the crisis in Ukraine lies with those who organized the coup d'état in Kiev on February 21, 2014...whatever the case, we must look for a way to solve the situation as it is today."[1] In his view, "What is needed is direct, fully fledged and equal dialogue between the Kiev authorities and the representatives of the people in southeast Ukraine. I believe that if we want to find a long term solution to the crisis, there must be an open, honest and equal dialogue."[2]

At the same time the Russian president expressed Moscow's support for the presidential election in Ukraine on May 25, 2014, even though Moscow had had many doubts before about holding it, given the situation in the country.

Relations between Moscow and the separatist movement in eastern and southern Ukraine are far from being clear and simple. Putin had tried to dissuade them from holding a referendum on their self-determination and to invite them for a dialogue and peaceful accommodation with the rest of Ukraine. He had also accepted the "roadmap" proposed by the OSCE Chairman and the Swiss President Didier Burkhalter. However, the secessionists in Donetsk and Lugansk did not want to listen to him, and on May 11, 2014, a referendum was held in Donetsk, and on May 18, 2014, in Lugansk. According to their organizers both elections brought overwhelming victories for the call for independence and the creation of two new statelets: Donetsk People's Republic and Lugansk People's Republic have been proclaimed.

Their future and further developments in Ukraine are, at the time of writing, difficult to predict. However, at the time a consensus had been growing among experts that the crisis there might still be resolved if different regions of the country were to grant broad local autonomy, going even as far as federalization of the political structures of the nation, and if the great power centers such as the US, the EU, and Russia stopped interfering in Ukraine's internal affairs. Because of the different geopolitical interests of the powers involved, such a solution would not be easy to implement. The Ukrainian events are still unfolding.

---

1 "Russian President Vladimir Putin, press statement, OSCE meeting," Moscow, May 7, 2014.
2 *Op. cit.*

These Ukrainian problems are not quite the focus of this book. I have included their brief description only in relation to the framework of an analysis of Russia's place in the world and in order to point to Russia's struggle for survival as a dominant motif of its geopolitics and history.

From the point of view of Russian and, I think, perhaps also European and even global interests, the present situation might be even worse than during the former Cold War period (1947–1989). It reflects major relative weaknesses of the Russian Federation relative to the Soviet Union and as well the American political and ideological hegemony over all Europe. In 2003, before the second American war against Iraq, the situation was still different, and both French and German politicians led a vigorous opposition against it. There were demonstrations against the war in most European cities, and the largest of them took place in London, England.

During the last decade many things have changed:

1. The collapse of the Euro and the impact of the global economic crisis which, though it started in the US, was more painfully felt in Europe;
2. The return of France to NATO and the American fold;
3. The growing influence of some Eastern European states which were once part of the Soviet bloc but now were admitted to the European Union and NATO; this "New Europe" became very hostile to Moscow and pro-American;
4. Last but not least the progressing Americanization of the old continent made it far less independent and probably more a part of a semi-global empire.

Though some of the European nations, such as Germany, and to the lesser extent France, Italy, and the Czech Republic, are reluctant to follow Washington's line on the Ukrainian crisis and its new Cold War with Russia, they now have neither the strength nor the courage to stand up to the only existing superpower. Although public opinion in Europe is divided and German business people want to avoid further conflicts with Moscow,[1] this seems to have little political impact. We do not know the content of the discussions among the Western political and economic elites at their Bilderberg meeting in Copenhagen in May 2014, however, the leaders of the June 5, 2014 meeting of the G7 in Brussels again threatened Moscow with fresh sanctions.[2] President Putin's visit to France and his talks with the Western leaders, including US President Obama, on June 6, 2014, did not

---

1 Bernd Ulrich, "Deutschen und Russland: Wie Putin Deutschen und Russland: Wie Putin spaltet," *Die Zeit*, April 10, 2014.
2 "Obama's European allies threaten more sanctions on Russia over Ukraine," *Los Angeles Times*, June 5, 2014.

bring many positive results. According to Ben Rhodes, a deputy US national security advisor, Obama told Putin that the May 25 election of the new Ukrainian President Petro Poroshenko was "an opportunity that should be taken"[1] and that "de-escalation depends on Russia recognizing Poroshenko as the legitimate leader of Ukraine, ceasing support for the separatists in eastern Ukraine, and stopping the provision of arms and materials across the border."[2]

On June 7, 2014, in his inauguration speech, President Poroshenko repeated similar demands and did not promise any real concessions to the Russophone population of the eastern and southern regions of the country. According to him, Ukraine should remain a unitary state and there would be neither official status for the Russian language nor political talks with the rebels in these regions. In fact the new Ukrainian President asked for their full and unconditional surrender, with only a vague promise of amnesty for those "with no blood on their hands,"[3] though he stressed that he did not want war or revenge on separatists in eastern Ukraine.[4] He has also stressed that Crimea will forever belong to Ukraine. It is possible that Poroshenko, who had previously made some conciliatory statements, found himself in a tight political position with little room for maneuver. He is obviously dependent on the Maidan people who control the state security sector and the oligarchs who brought him to power, and he cannot deviate much from the political line of his US protectors. However, both his official stand and the continuing military operations in eastern Ukraine seem to remove any chance for a peaceful solution of the conflict.

Russian President Putin also has serious problems of his own. In addition to attacks and demonization from the West, he also needs to face Russian public opinion, which feels solidarity with the Russophone people of eastern and southern Ukraine. They would not forgive him if he left the latter to their own fate. In addition as even some Russophobic scholars have to admit, "the separatist movement which Russia now supports was home grown in Ukraine."[5] The Donetsk People's Republic, and the so called "New Russia"

---

1 "Obama, Putin talk briefly at D-Day 70th anniversary event," *Los Angeles Times*, June 6, 2014.

2 *Op. cit.*

3 The English language translation of Ukrainian "President Petra Poroshenko's inaugural speech in Verkhovna Rada," *Kyiv Post*, June 7, 2014. See also "Poroshenko's Inauguration Speech a Declaration of War on Southeastern Ukraine," *nsbc*, June 7, 2014 and Daniel McAdams, "Washington Post at War with Reality on Ukraine," http://ronpaulinstitute.org/archives/peace-and-prosperity/2014/june/08/washington-post-at-war-with-reality-on-ukraine.aspx, June 8, 2014. As Daniel McAdams noted, Poroshenko's speech "was an iron fist in a velvet glove."

4 *Op. cit.*

5 Matthew Parish, "An Enquiry Concerning the Donetsk People's Republic – Analysis," June 8, 2014.

movement for the establishment of a "proto-state" [where Russian language and culture would dominate] out of swathes of eastern and southern Ukraine are born from native Ukrainian movements for dissolution of the country."[1] According to one of them, "Moscow latched onto pre-existing secessionist sentiment which it may now prove difficult to abandon."[2]

Despite the somewhat relaxing of the atmosphere during Putin's meetings in France, the situation remains serious. The Russian leadership has been more accommodating to the West and supportive to the new Ukrainian president than many anticipated.[3] However, Poroshenko rejected Ukraine's federalization and the granting of official status for the Russian language; Ukraine continues its military operation in the eastern region; and the number of civilian casualties is growing. As Dmitri Trenin, Director of the Carnegie Center in Moscow, notes: "Russia's unequal competition with the US will go on. Sooner rather than later, whatever Russia does or does not do, except for a complete surrender, the United States will keep more sanctions on it, including in the banking sector, and will lean harder on Europe and Japan to further tighten their technology transfer to Russia."[4]

No one in the West now pretends that Russia is, or could be, "one of us."[5] It is not even permitted to be perceived as one of the different but still recognized and accepted international partners such as China, Saudi Arabia and many other nations. Russia has now started to be seen more as a part of the world of "evil," alongside North Korea and Syria.

Although Washington policy is not necessarily shared by its European or other allies, they are now too weak and divided to represent any potential counterbalance or bridge for possible more friendly accommodation. Since February 2014, both Russia's place in the world and the international system as a whole has started to undergo accelerated and potentially dangerous changes. Further developments are still unpredictable, and one can only hope that the Party of War in Washington, D.C. will not prevail.

However, in my opinion the Ukrainian crisis itself is not the origin but rather one of the recent expressions and outcomes of the growing alienation between Russian and the West.

The collapse of the Soviet Union created a large vacuum of power in Eurasia, which the Americans wanted to fill. Now, for the first time in human

---

1 *Op. cit.*
2 *Op. cit.*
3 According to independent Russian analysts, the Russian leadership did everything possible to meet Western demands concerning the situation in Ukraine. Leibin Vitaliy, Valeriy Fadeev, "My ich ne Brosin," *Expert*, N 24(909) 09 June 2014.
4 Dmitri Trenin, "Russia vs. the West: End of the Round One," *Carnegie Moscow Center*, June 9, 2014.
5 *Op. cit.*

history, the US as a global hegemon wanted to acquire firm domination over "the world axial supercontinent"[1] which is the most important center of population and economic developments in the world. Their policy towards the successor state of the Soviet Union, the Russian Federation, was always ambiguous. As two Russian scholars noted in 1996, "The United States and NATO countries — while spurning Russia's self-esteem, to the greatest possible extent possible...firmly and consistently are destroying the geopolitical foundations which could, at least in theory, allow Russia to hope to acquire the status as the number two power in the world politics that belonged to the Soviet Union."[2]

Even at that time it became apparent that the new organization of the European space that was "being engineered by the West" was, in essence, based on the concept of supporting a number of "new, relatively small and weak national states through their more or less close rapprochement with NATO, the EU and so forth."[3] Concerning Russia, American aspirations went even further, going as far as projecting the disintegration of the Russian state and the destruction of its national ideas and traditions. In his 1997 article published in *Foreign Affairs*, former National Security Advisor Zbigniew Brzezinski suggested that Russia should "not engage in a futile effort to regain its status as a global power."[4] According to him, "a loosely confederated Russia composed of a European Russia, Siberian Republic, and a Far Eastern Republic — would be less susceptible to imperial mobilization"[5] and western and southern Russia would be drawn into the sphere of influence of an expanding European Union while Ukraine became a full member of the Euro-Atlantic Community.[6] For East and Central Asia, he predicted that they would enter the Chinese zone of influence. Brzezinski has been and still remains an influential member of the American establishment but the notion of partitioning Russia was not just his personal project. After the collapse of the USSR, other leading American politicians including Dick Cheney, who was then Secretary of Defense, aimed for similar, or even far more consequent destruction of the Russian state and nation.[7]

Between 1991 and 2000, the Russian Federation was in a deep socio-economic and political crisis and the majority of its population became

1 Zbigniew Brzezinski, "A Geostrategy for Eurasia," *Foreign Affairs*, Sept/Oct/1997.
2 A. Bogaturov and V. Kremenyuk, "Current Relations and Prospects for Interaction Between Russia and the United States," *Nezavisimaya Gazeta*, June 28, 1996.
3 A. Bogaturov and V. Kremenyuk, *Op. cit.*
4 Zbigniew Brzenzinski, *Op. cit.*
5 *Op. cit.*
6 *Op. cit.* See also Zbigniew Brzezinski, *The Grand Chessboard American Primacy and Its Geostrategic Imperatives*, Basic Books, 1997, pp. 87–122 (Chapter 4 "The Black Hole").
7 Robert Gates, *Duty: Memoirs of a Secretary of War*, 2014, p. 97.

impoverished due to the pro-capitalist economic reforms advised by the Americans. The former superpower was virtually on its knees and ready for almost all concessions and humiliations.[1] However, in spite of all Yeltsin's and later even Putin's pleas and proposals, the West never wanted to treat it as an ally and to integrate it into its political and military structures. Russia was left in the grey zone with an uncertain international status, neither friend nor foe. A situation like that was certainly difficult for Moscow, but because of Russia's weakness, it was indeed comfortable for the West.

The old Cold War (1947–1989) was not just a confrontation between Western capitalist democracy and Soviet state socialism. In its essence it was also a struggle between the American empire and the Russian nation, which was powerful at that time and dominated strategically important parts of Eurasia. The end of ideological confrontation and major social differences would not overcome the major geopolitical contradictions. Post-Soviet Russia was tolerated as long as it was desperately weak and submissive, and the Western powers seemed unchallenged. However, such a situation would not last forever.

In the 21st century Russia started to regain its strength, and the West came across a number of now internal and extended challenges and problems. Though only a few of them were either caused by or directly related to Moscow, Russia in contrast to China and even the Islamic world still remained a soft target, relatively easy to insult, attack and demonize. During all the post-Soviet period, though it had never been militarily defeated and conquered, it was still submitted to the treatment which a prominent Russian expert called "a Versailles policy in velvet gloves."[2]

---

1 In 1997 Zbigniew Brzezinski wrote that: "Russia, until recently the forger of a great territorial empire and the leader of an ideological bloc of satellites states extending into the very heart of Europe and at one point to the South China Sea, had become a troubled national state, without easy geographic access to the outside world and potentially vulnerable to debilitating conflict with neighbors on its western, southern, and east flanks. Only the uninhabitable and inaccessible northern spaces, almost, permanently frozen, seemed geopolitically secure," *The Grand Chessboard*, p. 96. Brzezinski was wrong to call Russia to be in the past "the forger." It was in fact the other superpower and if it were not the American leaders would not be willing to sign with Moscow the ABM Treaty on October 3, 1972. It was also incorrect to call the Russian Federation a "national state." It still includes a number of ethnic minorities, which are preserving their own language and cultural traditions. Last but not least President Putin is not a nationalist and "his regime seeks to maintain an equal distance from anti-Western nationalist and pro-Western liberals alike." (Andrei Tsygankov, "Putin is not a Nationalist," *Moscow Times*, June 24, 2014) However, Brzezinski description of Russia's geopolitical predicaments corresponded to realities of the period.

2 "Yevgeniy Shestakov, interview with foreign policy expert Sergey Karaganov, World is becoming less and less pro-Western," *Rossiyskaya Gazeta*, April 24, 2014.

In fact, despite all of post-Soviet Moscow's efforts to achieve more equitable relations with the West, that goal was not attained. The last Soviet leader, Mikhail Gorbachev, called for "Europe as a Common Home"[1] but this was not perceived as a serious proposal. The first president of the Russian Federation, Boris Yeltsin, later tried to fully integrate his country by joining NATO and making a direct alliance with Washington. Vladimir Putin, who succeeded him in office, more than once repeated similar efforts, supporting them by a number of unilateral concessions to Washington, which never achieved any positive results. The third Russian president, Dmitri Medvedev, followed the same path, announcing a "modernization alliance"[2] with the developed economies of the West and calling for new and more stable European security architecture in his speeches to German political, parliamentary and civic leaders in Berlin on June 5, 2008, and at the World Policy Conference in Evian, France, on October 8, 2008.

However, as the Director of the Carnegie Center in Moscow, Dimitri Trenin, admits: "All these efforts by the last Soviet leader and Russia's first three presidents have fallen far short of their expectations."[3] Consequently, according to a German scholar and member of the Bundestag: "As far as integrating Russia into a cooperative pan-European security system and developing a strategic partnership are concerned, the first 10 years of the new millennium amounted to a lost decade of estrangement, with crises and conflicts."[4] The election of Barack Obama as the US President and the ensuing "reset" policy he promised brought some temporary improvement here, but it was brief and limited to very selective examples of cooperation and did not include any major strategic changes.

As Moscow became stronger, it started to protest against encroachment on its vital interests and pressed Washington on its broken promises.[5] Western–Russian relations started to deteriorate, coming to remind analysts of the worst periods of the former Cold War.

The Western leaders have certainly never shown any serious interest in integrating Russia or even a readiness to ally with Moscow. Full integration with NATO or the EU was probably never possible. Even after the end of the Soviet Union, Russia has still remained too large in size and too independent-minded, a nation with a powerful nuclear arsenal and with

1 Council of Europe, "The Common European Home," speech by Mikahil Gorbachev, July 6, 1989.
2 Rolf Mützenüch, "Security with or against Russia? On the Russian Proposal for a European Security Treaty," 1 PG2/2010 p. 65.
3 Dimitri Trenin, "The Ukraine Crisis and the Resumption of Great Power Rivalry," Carnegie Moscow Center, July 9, 2014.
4 Rolf Mützenüch, ibid.
5 President Vladimir Putin's speech at the 34th Security Conference in München (Germany) on February 10, 2007, President of Russia Official Portal.

substantial material and intellectual resources. Its political and social elites see themselves as the successors of their Soviet and Russian Imperial predecessors and they wish to defend the traditional interest and great power status of their nation. After the end of the Cold War, with the West feeling that it was not facing any serious threat, the West might have seen an alliance with Russia as unnecessary and even as an obstacle for America's and the other Western nations' expansion in the enormous post-Soviet bloc territories. There was also no reason to invest in Russia and to help it in its economic development, unlike the case of Germany and Japan after World War II: they were rebuilt as strongholds against the Soviet Union and the threat of social revolutions in Europe and Asia.

Most of the American and other Western leaders anticipated that oligarchs protected by them and some other pro-Western forces in Russia would be able to preserve the political control of the nation which they acquired during Yeltsin's period, and because of their socio-economic interests would accept the surrender and subjugated status of Russia. Putin and his team's accession to power and their policy of national renewal and independence came as a great disappointment to them. Since 2011, their hostility and the anti-Russian campaign they launched rapidly gained speed, culminating in the 2014 Ukrainian crisis and the use by the Western media and politicians of the tragic crash of Malaysian Airlines Flight MH17 in Ukraine's Donetsk Region.[1]

In its efforts to rebuild itself and to regain international recognition, Moscow apparently hit a wall with the West. And alongside Western reluctance to accept Russia as an ally and real partner, the political class of the country is torn by internal divisions, as discussed above. Sovereignists and pro-Western Integrationists have never been able to come to a consensus and they have pulled the nation in different directions.[2]

---

1 Dimitri Trenin indicates that: "This may well be a turning point in the Ukraine conflict. The United States is using the threat of turning Russia into a pariah state to make Moscow end all support for the Donbass insurgents, so that Kiev can assume full control over the region." As je notices "the international investigation into the cause of MH17 crash has not properly begun, but the verdict has already fallen." Taking the cue from US President Barack Obama the Western leaders "made Russia responsible for the firing of the missile which killed almost 300 innocent people." Dimitri Trenin, "Midsummer Blues," http://carnegie.ru/eurasiaoutlook/?fa=56201

2 According to a senior Indian diplomat and political expert: "Russia can never be part of the Western world. It is too big and too different and too powerful and too unmanageable... It is about time the 'westernists' among the Moscow elites realize that all they have is a pipe dream." M.K. Badrakhumar "Putin it's your pay back time," *Indian Punchline - Reflections on Foreign Affairs*, July 20, 2014.

CHAPTER 3. RUSSIA IN THE MIDST OF THE UKRAINE CRISIS AND THE BATTLE FOR RUSSIA

Though the critical Ukrainian developments which started in the fall of 2013 were never completely free from foreign influences and involvement, they still had their own underlying domestic causes which had been deeply rooted in the country's history, and had their own meaning and importance. However, the ensuing international crisis over Ukraine, which might also be called the "Ukraine Crisis,"[1] had quickly acquired its own dynamics and importance, and involved a number of other geopolitical aspects and political forces.

I think the most important aspect, which is quite obvious to many observers, is the fact that what is at issue here is not so much the developments in Ukraine but the international status and socio-political system of Russia. Dmitri Trenin called it "the battle for Russia in which its position in this competition with the other powers is 'asymmetrical and very unequal.'"[2] Aligned against it are the American Superpower and its powerful allies such as the EU and Japan, with almost unlimited military, economic, and what has become no less important, soft power at their disposal. However, some analysts think that the results of this confrontation are still unpredictable, and according to Dmitri Trenin, "If Vladimir Putin manages to keep the Russian people on his side, he will win it."[3] If Putin were defeated, it would bring "another geopolitical catastrophe for Russia"[4]

---

1 Dmitri Trenin, "The Ukraine Crisis and the Resumption of Great-Power Rivalry," July 9, 2014, *Carnegie Moscow Center.*
2 *Op. cit.*
3 Dmitri Trenin, "A Battle for Russia," July 28, 2014, *Eurasia Outlook. Carnegie Moscow Center.*
4 *Op. cit.*

which could be a terminal one. The country would stop being a unified and relatively independent power center, lose its identity and probably disintegrate into a number of much smaller entities, which would be dependent on foreign countries.

What is at stake in the battle is not only the future of Russia but also the potential development of the whole international system. If Russia is able to survive and preserve its defensive positions, though for one or more decades the US would remain the leading power, the post-Cold War international system might be submitted to some changes. As a result of these changes regional powers such as the EU, Russia, China, and several others would become more assertive and influential. For the rest of the world Putin's defeat would mean the more intense and overwhelming American domination and further homogenization of global culture, leading to the rejection of previous values and the real implementation of the New, not only political but also social and cultural, World Order. The Ukrainian crisis which originally was local, or at most regional, in nature, transformed into Ukraine's crisis, with consequences that were international and unpredictable.

What were the roots and causes of such a dramatic, and for many observers, unexpected confrontation?

As I have already mentioned before, partial restoration of Russia's internal stability and external influence dismayed the American political class which particularly disliked Putin's project to establish the Eurasian Economic Community in order to ensure more multilateral economic cooperation between the Russia Federation and the other post-Soviet nations. Although the project was modelled on the EU example, it still ran against all American efforts to keep Russia divided and as much as possible isolated from the previous parts of the Soviet Union. Washington has always been very suspicious about a threat from the re-creation of its former rival, even if it were based on different political and economic premises. In the 1990s Dick Cheney, who was then the US Secretary of Defense and later would become the US Vice President, wanted the dismantlement not only of "the Soviet Union and the Russian Empire but of Russia itself, so it could never again be a threat to the rest of the world."[1] Though his suggestions could not be put into practice, the Americans have never trusted Moscow, and the 21st-century renewal of Russian political presence in the Middle East, particularly in Syria and to a lesser extent in Iran, increased American anxiety and possibly offended the personal pride of American leaders.

Another major reason for Washington's growing concern was Russia's constantly developing economic relations with the EU and other European nations. In fact, the Russian Federation became not only the main energy

---

1 Robert Gates, *Duty*, p. 97.

supplier to most of Europe, but also the third largest trading partner to the EU, and the EU became the first trading partner for Russia.[1]

After some difficulties caused by the economic crisis in 2008, mutual trade has resumed its growth, reaching a record level of more than $250 billion in 2012. At the same time it was estimated that up to 75% of Foreign Direct Investment stocks in Russia came from EU members.

Until the sectoral sanctions imposed in August 2014, Russia was Germany's eleventh biggest export market, with exports adding up to about $50 billion (Euros 37 billion).[2] Germany was also Russia's seventh biggest buyer of goods and services. Those economic relations were very profitable for Germany and this fact certainly contributed to the German business leaders' and several politicians' strong opposition to the imposition of economic sanctions on Moscow.[3]

Russia also had similar, though rather less advanced than in the case of Germany, economic ties with France, Italy, the UK, Spain, and a number of other European nations, including Denmark, Slovenia, Austria, the Netherlands, Greece, the Czech Republic and Poland. Although these types of relations do not need to have a direct impact on the foreign relations of the nations involved, the Americans still had some reasons to be concerned. The relations between foreign trade and international relations of the countries involved have never been a simple equation,[4] but the growing economic ties often facilitate political influence and cooperation. As the domination of Europe was the greatest *grand prix* of the World War II victory for Washington and the cornerstone of its global hegemony, the American leaders might have seen the further growth of Russian economic ties with the old continent as a kind of threat to their imperial interests. Any future potential rapprochement between the European nations and Moscow, could diminish the US' role as their protector from Russia and the guarantor of their political and socio-economic stability. If such a situation were to happen, the US' influence in Europe would decline and Washington's global

---

1   Russia-Trade-European   Commission,   http://trade.ec.europa.eu/doclib/docs/2006/september/tradoc_113440.pdf

2 Ibid. In 2013 the amount rose almost $267 billion, BBC News. "Russia trade ties with Europe," March 4, 2014.

3 "Only losers in economic war with Russia," *The Local* Germany News in English, August 8, 2014.

4 The best example for that might be the fact that between 2000-2012 the value of Polish exports to Russia increased tenfold and in 2012 grew by 59.9 billion (16% growth yearly), "Polish-Russia economic relations good, but not perfect," http://msp.gov.pl/en/polish-economy/economic-news/5252,Polish-Russian-economic-relations-good-but-not-perfect.html. However, Polish foreign policy has been hostile to Moscow. Since the beginning of the Ukrainian crisis Poland has been one of the EU's most hostile members towards Russia.

aspirations would be cut to size.[1] There had always been some people in Europe who dreamt about independence from US control, and even about a transcontinental Paris–Berlin–Moscow alliance.[2] Although after World War II they did not have the direct access to power, they might have been still able to use the economic developments to their political advantages.

These two major factors contributed to Washington's, and its allies', increased interest and involvement in Ukraine, which had always been seen as the most geopolitically sensitive spot for Russia.[3]

Western leaders must have been well aware of Ukraine's geopolitical and geo-strategic importance for Moscow. In 2004, US intelligence expert Peter Zeihan had already indicated that, "without Ukraine, Russia's political, economic and military survivability are called into question."[4] According to him, "It would not take war to greatly damage Russian interests, simply change in Ukraine's geopolitical orientation. A Westernized Ukraine would not so much be a dagger poised at the heart as it would be a jackhammer in constant operation."[5] However, although the Americans have always seen it "as in their best interest to slowly grind Russia into dust,"[6] the attempts for Ukraine's takeover needed to be postponed at that time. In 2004 the "Orange" Revolution in Kiev did not bring the expected outcomes, and Washington, being involved in Iraq, needed some "selective cooperation" with Moscow concerning Iran and other major strategic issues.[7]

During and after the Russian–Georgian War in 2008 the situation started to become tense again. As James Garden indicates, "the years 2008–2013 might, without exaggeration, be seen some years down the line as the West's 'March on Moscow.'"[8] On April 3, 2008, the NATO summit

---

1 According to the German analyst the "US/UK never would allow Russian-continental European relations to be dominated by an interdependence that had some 50% of continental Europe's energy security at its heart," Dr. Christof Lehmann, "The Atlantic Axis and the Making of a War in Ukraine," *New Eastern Outlook,* July 30, 2014. In Washington and London's perception, according to Dr. Lehmann, "it would challenge the US/UK's political, economic or military primacy and hegemony on the European continent."

2 Marc Rousset, *La nouvelle Europe. Paris-Berlin-Moscow. Le continent paneuropéen en face au choc des civilisations,* Paris (France): Godefray de Buillon, 2009.

3 According to Professor Stephen F. Cohen Russia thinks that their state originated in Kiev and that Ukraine entering NATO would be "hammering the final nail into the coffin of Russia as an independent great power." *Soviet Fates and Last Alternatives. From Stalinism to The New Cold War,* New York: Columbia University Press, 2011, p. 190.

4 Peter Zeihan, "Russia After Ukraine," www.stratfor.com, December 12, 2004.

5 Ibid.

6 Peter Zeihan, "The Russian Problem," www.stratfor.com, October 16, 2007.

7 Stephen F. Cohen, "America's New Cold War with Russia: Obama Congress and the media continue their dangerous one dimensional approach," *The Nation,* February 2013.

8 James Garden, "Who's really playing a zero-sum game in Ukraine?," www.russia-direct.org, July 1, 2014.

in Bucharest welcomed Ukraine's and Georgia's Euro-Atlantic aspirations and stated, "these countries will become members of NATO."[1] Because of opposition from France and Germany, and the outbreak of the Russian–Georgian War in August of the same year, it was impossible to implement this move at the time, but the anti-Russian information warfare and political campaign continued uninterrupted.

Without even mentioning the tensions around the civil war in Syria and Russia's involvement in the Middle East, it would be enough to note here both the information and political campaign against the Olympic Games in Sochi in the fall of 2013, where no serious American political interests might have been involved.

In 2014, US President Obama expressed his negative attitude to Russia and President Putin in his two official speeches,[2] and in an interview with the British journal *The Economist* on April 2, 2014. Obama said that Putin "represents a deep strain in Russia,"[3] which he characterized as a nation that "does not make anything"[4] [presumably in economic terms], "demographically dying out and represents just a regional challenge."[5] He concluded that, "We [the Americans] have to make sure that they don't escalate where suddenly nuclear weapons are back in discussion of foreign policy. And as long as we do that, then history is on our side."[6]

His dismissive opinions, which were often based on poor data and wrong premises,[7] were in fact nothing new in the American political elite's perception of Russia.[8] The Russian Federation, the successor state of the Soviet Union, formerly a powerful competitor for the US, has probably always been seen as unfinished business, the defeated but still not completely dominated and submissive nation on probation. The project to divide Russia into a number of smaller states and statelets was not just a figment of a marginal group's imagination.

The American political class' hostility to Moscow has always been stronger and more deeply rooted than in relation to China, Iran and even the so-called "Rogue States." After the collapse of the Soviet Union the prominent

1 Bucharest Summit Declaration, April 3, 2008, http://www.nato.int/cps/en/natolive/official_texts_8443.htm
2 Especially in his speeches on March 25 in Hague at the Nuclear Security Summit, and on March 26, 2014 at the EU-US Summit in Brussels.
3 *Economist*, August 2, 2014.
4 *Op. cit.*
5 *Op. cit.*
6 *Op. cit.*
7 Mark Adomanis, "3 Things Barack Obama Got Wrong About Russia," *Forbes*, August 4, 2014.
8 Gilbert Doctorow, "House of Cards and the Obama Administration Policy on Russia," http://us-russia.org/2549-house-of-cards-and-the-obama-administrations-policy-on-russia.html, August 7, 2014.

Harvard historian and expert on Russia, Richard Pipes wrote that, "It is desirable for Russia to keep on disintegrating until nothing remains of its institutional structures."[1] Columbia University economist Richard Ericson then suggested that any reform in Russia "must be disruptive on a historically unprecedented scale. An entire world must be discarded, including all of its economies and most of its social and political institutions, and concluding with the physical structure of production, capital and technology."[2]

Western leaders were seeing themselves as victors in the Cold War and Russia as the loser that had to pay a heavy price including both socio-economic and geopolitical aspects. Consequently, the 1990s became one of the darkest periods in all Russian history, and its very survival had seemed at that time to be uncertain. In fact Russia proved to be able not only to survive but even, up to a certain level, to recover. As one British commentator remarked: "It is a recovery the West has never forgiven."[3]

However, as I have already indicated, Russia's survival and its relative recovery do not imply social stability and international recognition, both of which represent an enormous challenge to the nation. The return of the Crimea to Russia and the popular reaction against Western pressures and information warfare caused an overwhelming rise of national patriotism and support for their leader, which have exceeded 80% of the public opinion.[4] It was like that in the summer 2014 before the new wave of Western sectoral sanctions against the country's economy. The impact of the sanctions on public opinion can still be seen, but because Russian society is now class divided, and different social groups might often have contrasting socio-economic interests, the recent national unity could be fragile, and the impact of the sanctions could contribute to increased division among the political and economic elites.

Another, and at least for now more severe, challenge has been brought about by the new Cold War with the American superpower and its allies, which collectively represent the Western center of the world. Although the confrontation between the global power center, which, in spite of all its geopolitical and cultural changes, is still seen as the West, and the nations which wanted to preserve their own political and economic sovereignty, was not a new phenomenon, its scale was still unprecedented.

Russia was by no means the only nation not willing to submit to Western political requirements, but only a few of them, such as relatively

---

1 Richard Pipes, "Russia's Chance," *Commentary*, 93 no.3, March 30, 1992.
2 Richard E. Ericson, "The Classical Soviet Type Economy: Nature of the System and Implication for Reform," *Journal of Economic Perspectives*, Autumn 1991, 5, no.4, p.25.
3 John Wight, "A recovery the West has never forgiven," www.rt.com, August 15, 2014.
4 "Putin's Approval Rating Soars to 87%, Poll Says," *Moscow Times*, August 6, 2014.

weak and peripheral Iraq and Libya, had been in a similar way condemned and consequently destroyed. Russia has always been seen as stronger than them, and still has at its disposal a substantial amount of nuclear weapons. As some observers indicate, "the extreme level of anti-Russian sentiment in the American media in connection with the civil war in Ukraine is surprising even to seasoned analysts of the media campaign against Russia under President George W. Bush,"[1] and all other previous conflicts. The way of treating Russia by the majority of Western politicians, journalists and other public opinion makers cannot be compared with their more nuanced and diplomatic approaches to the other nations, and is sometimes used only on the eve of major military conflict in a need to dehumanize the potential enemies. As Professor Tsygankov notes: "In the United States, there are influential segments of the political class who may differ in their agendas and ethnic roots, but who nonetheless converge in viewing Russia as the most important threat to the West.[2] The reasons for that include various historical and geopolitical factors, which have already been discussed before, and the bitter disenchantment and anger that at the end of the Cold War, Moscow did not want to submit to the neo-liberal economic policy promoted by Washington and NATO-centered security institutions in Europe and Eurasia. There are also some substantial differences in the background and behaviors of Russia and other nations not following American leadership, which are mostly of an African, Asian and Latin American background.

Russia had originated outside the Western European core of civilization and its integration into the European mainstream has never been completed. However, because of a number of geopolitical and socio-cultural factors it avoided being conquered and colonized like the rest of the non-Western world including China. Even the shocking outcomes of the Cold War and the collapse of the USSR were more the result of the internal crisis than of external pressures. Being a semi-peripheral, but at least partially European, and in traditional terms quasi-Western nation, Russia, its economic weakness notwithstanding, has always been a far more self-confident and outspoken challenger of the West than the other BRICS nations with their colonial past and memories of Western domination.

The Russian Federation is not and cannot claim to be a power at the level of the Soviet Union or even of the Tsarist Empire of the 19th and early 20th centuries, but it still remains, as President Obama admitted, a "regional power" which in addition is engaged globally and plays an important role in a number of other regions from Africa and the Middle East to the Far East and the Arctic. Moscow also does not forget its glorious historical past of

---

1 Andrei P. Tsygankov, "Russia has an inferiority complex, America has a superiority complex," *Russia Direct*, August 5, 2014.
2 Ibid.

being, for at least three centuries, a great European power, and in the 20th century a victor of World War II against Nazi Germany.

In the context of the unfolding "Western March on Moscow," some apparently unrelated developments would further aggravate the already tense relations. For the EU the main bone of contention became the issue of the Russian gas supply to Europe and Moscow's refusal to agree on the EU Third Energy Package, which Brussels tried to impose on Russia in December 2012.[1] As a British scholar wrote, the Third Energy Package constituted "an EU attempt to curb its energy relations with Gazprom and Russia, or at least to narrow Gazprom's room to maneuver."[2] Its possible effect would be to impose on Russia legal principles and economic arrangements that though favorable for the EU, certainly did not correspond to the Russian economic needs and political prestige. The European Commission, because of Russian economic difficulties and relative technological inferiority, "certainly knows itself to be in a powerful position vis-à-vis Russia."[3] However, Moscow had good reason to refuse to submit to the pressure.[4] The Brussels proposal was hardly compatible with Russian economic interests and would subject Russia's pipeline network to multilateral regulations.[5] Another, and perhaps no less important cause of the worsening of Brussels–Moscow relations was the fact that by 2004 admission to the EU was granted to former Communist countries of Central and Eastern Europe, including the Czech Republic, Estonia, Hungary, Latvia, Lithuania, Poland, Slovakia, and Slovenia. This admission brought into the EU a bloc of mostly very pro-American and often anti-Russian group influence, which according to various analysts "hijacked" Brussels' Eastern policy, which had previously been rather cooperative and conciliatory. It is possible that partly for that reason Brussels did not want to accept Putin's proposal to include Russia in its negotiations on the Economic Association Agreement with Ukraine in Fall 2013.

All those disagreements notwithstanding, without the support and engagement of the Americans, the EU would never have taken on the risk of a major confrontation with Moscow.

However, unfortunately for world peace, the US leaders became even more displeased with post-Soviet Moscow's political posture and behavior

---

1 In Dr. Christof Lehmann's opinion the War in Ukraine "became unavoidable in December 2012 when the European Union and Russia failed to agree on the EU 3rd Energy Package," "The Atlantic Axis and the Making of a War in Ukraine," *New Eastern Outlook*, August 19, 2014.

2 Lisa Pick, "EU-Russia energy relations: a critical analysis," *POLIS Journal*, vol. 7, Summer 2012.

3 *Op. cit.*, p. 333.

4 *Op. cit.*, p. 334.

5 Ibid.

in 2013. At that time there were at least three major causes of Washington's irritation:

1. The first was Russian opposition to the forceful change of the Syrian regime and the successful conclusion of the Syrian agreement on chemical weapons led by Moscow.

2. The second was the American elites' dissatisfaction caused by Russia's new economic and social developments and the apparent strengthening of the nation 'defeated' in the Cold War. As the Russians intended to make the Sochi Winter Olympic Games (7–23 February 2014) a symbol of their real or pretended renewal, they became the object of vicious attacks from the Americans and their allies' media and politicians, which were in fact, unprecedented in all previous history of Olympic tradition.[1]

3. The third and probably the most direct irritant was the case of an American computer professional and a former contractor of the US' National Security Agency who from June 5, 2013, had started to disclose a secret American surveillance program and received temporary asylum in Russia on August 1, 2013.[2] Although Snowden had never been a Russian spy and his stay in Russia had been forced on him by the cancellation of his US passport during his trip from Hong Kong, via Moscow, to Havana, in this case almost all American political elites considered Russia to be responsible, and one of the outcomes of that was President Obama's decision to cancel the Moscow summit with his Russian counterpart Vladimir Putin, which had then been prepared.[3] It was the first time an American leader had called off such a meeting. As at that time, a US administration official admitted, although "Snowden was obviously a factor, this decision was rooted in a much broader assessment

---

1 The 2008 Summer Olympic Games in Beijing, China, did not cause any protest from the West and it was attended by the US President, George W. Bush, and a number of other Western officials.

2 The well respected American international lawyer Professor Richard Falk indicated that because Snowden was accused of a "quintessential political offense, Russia returning him to the US would have been morally and politically scandalous." According to Professor Falk "President Vladimir Putin, considering the nature of the Snowden disclosures about the global reach of American surveillance systems, acted with exceptional deference to the sensibilities of the US. Instead of merely pointing out that Snowden could not be transferred to the US against his will, Putin went out of his way to say that he did not want the incident to harm relations with the United States, and even went so far as to condition Snowden's asylum on an unusual pledge that he refrain from any further release of documents damaging to American interests." Richard Falk, "Snowden Asylum: It's the law stupid," http://msnbcinternational.com, August 5, 2013.

3 Peter Baker and Steven Lee Myers, "Ties Fraying, Obama Drops Putin Meeting," New York Times, August 7, 2013.

and deeper disappointment."[1] Although Benjamin J. Rhodes, the US president's deputy national advisor stated that "we [the US] are not in any way signalling that we want to cut off this relationship,"[2] Aleksei K. Pushkov, chairman of the Russian Parliament's foreign affairs committee, was probably right in saying that the move heralded the end of the Obama administration's "reset" policy and that "the bilateral relationship has come to an impasse."[3]

At the beginning of 2014, in spite of all those problems and the hostile Western media campaign, Vladimir Putin had at least two reasons to feel satisfied. Much maligned ahead of their start the Sochi Olympic Games proved to be very successful and were praised even by his political enemies in Russia. What was no less important, Putin was able to influence the Ukraine President Victor Yanukovych to postpone his signing of the Ukraine–European Union Economic Association Agreement and to accept Russia's financial help. He had offered the Ukrainian leader quite favorable economic conditions, but he had probably hoped to preserve the historical links between Moscow and Kiev.

Notwithstanding all the challenges at the beginning of 2014, Russia's international situation did not seem bleak, and some people might even have seen the country as a reborn and rising power. The coup d'état in Kiev on February 21/22, 2014, and the ensuing events including the establishment of the new government in Kiev which was hostile to Moscow, and the civil war in Eastern Ukraine, created a new and much more dangerous situation. Russia's defensive steps such as annexation of Crimea and limited support to the Russophone rebels in Eastern Ukraine brought its relations with the West close to a state of war and made its international standing more precarious.

All those developments and the resultant political tensions with their numerous social and economic implications created, for Moscow and Europe alike, the greatest challenge since the end of the Cold War in the late 1980s and, perhaps, even since the end of World War II in 1945. During the Cold War, the 1947–1988 period, the international system with its bipolar structure, and since the 1950s the mutually acknowledged role of the nuclear deterrent,[4] seemed to be more stable and predictable than the present uni-multipolar one, the nature of which is not as easy to determine and which is in the process of constant change and transformation.

---

1 *Op. cit.*
2 *Op. cit.*
3 *Op. cit.*
4 The Soviet Union conducted its first weapon test of an implosion-type nuclear device on August 29, 1949. Moscow acquired nuclear weapons about five years later than the US. Their further development and deployment were even more delayed, but the military deterrent had already been established.

Following the end of the Cold War period and the beginning of the Washington-dominated unipolar system which represented a unique attempt to establish global control by one nation, which though enormously wealthy and powerful was isolated by two oceans from the rest of the world and a relatively a new one. American hegemony was largely based on their apparently then unlimited financial resources and on their domination of Europe achieved after World War II which at that time was still "the world's geopolitical center of gravity."[1] Its legitimacy was also supported by skilful manipulation of soft power and the spread of the American developed pop-culture which, in spite of being seen by many European and Asian intellectuals as simplistic, still attracted millions of young people from all continents.

However US global domination, which may have been overextended, has never been deeply rooted. The declining value of the US dollar began to be noticeable with the end of the Bretton Woods System in 1971–73 and since then it has continued further.[2] This could not go on without some political consequences. The US dollar has remained the major international currency, but new economic powers such as China and other BRICS countries, including Russia, have started to rise up and ask that their needs and interests be taken into account. Although it is still impossible to challenge the major importance of the United States, its previously almost unlimited power has begun to encounter a number of new problems.

One of them is the fact that Europe has lost its geopolitical importance and that the economic and cultural globalization initiated by the US made the world both more American-like but also more difficult to control. Among the most important aspects of the process were the question of Russia's survival, and Moscow's attempts to regain its role and status as an independent political and cultural power center.

As Dmitri Trenin noted, "The Ukrainian crisis that erupted in early 2014 brought to an end the post-Cold War status quo in Europe."[3] Although Moscow's reaction to the violent change of the government in Kiev, which was supported and immediately recognized by the West, was caused by its "greatest fear which at that time would have been the loss of its naval base

---

1 Luis Simon, "A post-European world? American-Russian Relations in Perspective," http://www.eurostrategy.org, April 20, 2014.
2 According to the Bretton Woods system, the external values of foreign currencies were fixed in relation to the US dollar, whose value was then expressed in gold at the congressional set price of $1. 35 per ounce. Since the 1960s the US did not have enough gold to cover the value of dollars in circulation and President Richard Nixon suspended the dollar's gold convertibility. Since 1999 it has fallen from about 123 mg of gold to less than 21 mg today.
3 Dmitri Trenin, "Ukraine Crisis and the Resumption of Great Power Rivalry," Carnegie Moscow Center, July 9, 2014.

and single warm water port in the Crimea,"[1] and as even President Obama then said, "reflected weakness and not strength,"[2] Washington and its allies started to call Russia "Enemy Number One" and a "revisionist" power. Some of the possible real causes of such behavior on the part of the West have already been mentioned. However, in addition to all the specific reasons for their hostility to Russia, the Western leaders also wanted to punish Moscow in order to provide an example of their power and to intimidate the other non-Western nations.[3]

It is also possible that the whole international crisis around Ukraine was largely initiated and provoked for that purpose. The Western leaders must have been well aware of Russia's possible reaction to their efforts to make Ukraine part of their zone of influence and Moscow's contingency plan concerning Crimea in case a pro-Western coup should occur in Kiev.[4]

This method of intimidating non-Western nations is by no means limited to Russia; Ukraine and almost all countries in the world are now interrelated. According to Anne Marie Slaughter, a professor at Princeton, "The solution to the crisis in Ukraine lies in part in Syria. Obama's climb-down from his threatened missile strikes against Syria last August emboldened Russian President Vladimir Putin to annex Crimea.... It is time to do it. A US strike against the Syrian government now would change the entire dynamic..., shots fired by the US in Syria will echo loudly in Russia."[5]

As I have already discussed, Russia might be more sensitive and outspoken than the other post-colonial non-Western nations, but still, with regard to the crisis in Ukraine it obviously acted in self-defense and probably with the most possible caution and moderation.

In annexing Crimea (apart from being forced into it, in order to ensure the security of the Russian navy), Putin did not follow the appeal of Russian nationalists — which was supported at some point by the majority of Russians (57%) — to intervene militarily in the domestic civil war in Eastern Ukraine. Against the hostilities of the present Ukrainian leaders and the Americans supporting them, Putin consistently called for peaceful negotiations and a solution among the conflicting parties. On September 3, 2014, he presented a 7-step plan to stop hostilities in Eastern Ukraine,

---

1 Mary Dejevsky, "Fear not ambition, is what fuels Moscow in Ukraine," *Guardian*, July 7, 2014.
2 *Op. cit.*
3 Sergei Karaganov, "Dolgaya Konfrontaciya," www.SVOR.ru, September 4, 2014. There is also a slightly altered English version of this article "Russia and the US: A Long Confrontation," *Russia in Global Affairs*, September 23, 2014.
4 James Garden, "Who's really playing a zero-sum game in Ukraine."
5 Anne Marie Slaughter, "Stopping Russia Starts in Syria," *Project Syndicate*, April 23, 2014. Moscow has recently warned Washington against air strikes on Syria. Karl Kincaid, "Do not launch air strikes on Syria, Russia warns Obama," *Irish Independent*, September 12, 2014.

providing for "full and objective international control over a possible ceasefire including observation and monitoring, exclusion of use of combat aircraft against civilians and villages, prisoner/captive exchange via an all-for-all formula, without preconditions, humanity corridors for refugees' movement and delivery of humanitarian aid across the Donetsk and Lugansk Regions and direct repair-crew access to destroyed social and transit infrastructure with supportive aid."[1] Because of his initiative and in spite of all obstacles and the Kiev's government reluctance, the ceasefire for Eastern Ukraine was finally agreed and signed at the Minsk peace talks on September 5, 2014.[2] As a prominent British journalist and expert on Russia commented: "Fragile [the ceasefire] may be, but the terms of the Minsk agreement, and the route to peace that it charts, represent the best chance there has been to end the fighting, and there are compelling reasons not to give up on them quite yet."[3]

Unfortunately, the American and the EU reaction to the ceasefire was to ratchet up economic sanctions several times and to tighten restrictions on major Russian banks and corporations.[4] In a marked difference with the first two rounds of anti-Russian sanctions from March and April 2014, which were mostly directed against a number of individual politicians and business people in Russia, in the third round the US extended the sanctions to two major Russian energy corporations, Rosneft and Novatek, and two major banks: Gazprombank and Vneshnekonombank. Going even further on September 12, 2014, Washington imposed sanctions on Russia's largest private bank (Sberbank), a major arms maker (Rostec), and its biggest oil companies (Gazprom, Gazprom Neft, Lukoil, Surgutneftegaz, and Rosneft) with regard to arctic deep-water and shale exploration.[5] The EU acted even earlier. On July 31, 2014, Brussels introduced the third round of sanctions which were directed against the major sectors of Russia's economy.[6] These sanctions by the major Western power centers were followed by sanctions by almost all of their partners, such as Canada, Japan, Australia, and even Norway and Switzerland.

The additional round of sanctions introduced by Brussels after the Minsk armistice agreement on September 5, 2014, was intended to block loans for five of Moscow's major state banks and to harm EU member nations'

---

1 "Ukraine ceasefire: Putin lays out 7-step plan to stop hostilities in E. Ukraine," RT, September 3, 2014.

2 "Ukraine ceasefire agreed for east of country at Minsk peace talks," *The Guardian*, September 5, 2014.

3 Mary Dejevsky, "This ceasefire is Ukraine's best hope," *The Guardian*, September 7, 2014.

4 "How far do EU-US sanctions on Russia go?" BBC New Europe, September 15, 2014.

5 Arshad Mohammed and Bill Trott, "US Intensifies sanction on Russia," Reuters, September 12, 2014.

6 http://eur-lex.europa.eu/legal-content/EN/TXT/pdf

business with oil and defense industries in Russia.[1] The EU sanctions will block the export of services and deep-water technology for Russia's oil industry.[2] The financial sanctions have also affected such Russian major corporations as Rosneft, Transneft, and Gazprom Neft, the oil subsidiary of gas giant Gazprom.[3]

As European Policy Center analyst Paul Ivan remarked, the most important sanctions "target several top Russian oil producers and pipeline operators.[4] They would bar them from raising capital and borrowing on European markets." As some of them have also been sanctioned by the US, "it is a bit of Europe catching up with what the US has been doing."[5]

However, even the European Policy Center analyst was rather skeptical whether the sanctions made sense politically and could be effective. He said, "The Russian economy can enter into recession and contract," but "the Russians have a very high threshold for pain. Putin's popularity would decrease a bit, but not enough to provoke a change in policy."[6]

The political causes and economic impact of the sanctions might be disputed.[7] I think that their importance should be neither neglected nor exaggerated.[8] Russia is a very large country, rich in natural resources (the 6th largest economy in the world), and the US and its allies (the West) are not the only possible providers of goods and services. It is also possible to get the necessary loans and investment capital from China or some other non-Western sources. In my opinion the most disturbing feature of these sanctions, especially the third round, was their timing.

In September 2014, the new Western sanctions hit Russia despite the ceasefire in Ukraine, the exchange of prisoners, the apparently successful Minsk meeting between Putin and Poroshenko, and Putin's peace plan in Ukraine that began to be implemented in spite of all obstacles. Quite a few bloggers asked "why these nonsensical sanctions are being implemented

---

1 "Ukraine Crisis: New EU sanction on Russia go into effect," BBC *News Europe*, September 12, 2014.

2 *Op. cit.*

3 *Op. cit.*

4 "EU tighten sanctions against Russia," Focus News Agency, Brussels, September 9, 2014.

5 *Op. cit.*

6 *Op. cit.*

7 Andrei Tsygankov, "Why Western Sanctions Won't Make Putin Change His Strategy," *Moscow Times*, April 27, 2014. See also Lada Ray, "Predictions: The Real Reasons for West's Anti-Russian Sanctions," September 16, 2014, http://futuristrendcast.wordpress.com/2014/09/16/predictions-the-real-reasons-for-wests-anti-russian-sanctions/

8 Ivan Kapitonov, "Why the Kremlin is not very concerned with energy sanctions. The new energy sanctions imposed by the West could force Russia to turn to other partner or technologies to compensate for the lost potential of Arctic and shale prospecting projects," *Russia Direct*, September 19, 2014.

now. Instead of encouraging the peace process in Ukraine, they are bound to discourage it."[1]

Dmitri Trenin, when asked about this apparent paradox, admitted that "imposing sanctions amidst the ceasefire agreement and the exchange of prisoners of war will bring about dissonance."[2] However, according to him, "this step was not unpredictable and few in Russia, at least among the expert community, expected sanctions to be alleviated with the implementation of the peace plan."[3] For Trenin and for many other Russian analysts, Western and Russian based, including Sergei Karaganov, "the Ukraine crisis was not an isolated spat or tragic misunderstanding, but rather the last straw for both sides. The failure to achieve an acceptable post-Cold War settlement produced an unanchored relationship between the West and Russia."[4]

Both this failure and its possible consequences had not been unpredictable. During the previous years a number of analysts including George F. Kennan, a former American diplomat and an expert on Russia, indicated the negative trend of development and warned of its potential outcomes. In 1998 Kennan argued that "NATO expansion set up a situation in which NATO has to either expand all the way to Russia's borders, triggering a new Cold War, or stop expanding after these three countries [Poland, Hungry, the Czech Republic] and create a new dividing line through Europe."[5] He considered that also to be "the beginning of the new cold war,"[6] and predicted that "the Russians will gradually react quite adversely."[7] As he said, "Of course there is going to be a bad reaction from Russia, and then [the NATO expanders] will say that is how the Russians are — but this is just wrong."[8]

George Kennan was then a much-respected figure and his opinion was at that time shared and supported by many influential Americans. Susan Eisenhower (the granddaughter of President Dwight E. Eisenhower) gathered a group of 49 military, political, and academic leaders, who together signed an open letter to President Clinton on June 26, 1997, that called the plan to expand NATO "a policy error of historic proportions."[9]

---

1 Lada Ray, *Op. cit.*
2 Trenin, "Russia-West rivalry over Ukraine is higher priority than security," *Russia Direct*, September 15, 2014.
3 *Op. cit.*
4 Dmitri Trenin, "The Ukraine Crisis and Resumption of Great Power Rivalry," *Russia in Global Affairs*, July 14, 2014.
5 Thomas Friedman, "Foreign Affairs; Now a Word from X," *New York Times*, May 2, 1998.
6 *Op. cit.*
7 *Op. cit.*
8 *Op. cit.*
9 Eugene J. Carrol Jr., "NATO Expansion Would Be an Epic Fateful Error," *Los Angeles Times*, July 7, 1997.

In 2009, even while working for an American NGO, Dmitri Trenin admitted that "the West lacked the will to adopt Russia as one of its own."[1] By this time that had already been obvious to any careful observer, and the causes could be traced back to the beginning of the post-Cold War era — in spite of all efforts made by both Yeltsin and Putin's administrations, already been discussed above, and their opening wide the Russian border to Western capitalist penetration which proved to be often extremely harmful for the nation. [2]

After the dissolution of the Soviet Union in December 1991, the West started to see Russia as a special case which was very different from that of other post-Communist nations. As Trenin noted at the time, "armed with nuclear weapons, its great power mentality shaken but unbroken, and just too big, Russia would be granted privileged treatment, but no real prospect of membership in either NATO or the EU. The door to the West would officially remain open, but the idea of Russia actually entering through it remained unthinkable."[3]

The privileged treatment mentioned by Trenin in fact amounted mainly to putting this great country on probation, submitting it to various forms of control and supervision and an overwhelming important concern "that Russia would pursue a generally pro-Western [foreign] policy."[4]

In practice, it often meant a most humiliating submission to Western wishes and running against its vital national interests, such as the cases of the bombardment of Serbia, the destruction of Yugoslavia, and NATO's eastern expansion.

The whole Western approach to post-Soviet Moscow was in fact similar to, though not as open and brutish as, the treatment of Germany when it was defeated in World War I by the victorious "Entente." It was, as Sergei Karaganov writes, "a Versailles policy in velvet gloves."[5]

After World War II, the Western European nations lost their political importance and the US leaders have always believed in their unquestionable superiority and the overwhelming power which they might have at their disposal. After September 11, 2001, Russian President Vladimir Putin proposed to Washington that Moscow would recognize the global

---

1 Dmitri Trenin, "Russia Reborn," *Foreign Affairs*, November/December 2009, p. 64.
2 According to the American economist Professor Michael Hudson, the economic and social result of submission to the West was not "bringing about Western European or American style capitalist development" but "the world's largest resource grab since Europe's conquest of the New World five centuries ago," Michael Hudson, "The New Cold War Gambit," May 13, 2014.
3 Dmitri Trenin, "Russia Leaves the West," *Foreign Affairs*, July/August 2006, p. 89.
4 Yevgeniy Shestakov, interview with foreign policy expert Sergei Karaganov, "World is becoming less and less pro-Western," *Rossiyskaya Gazeta*, April 24, 2014.
5 *Op. cit.*

leadership of the US in exchange for American recognition of "its role as a major ally, endowed with a special responsibility for the former Soviet space."[1] Washington rejected the offer, which it considered to be "made from a position of weakness,"[2] and intensified its direct political and military expansion along the Russian borders.

In fact it could hardly have been otherwise. Washington followed its Deputy Secretary of Defense Paul Wolfowitz's doctrine of the quest for global spectrum domination,[3] and the Russian leaders could not set aside their national interests and long political history. And yet, according to Dmitri Trenin, until mid-2006 Russia had been willing to see itself as "Pluto in the Western solar system, very far from the center but still fundamentally part of it."[4] However, largely because of the George W. Bush administration's foreign policy Moscow came to the conclusion that furthering its policy of appeasement and searching for reward from the West was not a practical option and could not bring the expected results. The Kremlin's new approach to foreign policy was based on its unpleasant experience that, as a great power and a very large country, "Russia is essentially [at least among the Western political elite] friendless; no great power wants a strong Russia, which would be a formidable competitor, and many want a weak Russia that they could exploit and manipulate."[5]

Not being a small or middle-sized European entity like the other post-Communist nations, and with all its imperial history and still enormous resources, Moscow had neither the will nor the need to become just one more American vassal and a part of their global empire.

Opting for a more independent foreign and domestic policy, Moscow did not intend to become an anti-Western power. In 2006 Trenin argued that "Today's Russia may not be pro-Western, but neither is it anti-Western,"[6] and a Sino-Russian alliance, the possibility of which has always caused great concern in the US, "could only occur as a result of exceptionally short-sighted and foolish policies on Washington's part."[7]

---

1 Trenin, "Russia Leaves the West," *Op. cit.*, p. 90.
2 *Op. cit.*
3 The classic statement of the US goals by Wolfowitz himself admits: "Our first objective is to prevent re-emergence of a new rival, either on the territory of the former Soviet Union or elsewhere. This is a dominant consideration underlying the new regional strategy, and require that we endeavor to prevent any hostile power from dominating a region whose resources would under consolidated control, be sufficient to generate global power...," quoting from a Department of Defense planning document, "Prevent the Re-Emergence of a New Rival," February 1992, in P.E. Taylor, "US Strategy Plan Calls for Insuring No Rivals Develop. A One-Superpower World," *The New York Times*, March 8, 1992.
4 Dmitri Trenin, "Russia Leaves the West."
5 *Op. cit.*
6 *Op. cit.*
7 *Op. cit.*

Writing in the fall of 2007, even such an astute analyst as Trenin was unable to foresee all the future conflicts and developments caused by the increasing globalization and the way events in geographically remote areas and apparently unrelated issues interact with and influence each other.

The post-Soviet Ukraine had always faced numerous ethnic, socio-economic and political challenges. However, most of them, even the most potentially disruptive ones, seemed to be either latent or only of local importance. As late as in spring and summer of 2013, they seemed unlikely to generate a major international crisis, and the Western public paid them rather little attention.

The important issue of the Russian gas supply to Europe, and Moscow's refusal to agree to the Third Energy Package proposed by Brussels in the winter of 2012, could not by itself have led to the Ukraine crisis with all its threatening global repercussions. I do not agree with Dr. Lehmann's opinion that the war in Ukraine then became unavoidable. This disagreement might have created additional preconditions for the crisis, but it could not have provoked such a major geopolitical confrontation. Without the initiative and active support of the US, the EU would never have taken the risk of a major political confrontation with Moscow. The main role was, and probably had to be, taken by Washington, which was influenced by developments in the Middle East and their global systemic implications.

In my opinion the origins of the Ukraine crisis must be traced back to the situation in the Middle East in 2012–2013 and the developing of the "Arab Spring" and the civil war in Syria. Although these events seemed not to be directly related to Ukraine's problems, they consequently involved Moscow and Washington in a complex struggle, the results of which might have been decisive both for the international status of Russia and the shape of the whole international system.

As Dmitri Trenin rightly indicated, "To Moscow, Syria is not primarily about Middle Eastern geopolitics. Rather, from a Russian policy perspective, Syria — much like Libya, Iraq, or Yugoslavia previously — is about the world order. It is about who decides whether to use military force? Who decides the actors for use of that force? And who decides under what rules, conditions, and oversight military force is to be used?"[1] Keeping in mind its weakness in relation to the US Superpower and all its internal vulnerabilities, Russia has also always rejected outside military intervention without a UN Security Council mandate and the concept of regime change under foreign pressure[2] (R2P).

---

1 Dmitri Trenin, "For Russia, Syria is not about Syria," *Daily Star* (Lebanon), 03/10/2014.
2 *Op. cit.*

For all these reasons in the fall of 2013 Moscow wanted to prevent the American military intervention in Syria. In September of that year, Russian President Putin appealed to the American people asking for caution in Syria,[1] and Russia submitted its plan for Syria's chemical disarmament which had already been approved by the Syrian government.[2]

The fact that the Obama administration accepted the proposal and that the war was then, at least temporarily, avoided was probably the greatest diplomatic victory that Moscow had had since the decline of the Soviet Union. According to the well-known American political analyst George Friedman, for the first time since the early 1990s, the Russian Foreign Minister was able to sit with the US Secretary of State as an equal.[3] At that time, it seemed to some that the agreement which Sergei Lavrov and John Kerry signed in Geneva on September 13, 2013, was going to open a way to solve not only the Syrian chemical weapons problem but perhaps provide an opportunity for better Washington–Moscow relations.

However, the path to those two very desirable goals proved to be a rocky one and the optimists' expectations did not take sufficiently into account the two factors that were probably most important: the attitudes of the American political elites and the mechanism of the present international system. Although President Obama's administration had accepted the Russian initiative and at least postponed the military attack on Syria, in the US and in some other American ally nations they have been, and still are, very powerful forces which want to go to war there. According to the prevailing consensus of the American political class, the Baathist regime in Syria had to be overthrown.[4] With Russian help the Americans wanted to disarm the existing Syrian state, but they were not going to stop arming and

---

1 "A Plea for Caution From Russia, What Putin Has to Say to Americans About Syria," *The New York Times*, September 11, 2013.
2 "Syrian chemical weapons: Russia hands disarmament plan to US. John Kerry and Sergey Levrov to discuss proposal at two days of talks in Geneva," *The Guardian*, 11 September 2013.
3 George Friedman, "Strategy, Ideology and the Close of the Syrian Crisis," www.stratfor.com, September 17, 2013.
4 The consensus was probably established after several American efforts to get Syrian acceptance for protecting Israeli interests in the Arab-Israeli settlement. In March 2000 during his meeting with US President Clinton in Geneva, the Syrian leader Hafez al Assad staunchly held to his view that there must be a full Israeli withdrawal from the Golan Heights to the Israeli-Syrian frontiers that existed on June 4, 1967 before the Arab-Israeli war of that year. According to him, there were two basic principles for a peaceful settlement in the region: "Israel must fully withdraw from the territories its acquired in 1967 and Palestinian rights must be restored." None of these demands were acceptable to Washington. Jane Perlez, "In Geneva Clinton Bet That Assad Would Bend, and Lost," *New York Times*, March 28, 2000. See also: William J. Clinton XLII President of the US: 1993-2001, "The President's News Conference With President Hafez al Assad of Syria in Damascus," October 27, 1994.

supporting the Syrian rebels and their allies in the region. In the fall of 2014, the Americans started to bombard Syria, presenting that as a struggle against the ISIS Islamic terrorists which they had previously helped to establish. Their plan for the future of Syria seems to be similar to that of Libya or even Somalia, and the impact that will have on the whole region is impossible to predict. It is hard to believe that it could be a positive one.

The hoped-for improvement in American–Russian relations did not materialize. The apparent success of Russian diplomacy caused anger and bitterness in US politicians who had never wanted to recognize Russia as "a partner in the world arena who is valuable in itself."[1] As the director of the Carnegie Moscow Center Dmitri Trenin then commented, "The United States expects deference, Russia insists on independence. For Washington, partnership with Moscow means splitting the difference and the necessary compromise."[2] The US, which originated as a country relatively isolated from the rest of the world, and which in the 20th century in the aftermath of the two great European wars (World War I and World War II) became a global superpower, has neither the experience nor the patience for that.[3] America did not want to perceive Russia as an equal partner or even as a state with legitimate national interests. Because of that, the West has not stopped its historical attempts "to foster the geopolitical disintegration of the Eurasian space"[4] and the 'march on Moscow' was accelerated.

Almost exactly two months after the Geneva agreement on the chemical disarmament of Syria, the Ukraine crisis started. Since the very beginning, this crisis was incomparably more threatening for Russia than the Syrian one, which is going still to continue though it has become less important for the Western media and probably even the Western leaders.[5]

Today's gravest political crisis since World War II, which was rightly called "a battle for Russia,"[6] has begun. Its roots do not lie only in the worldview and interests of the American political class and the Europeans

---

1 "Interview with Dmitri Trenin, director of the Moscow Carnegie Center," by Sergey Strokan, *Kommersant*, September 18, 2013. "Rossiya Yedinstvennaya Derzhave, gotovaya protivasostoyatsya SS" ("Russia the only country ready to stand up against the USA").

2 Dmitri Trenin, "The Snowden case as the Mirror of US-Russia Contentions," Carnegie Moscow Center, August 2, 2013.

3 D.B. Kanin, S.E. Meyer, "America's Outmoded Security Strategy," *Current History*, January 2012, p.22.

4 Richard Sakwa, "Russia new normal: From troublemaker to problem solver," http://www.russia-direct.org, August 20, 2013.

5 There are even now voices calling for America's acceptance of Assad. See for example Behzod Yaghmaion, "The Inevitable Emergence of Assad as a US Ally. The only option for the United States to defeat the Islamic State and end the refugee crisis," *Globalist*, October 4, 2014.

6 Dmitri Trenin, "A Battle for Russia," http://carnegie.ru/eurasiaoutlook/?fa=56261, July 28, 2014.

following them. It is even more difficult to lay blame on Russia's reactions, which were mainly defensive and overall modest. What was behind all these developments was a new major systemic transformation. The international system as a whole is passing through a slow but difficult transition period from the post-Cold War "unipolar moment" to a possible, but as yet not easy to determine, multipolarity.

Such historical periods have always abounded with conflicts and uncertainties. According to a leading Russian liberal professor, Alexei Arbatov, "In the early 1990s, the US had a unique historical chance to lead the creation of a new multilateral world order together with other centers of power. However, it unwisely lost this chance. The US suddenly saw itself as the only superpower in the world."[1] Arbatov, who has always been very pro-Western and has defended Washington's policy, is now willing to admit that the first two decades after the end of bipolarity have convincingly shown that a unipolar world brings no stability or security. Monopoly both at national and international levels inevitably leads to a legal nihilism, arbitrary use of force, stagnation and ultimately defeat.[2]

In spite of all those problems, which are now hard to deny, the American political class wants to preserve and further expand its hegemony and is not willing to compromise.[3] The crisis in Ukraine has been a reaction to America's lack of success in Syria and the Middle East and the Russian role in that region which hurts America's ego.

Since the fall of 2013, Washington and its European allies have been driving Ukraine into their realm of influence. The West hit Russia in one of its most vulnerable spots and the end of the new conflict is impossible to predict. As of now, the West has achieved numerous strategic goals and pushed Russia into a corner. It might not see any convincing reason to accept Russian proposals and may reject all of Moscow's efforts to find a compromise. However, it is by no means certain that having the West establish lasting control of the whole Ukraine and further expand into Russia are realistic and beneficial for the interested parties.

During its over 1000 years of history, Russia has probably never been under such stress and under so many direct and indirect threats as now. I think that even the horrible period of World War II, which in Russia is called "The Great Patriotic War" (1941–1945), seems by comparison to be less dangerous and less threatening for national survival. Both the Nazi-led anti-Soviet coalition and the military technologies of the period were, in

---

1 Alexei Arbatov, "Collapse the World Order? The Emergence of a Polycentric World and its Challenges," *Russia in Global Affairs*, September 23, 2014.
2 *Op. cit.*
3 Andrei Tsygankov, "Amerikanskoye videnie mirovayodka: vsye pod kontrolem," http://www.globalaffairs.ru, September 3, 2014.

practice, very minor compared to the military means now available to the American superpower and its allies. The US-led coalition includes in its ranks all the developed capitalist nations from European Union members to Canada, Japan and Australia, and NATO forces are already present in direct proximity to Russian centers, including its former capital St. Petersburg. US troops are moving to Poland and there is constant and growing Western naval presence on the Black and Baltic Seas.

Located on the Eurasian lowland and devoid of natural boundaries, Russia has been a frequent object of eastern, western, and southern aggressions.[1] Its almost miraculous historical survival was largely the outcome of certain other specific geopolitical and human features, such as the great size of its territory, the harsh climate, and the strength and patriotism of its people under the leadership of generally accepted autocratic leaders. Even the greatest haters of Russia have usually accepted that its people are able to withstand a lot of suffering and to stand up to enormous predicaments.

Indeed, it was like that for many centuries, but it is far from certain that it is still that way now. Modern/post-modern technologies and the new military devices have made the role of space and climate secondary, and because of all the last century's wars and social disasters, the population of the country is much smaller and more internally divided than in the past. The Russian people suffered heavy casualties during the Bolshevik revolution and the ensuing civil war and both World Wars. During Yeltsin's presidency, pro-capitalist socio-economic reforms led also to great economic and demographic catastrophes.[2] Under optimal circumstances, recovery from them would require at least two more generations. The new foreign aggression or even a prolonged period of suffocating economic sanctions and information warfare might lead to the final breakdown and the end of that Russia which we know from history and geography.

Present-day Russia is not as nearly equal to the US in power, and it cannot represent any real threat to American security. However, Washington still "regards Moscow as a force that inhibits what the US considers to be the

---

1 George Friedman, "The Geopolitics of Russia: Permanent Struggle," www. stratfor.com, October 15, 2008. See also Peter Zeihan, "The Russia Problem," www.stratfor.com, October 17, 2007. As Zeihan correctly indicated, "The Russian geography is problematic. It lacks oceans to give Russia strategic distance from its foes and boasts no geographic barriers separating it from Europe, the Middle East or East Asia. Russian history is a chronicle of Russia's steps to establish buffers and these buffers being overwhelmed."

2 Although the issue has already been mentioned before, I would recommend the reading of Naomi Klein, *The Shock Doctrine. The Rise of Disaster Capitalism*, New York: Metropolitan Books, 2007, pp. 218-245. However, I do not agree with her putting at the same level Russian privatizations and the destruction of the social institutions with the Pinochet's Chile. The historical backgrounds of both countries were very different and Yeltsin's time reforms were for Russia incomparably more harming than Pinochet's harsh rule in Chile.

proper functioning of the international system."[1] According to the liberal Russian analyst cited before, Washington just wants to discipline an insufficiently obedient vassal, "to curb him and prevent from questioning the order of things."[2] In my opinion, Washington's present aspirations go even further. As Sergey Karaganov indicated, the course embarked upon by the Americans, to contain or even discard Russia "seems to be aimed at regime change."[3] According to Karaganov, "To all intents and purposes this is a course that means destroying the country because the current Russian regime was created entirely organically and is supported by the majority of the population."[4] The American political class would probably have no moral obstacle to destroying Russia, but as long as Putin still has strong social support in the country, it would probably prefer to use the weapons of economic sanctions to nourish popular discontent and then foster a new color revolution or something similar to the Ukrainian Maidan in Moscow. As a faster alternative, it might be willing to persuade some Russian politicians or wealthy businessmen to organize a coup, including killing Putin and his supporters. A way to do that has already been suggested by former Special Assistant to the Director of Central Intelligence Agency and Vice Chairman of the CIA's National Intelligence Council Herbert E. Meyer.[5]

Even without resorting to any such drastic means, Russia has been put in a very difficult situation, and the impact of today's tensions might be catastrophic.

Without any real proof or evidence, Washington used the tragic crash of Malaysian Airlines Flight 17 as a pretext to tarnish Moscow. The West has named Russia, and specifically President Putin, as the main culprit. In any case the disaster was a great misfortune both for Moscow and the rebels in Eastern Ukraine, who certainly did not need any more bad press in the West.[6]

---

1 Fyodor Lukyanov, "Russia's Asymmetrical Response: Global Aikido," in Paul J. Saunders, editor, *Cast of a New Cold War. The US-Russia Confrontation Over Ukraine*, Washington D.C.: Center for National Interest, September 14, 2014.

2 *Op. cit.*

3 Yevgeniy Shestakov interview with foreign policy expert Sergey Karaganov, "World is becoming less and less pro-Western. Current American policy is aimed at change of regime in Russia," *Rossiyskaya Gazeta*, April 24, 2014.

4 *Op. cit.*

5 Herbert E. Meyer, "How to Solve the Putin Problem," *American Thinker*, August 4, 2014.

6 Ukraine, the Netherlands, Australia and Belgium on August 8, 2014 signed a non-disclosure agreement of date obtained during the investigation of the death of the Boeing 777. The data loss of flight MH17 in Donetsk region will be published only with the consent of all parties who participate in investigation. Any of the signatories has the right to veto the publication of the results of the investigation without explanation. It seems obvious that intermediate results of the investigation directly prove the innocence of Russia and/or the Eastern Ukrainian rebels for the tragic event and that not satisfied the countries

This was also the pretext used to force the EU countries to adopt the third and most painful round of sanctions against Russia.[1] As a result of that, as liberal Russian analyst Igor Yurgens says, "Russia faces US and EU economic machines comprising 800 million people on both sides of the Atlantic who together produce half of the world's wealth."[2] In his view, "accounting for just 2% of global GDP, Russia can hardly win such a boxing match — particularly since more than 50% of Russia trade turnover is with the European Union."[3]

The Western military superiority is no less overwhelming. NATO members spend over ten times more than Russia on defense; they possess superior military equipment and are able to maintain that superiority while spending less on defense as a share of their GDP than Russia.[4] The US is the biggest military spender in the world, but even European NATO members spend over three times more than Russia does.[5]

According to former Russian Finance Minister Alexei Kudrin, in addition to squeezing the country militarily and forcing Europe to impose economic

signatories. Granting the present Ukrainian government the right to veto of the results publications preclude any chance of questioning the official Western version. The only country, which refused to sign this agreement, was Malaysia itself. The incident with a Malaysian passenger plane in Donetsk region of Eastern Ukraine has been used to push ahead with the sectoral economic sanctions against Russia and some Western media called Putin a mass killer of innocent children on the flight. Shortly after the event on July 21, 2014 Dmitri Trenin of the Carnegie Moscow center rightly noted: "The international investigation into the cause of the MH17 crash has not yet properly begun, but the verdict has already fallen. This may well be a turning point in the Ukraine conflict. The United States is using the threat of turning Russia into a pariah state to make Moscow stop all support for the Donbass insurgents, so that Kiev can assume full control over the regime.... Some in the West even hope it might be the beginning of the end of Putin's Russia. The EU is likely now to impose new sanctions on Russia." Dmitri Trenin, "Midsummer Blues," *Eurasia Outlook*, July 21, 2014.

1 On October 3, 2014 US Vice President Joe Biden in his speech at Harvard University's Kennedy School of Government stated, "We relied the major development countries to impose real cost on Russia." Talking on the EU nations he admitted, "it is true that they did not want to do that. But again, it was America's leadership, the President of the US insisting, often times almost having to embarrass Europe to take economic hits to impose costs. And the results have been massive capital flight from Russia, a virtual freeze on foreign direct investment, a ruble at an all-time low against the dollar, and the Russian economy teetering on the brink of recession," The White House. Office of Vice-President, "Remarks by the Vice-President at the John F. Kennedy Forum," Harvard Kenned School. Boston, Massachusetts, October 3, 2014.

2 Igor Yurgens, "Targeted Sanctions with An Unclear Target," in Paul J. Saunders, editor, *Op. cit.*

3 *Op. cit.*

4 Slobodan Lekic, "Despite Cuts, NATO Still Accounts for Most of the World's Military Spending," *Stars and Stripes*, February 25, 2014.

5 *Op. cit.* For more detailed data proving that point see: the International Institute for Strategic Studies, The Military Balance 2013, London: Routledge, 2013.

sanctions against Russia, Washington has probably used another weapon against Moscow again: by persuading Saudi Arabia to cause a drop in oil prices.[1] After Saudi Arabia, which certainly has great influence on the price of oil worldwide, decided to extend a big discount to its Asian customers, there was an immediate decline in oil prices. Russian Finance Minister Anton Siluanov predicted that the Russian budget would have a shortfall of 500 billion rubles (nearly $12.5 billion) if oil prices dropped to $87 per barrel and dollar exchange rates went as high as 40 in 2015.[2] The drop of oil prices might be even more dangerous for Moscow than the European economic sanctions.

Russia's present economic predicaments are nothing new. The economy has always been a weak spot for this large and otherwise powerful nation. Russia was for various reasons less economically advanced by the 16th century, and it entered the emerging world capitalist system as a provider of raw materials, exporting low-value-added products while importing high-value-added ones. In spite of all the often draconian political and social measures of the Soviet period and skilful macroeconomics regulatory measures, the problem of "catch-up development" has not been solved. In 2013, oil and gas comprised 68% of all Russia exports, with crude oil and petroleum products netting them almost four times as much revenue as natural gas.[3] Although Russia also has some highly-developed economic branches, especially in the airspace and atomic industries (it is the third largest generator of nuclear power in the world and fourth largest in terms of installed capacity),[4] the fact of being predominantly dependent on the export of gas and oil makes this country's budget and all social life there highly dependent on the fluctuating international prices of natural resources. As the Russian national budget derives some 45%[5] of revenues from oil taxes, cheap oil could be seen as a potentially serious national security challenge. Unfortunately for Russia, crude prices have fallen more than 23% since June 2014, depressing the ruble and causing shortfalls in the national budget. According to Russian Deputy

---

1 Alexei Kudrin is a liberal economist who is seen by some in the West as being a leading opponent of Putin's policy. However, he stated recently that he does not rule out the idea that the US and Saudi Arabia teamed up against Russia to dump oil on the world market. A similar manipulation in the late 1980s contributed greatly to the collapse of the Soviet Union. Pavel Koshkin, "As the price of oil drops, so do hopes for Russia's economic future," *Russia Direct*, October 2013.

2 Andrei Tsygankov, "Amerikanskoye vidyeniye Mirovoporyadka: vsye pod kontrolem," http://www.globalaffairs.ru, September 4, 2014.

3 Rob Wile, "Here's How Dependent Russia's Economy is on Oil and Gas," *Business Insider*, July 23, 2014.

4 EIA, US. Energy Information Administration "Russia," report revised on March 12, 2014.

5 Carol Matlock, "Will Cheap Oil Choke the Russian Economy?," www.businessweek.com/articles, October 13, 2014.

Finance Minister Tatyana Nesterenko, the country's draft budget for 2015 was based on $100 barrel oil, but the price is now at about $88/barrel, the lowest since the end of 2010.[1]

Nonetheless, Moscow has quite a large capital reserve both in gold and foreign currencies[2] so the situation, at least for now, is still not dramatic and the Western media largely exaggerate the situation.[3]

I am not an economist, and in view of the often contradictory information available I cannot fully grasp and properly analyze all the causes and outcomes of the present Russian economic predicament. In addition, as I have already stressed, the relations between economic and political factors are far from simple. However, no one can deny that both the Western sanctions and the drop in oil prices are having an impact on Russian society. In early September 2014, Sberbank, which is the leading bank in Moscow, was added to the list of Russian state banks excluded from the Western debt market; this made it almost impossible for Russian companies to raise money from Western sources.[4]

China is a major economy that refuses to follow Washington's line and impose sanctions against Moscow; and yet there are even some Chinese banks, with their well-established links to the US financial market, who are reluctant to lend to those Russians who find themselves under Western sanctions.[5] Similar fears and cautiousness may be observed among some other major non-Western lenders.

Even so, both economic and political relations between Russia and China are strong and as Trenin writes, "There are truly excellent prospects for Sino-Russian economic cooperation."[6] On May 21, 2014, the two countries signed an "epochal" (Putin's definition) 30-year, $400 billion deal for Gazprom to deliver Russian gas to China; this indicated Russia's shift towards Asia and strained relations with the West.[7] A British commentator wrote that this deal

---

1 *Op. cit.*
2 As of September 1, 2014, the Reserve Fund stood at $91.7 billion and the National Welfare Fund at 83.3 billion. The Reserve Fund according to its current requirements can be invested only in the US dollar, Euro, Pound Sterling and a debt securities of a small group of Western countries and a few international institutions. "Finance Minister Pledges to Uncork Reserves to Help Sanctions – Hit Russian Banks," Reuters, *Moscow Times*, September 28, 2014.
3 "Novak: oil price drop no 'tragedy,'" *Russia Beyond The Headlines*, October 17, 2014.
4 Chris Weafer, "Guest post: there is cause for optimism over Russia's crisis," *Financial Times*, October 17, 2014.
5 Dmitri Trenin, "Russia's growing China connections," *China Daily*, October 13, 2014.
6 *Op. cit.*
7 "Russia signs 30-year deal worth $400 bn to deliver gas to China," www.theguardian.uk, May 21, 2014.

"could ignite a shift in global trading,"[1] especially given that both countries are trying to put an end to the dollar's dominance as a petrocurrency.[2] In 2014 the European economy declined in a triple-dip recession largely because the US forced Europe to implement sanctions against Russia, sanctions which are harming the export-driven German and French economies; but China is willing to export both agricultural products and oil and gas equipment to Russia. In addition Moscow can pay for them in either Russian or Chinese currencies, rubles or renminbi, thus accelerating the de-dollarization of bilateral commercial relations.[3] The trade turnover between the two nations is increasing every year and in 2015 was expected to grow to $100 billion.

In order to facilitate further development, The People's Bank of China (PBOC) released a surprising announcement on October 13, 2014, stating that the central banks of China and Russia had signed a 3-year, 150 billion yuan, bilateral local-currency swap deal.[4]

Meetings between Chinese and Russian political leaders are also expanding mutual cooperation. In 2014 Russian President Putin met with Chinese President Xi nine times, and on October 12, 2014, China's Premier Li Kequang went to Russia in order to attend the 19th China–Russia Prime Ministers' Regular meeting. He met Russian Premier Dmitri Medvedev and signed a package of deals ranging from satellite navigation and high speed rail construction to youth exchanges and academic cooperation.[5]

High-level meetings have been vital to the creation of momentum and to sustaining it, but the implementation of all these great projects will require hard work and mutual understanding between the two peoples. Besides, neither China nor any other Asian connection will make Russia into an Asian country. Trenin correctly indicates that his country "will remain what [it] has always been: an Eastern European civilization, spanning northern Eurasia from Baltic to Pacific."[6] However, the increased links with Asia should provide Moscow with a new strength to help it survive its present

---

1 Liam Halligan, "Russia-China gas deal could ignite a shift in global trading," *The Telegraph* (UK), October 23, 2014. This deal and partial replacement of the Petrodollar by the other currencies caused a reaction by the American scholar Professor Michael Snyder in his article, "Who Needs the United States? Not Russia and China," *New York Times*, May 21, 2014. See also one of his earlier articles: "De-Dollarization: Russia is on the verge of Dealing a Massive Blow to the Petrodollar," *Economic Collapse*, May 13, 2014.

2 *Op. cit.*

3 "China-Russia economic cooperation sustainable, inclusive: Chinese vice-premier," *Xinhuanet, English news cn12014–10–12–13.47*

4 Tyler Durden, "China, Russia Sign CNY150 Billion – Local Currency Swap as Plunging Oil Prices Sting Putin," http://www.zerohedge.com/news, October 13, 2014, and PBOC website.

5 "Chinese premier arrives in Russia for official visit," *Xinhuanet_Englishnews. cn/2014–10–12–182139*

6 Trenin, *Op. cit.*

difficulties with Brussels and Washington, and enable it to find a new equilibrium in relations with them based on the outcome of the current rivalry.

In spite of all the efforts of the Obama administration, Russia is still not internationally isolated, at least not from Asia and Latin America. There are also some other developments that are positive for Moscow, both in Russia itself and in Europe.

In September 2014, Russian industry and agriculture showed the fastest growth since 2012. As a part of the difficult economic transition to import substitution, in September 2014 retail and investment numbers declined, but agricultural production increased by 16.8% year-on-year in September and 7.7% in the first nine months of the year (2014). It seems that combined with strong industrial output growth in September 2014 (2.8%) driven by import substitution, this should lead to improvement in basic sector output.[1]

The combination of the sanctions with the drop in oil prices has also some positive outcomes for Russia. Oil prices are now lower but, at least partly because of the sanctions, so is the Russian currency. As oil revenues are mainly calculated in dollars, this means Russia's tax receipts from the oil trade, which are so crucial for the state budget, are not much different than they were before. Russian oil companies earn dollars abroad but spend rubles domestically, and their production budget has not been greatly affected. As Chris Weafer of Macro-Advisory notes: "At that oil price and ruble exchange rate, the federal budget would likely run a deficit of approximately 2.5% of GDP. Hardly the sort of scenario which would crash the economy or kill public support for the president."[2] In the view of Russian economists, as expressed by Alfa-Bank's chief economist Evgeniy Gavrilenkov, "the [Russian] economy is adjusting to the new environment. Economic growth has slowed, but it is not stagnating or contracting."[3]

The American and Russian experts might dispute the results of the economic sanctions but they all agree that Washington–Moscow relations are at their rock bottom.

The geopolitical and economic factors are here strictly inter-related and the West, or more exactly the American power elite and its allies, are making abundant use of their economic might to regain control over Russia and the whole international system. The officially undeclared economic war against Moscow could be now more successful than during the Cold War

---

1 "Russian agriculture production soars after food sanctions," *Business New Europe*, October 21, 2014. See also "Putin's import substitution policy is working," *Business New Europe*, October 21, 2014.

2 Chris Weafer, "Comment: Life in Russia with $80 oil," *Business New Europe*, October 17, 2014.

3 "Putin's import substitution policy is working," *Business New Europe*, October 21, 2014.

(1947–1989) period. The Soviet Union had a very different socio-economic system then and was largely isolated from the capitalist markets. The Soviet state legally owned and directed almost all of the economy of the country and those international trade and financial transactions still existing were under its strict control. Until Gorbachev and Yeltsin's time, there was also no substantial group of people with a vested interest in economic ties with the West. Since the 1990s, Moscow's opening to globalization has made the nation far more vulnerable to the global market and international financial pressures. Its present economic situation is far from tragic, but Russia has have already had to spend $60 billion from reserves to support companies suffering financial loses due to Western sanctions.[1] Although mathematically Russia still has enough reserves to hold out for at least two years before Western sanctions start to suffocate its economy,[2] it remains under threat from "the sleeping dragon of investor panic,"[3] which might be easily stimulated by the ongoing information warfare. Former Russian Finance Minister Alexei Kudrin predicted that the Western sanctions would last a minimum of one year (possibly to March 2015)[4] or two, depending on the settlement in southern and eastern Ukraine.[5] It might be a long and trying period for the Russian economy and the internal stability of the nation. In fact, all these predictions proved to be too optimistic.

Both the Russian president, Putin, and the Russian political class for a long time expected that European opposition against the disruption of economic links with Russia would render the sanctions either impossible or ineffective in practice.[6] Opposition to sanctions against Russia came not only from some rather marginal left- or right-wing parties, such as the French Front National or Die Linke in Germany, but, especially in Germany and though to a lesser extent in France, from many influential business leaders, politicians and intellectuals, including three former chancellors and the former president of Germany. Professor Hans-Werner Sinn gave expression

1 M.K Badhrakumar, "Russian economy skids on oil slick," *Indian Punchline Reflections on Foreign Affairs*, October 23, 2014.

2 According t the independent analysts Russia has the stockpile of $472 billion hard currency reserves and nearly $1.5 trillion of assets overall. "It is more than enough to keep banks, firms and the economy going as the West tries to punish Moscow over the Ukrainian crisis," Maxim Shemetov, "Unless investors Panic, Russia's Reserves Will Withstand Sanctions," Reuters, August 1, 2014.

3 *Op. cit.*

4 "The anti-Russian sanctions imposed by the European Union will not be scaled back or rescinded until mid-March of next year, an EU diplomatic source told RIA Novosti, Moscow," October 29, 2014, RIA Novosti.

5 M.K. Badhradkumar, *Op. cit.*

6 "Russia counts on EU's 'friends,' to avert further sanctions," http://www.euractiv.com/sections/global-europe/russia-counts-eu-friends-avert-further-sanctions-303091, June 26, 2014.

to their opinions in an article addressed to the American public.[1] European opposition to the sanctions was grounded in various political, moral but also economic considerations. While American–Russian links have been quite modest,[2] for the European nations Russia has become a major commercial partner and the Eurozone did 12 times as much trade with Russia as the United States did [in 2013]."[3]

The major European economies, particularly Germany, only finally accepted anti-Russian sanctions after flight MH17 was shot down over eastern Ukrainian airspace on July 17, 2014. Though the cause of the tragedy is still under investigation,[4] American media and politicians instantly blamed it on Russia and even President Putin himself. Because of the following huge information/disinformation campaign, it became politically impossible to oppose the sanctions.[5] As one leading economic analyst has indicated: "the supine diplomacy of Japan and some European countries having the most to lose from the break with Russia demonstrate the degree of dominance in Washington."[6]

The Western sanctions were obviously politically motivated and their results are, at least until now, more political than economic. Despite dire forecasts for its economy, Russia has recently risen an unprecedented 30 positions in the World Bank's annual "Doing Business" survey for 2015.[7] The country received 62nd place out of 189 ranked nations, ahead of China at 90, Brazil at 120 and India at 142. Though Russia is still lagging behind many developed capitalist nations, and the World Bank noted its worsening business climate for the category of "trading across borders" (which might be related to the existing political situation),[8] overall progress and the fact of its official recognition by the Western-dominated institution might be seen as a remarkable success. However, the improvements in business

---

1 "Why We Should Give Putin a Chance. Russia's annexation of Crimea violated international law, but the West triggered the crisis in Ukraine," *Wall Street Journal*, May 2, 2014.

2 2013 was estimated at $40 billion.

3 Liam Halligan, "Why the West will surrender in its new cold war with Russia," *The Spectator* (UK), October 18, 2014. According to Russian President Putin, during the first six months of 2014, Russian trade with the EU totaled over $260 billion. Meeting of the Valdai Discussion Club, October 24, 2014, President of Russia, www.kremlin.ru

4 "MH17 prosecutor open to theory another plane shot airliner," *Der Spiegel*, Amsterdam, October 27, 2014 (Reuters).

5 Liam Halligan, *Op. cit.*

6 Eric Kraus, "The Bear and Dragon Chronicles – Western Myopia," http://russia-insider.com/en/china_politics_business_opinion_media_watch/2014/11/02/10-36-57am/bear_and_dragon_chronicles_-, October 28, 2014.

7 Sam Skove, "Russia Climbs 30 Places in World Bank Business Ranking," *Moscow Times*, October 30, 2014.

8 *Op. cit.*

activities cannot take away the lurking external threats to the country's macroeconomic development and its political future.

I believe that Yevgeny Primakov, a prominent scholar and former Premier of Russia, was right in saying that, "The aim of the anti-Russia sanctions is to weaken Russia, corner us, put into practice the idea of a 'color revolution' in our country."[1] He was by no means the first to point that out. More than three months earlier, Dmitri Trenin had observed that "It is no longer the struggle for Ukraine, but a battle for Russia."[2] This battle is still on, and its results will be important not only for Russia itself but most likely for the whole international order.

The problems of Russia and the present international system were debated at the 11th Valdai International Discussion Club October 22–24, 2014. The Russian and Western experts (and, in the case of the West, politicians, mostly retired), gathering there received bad press in the American media and even in a number of European countries. It was nevertheless a meeting worthy of attention of those people who, in spite of their different views, are still willing to share common concerns about the future. During and even after the long meeting on October 24 with Russian President Putin, the atmosphere was calm and open, despite the current political tensions and the Russia–West confrontation. Watching all the proceedings on my computer, I was particularly impressed by the remarkable lack of rudeness, insults and arrogance, which are unfortunately so frequent in Western political debates and media. Although the opinions of the participants often sharply differed and neither a consensus nor common suggestion how to solve the problems was achieved, it was still a very interesting and instructive debate. While in attendance, the former French Prime Minister Dominique de Villepin stressed that "a serious dialogue is possible, provided it is based on respect for existing differences and the principles of the countries' independence and equality."[3]

The speeches and discussions during the three consecutive sessions focused on the present economic and political international system and the situation and role of Russia in its framework. In addition, the issues of zones of special interest (in the American tradition, the Monroe Doctrine) and sanctions against Russia generated major debate. Some argued that the Monroe Doctrine was a thing of the past and that the US no longer followed it, but some participants suggested that if that were true it would be so

---

1 "The goal of Western economic sanctions is a "color revolution" in Russia, Russian Academy of Sciences presidium member, academician Yevgeny Primakov is convinced," TASS, October 29, 2014.

2 Dmitri Trenin, "A Battle for Russia," http://carnegie.ru/eurasiaoutlook/?fa=56261, July 28, 2014.

3 http://valdaiclub.com/valdai_club/73620.html

only to the extent that the US, as a global superpower, no longer needed the Doctrine because the US now considers the whole world as more than its "zone of special interest" — in fact, as its sphere of dominance. It was suggested that after 1989, the Russian Federation represented something similar to a Monroe Doctrine for the post-Soviet space, and that this is a reality of international relations which more and more major players seek to follow. Concerning the sanctions, the consensus was that they have ripple effects not only for the targeted country but also for the countries imposing the sanctions, especially the European nations (the US is in more favorable and well-protected position). However, in the future the US might also be affected, if the other countries are able to leave the dollar zone and create their own alternative economic and financial systems.

Most of the experts indicated that they consider the international system to be in a period of international crisis. However, there was no agreement on the causes and extent of the crisis, and there was also no common opinion how to overcome it.

Since the end of the Cold War many people have expected that a new international system based on economic globalization would take shape on its own, without any political intervention by the main actors. However, this concept of liberal internationalism and the idealization of the rule of the market did not prove to be completely practical and applicable. States and their political interests are proved still major actors and the recent sanctions against Russia have challenged previous economic systemic premises. The role of the US as leader of the unipolar world was questioned by many Eastern and Western participants,[1] but no consensus or practical suggestions were found to address that issue.

The most important point of the last Valdai Club meeting was Vladimir Putin's speech of October 24, 2014. Though the speech was attacked by the Western media as anti-American,[2] the speech's criticism of Washington's policy was a rather secondary issue and Mikhail Gorbachev said "it was the best and most significant speech Putin has ever made."[3] The Russian leader

---

1 One of the strongest voices on this issue was opinioned by a *Guardian* columnist and associate editor, Seumas Milne, "A real counterweight to US power is a global necessity. Conflicts in the Middle East and Ukraine will spread without effective restraint on western unilateralism," *The Guardian* (UK), October 29, 2014.

2 See for instance Kellon Howell, "Putin blasts US in Cold War inspired speech:" 'the bear...will not surrender,' *Washington Times*, October 25, 2014. One needs to keep in mind that this journal is considered as a quite moderate.

3 "Gorbachev endorses Putin's views on the West," *Intelligence* (UK). While asked about Putin's Valdai speech, Gorbachev told RIA Novosti on October 25, 2014, "The speech was fantastic. I don't think there has been such a speech in all the years of Putin's rule. Perhaps also the situation demands this. Basically, I agree with all the ideas expressed by him," *Op. cit.*

may have been offended by the severe economic sanctions and information warfare waged against his country, but he kept his focus on what he considers to be global problems and Russia's role among nations.

Putin's speech, apparently well prepared and structured, is not easy to summarize, but it is easy to misunderstand and attack. The New York Times described it as "perhaps his strongest diatribe against the US," and Fox News reported that "Putin Blasts US in his Speech Blaming West for Conflict in Ukraine." Numerous others made even stronger accusations.

In fact in his three-hour appearance the Russian president repeated again his well-known objections to US foreign policy but, in contrast to many Western speeches and publications, his long talk was neither aggressive nor insulting and can hardly be characterized as a "diatribe." He mentioned the Ukrainian issue only briefly and in the much broader and in my view well-argued context of political and cultural relations.

What were the causes of such a strong Western reaction? What was the substance of Putin's controversial address and what was its real meaning?

The Russian liberal and usually rather pro-Western analyst Fyodor Lukyanov indicates that with the exception of "a couple of scathing metaphors such as 'master of the taiga' [in relation to Russia] and the geopolitical 'nouveaux riches' not being able to deal with the enormous power and wealth cast upon them [which might as well have been a reference to the US], in essence the speech was more that of an analyst than a publicist."[1]

As the theme of the last Valdai Club session was the present shape of the international system, "New Rules or Game Without Rules," Putin started by recalling that we are living in a time of general transformation which includes not just the political, but all aspects of individual and social life on our planet. This kind of change "has usually been accompanied, if not by global war and conflict, then by chains of intense local-level conflicts."[2] Therefore, it is not surprising that "the world is full of contradictions today... and global politics is above all about economic leadership, issues of war and peace and the humanitarian dimension, including human rights."[3] As an almost inevitable outcome of that, the current system of global and regional security has been seriously damaged and there is now no guarantee that it can protect the world from upheavals. One of the reasons for that might be the fact that many of the present institutions were created in the period after

---

1 Fyodor Lukyanov, "Playing by the rules and without rules," http://eng. globalaffairs.ru/redcol/Playing-by-the-rules-and-without-rules-17078, November 4, 2014.
2 "Putin speech to Valdai Club," http://eng.kremlin.ru/news/23137, October 24, 2014.
3 *Op. cit.*

World War II; they have become somewhat outdated and might require some reforms and updating. But Putin believes that the main cause of the problems is the fact that "the Cold War ended, but it did not end with the signing of a peace treaty with clear and transparent agreement on respecting existing rules or creating new rules and standards."[1]

Though the Russian president spoke mainly in general terms, he touched on a number of current challenges including political and economic confrontations, arbitrarily imposed sanctions, nuclear disarmament, and the conflicts in Ukraine and the Middle East. As a way to get out of the impasse he proposed a renewal of the international system based on respect for international law and multilateral consensus. Putin criticized American unilateralism and Washington's tendency to impose its will, and its socio-political and cultural models, on the rest of the world, but he explicitly called for the restoration of Russian–American dialogue, including an open discussion on strategic nuclear weapons.[2]

However, at the same time Lukyanov, an analyst whom I have cited before, perceived "a touch of fatalism in the president's tone."[3] Given the fact that the US president had called Moscow's support for the rebels in Eastern Ukraine an act of aggression and a global threat alongside the Ebola virus in West Africa and the ISIS terrorism in Syria and Iraq,[4] and given the imposition of heavy economic sanctions on Russia, Putin could hardly have been very optimistic. "The Russian president now believes that there is no use even trying to persuade the other side, especially the US,"[5] and thinks the sanctions will remain in place no matter what happens in Ukraine.[6] At a time when, according to two leading American experts on Russia, "most in Washington want to treat Putin as if he were Slobodan Milosevic, Saddam

---

1 *Op. cit.*
2 The liberal Russian scholar Igor Ivanov, who has always been in close touch with the Western elites and, during Yeltsin's presidency was the Foreign Minister for Russia commented about that: "The lack of contact, breakdown of the dialogue, and substitution of diplomacy with hostile rhetoric's never did anything to solve problems between states. I would like to hope that the hand extended by Vladimir Putin to our American partners will not be left to hang in the air," Igor Ivanov, "From Munich to Sochi," *RIAC*, November 6, 2014.
3 Lukyanov, *Op. cit.*
4 "Obama condemns Russia, calls for action against ISIS and Ebola," Everett Rosenfelt, *CNBC*, September 27, 2014. Also, according to Russia's Foreign Minister Lavrov: " We [the Russians] earned the second place among the threats to international peace and stability," "Russia tops ISIS threat, Ebola worst of all?" *RTU*, September 24, 2014.
5 Anastasia Borik, "Russian foreign policy is not aggression, it's fatalism," *Russia-Direct*, November 6, 2014.
6 *Op. cit.* Dmitri Trenin has already indicated the similar bleak prospects in his articles in Summer 2014.

Hussein, or Muammar al-Gaddafi,"[1] there is not much reason for him to be trusting and optimistic.

Right at the beginning of his speech Putin warned the audience that "some of what I say might seem a bit too harsh,"[2] but he added that "if we do not speak directly and honestly about what we really think, then there is little point in even meeting in this way."[3] He contrasted Valdai Club meetings with "diplomatic get-togethers where no one says anything of real sense...."[4] According to him the reason for the present meeting was not to trade barbs but to attempt to get to the bottom of what is actually happening in the world. He also indicated that the bygone era of a solid international system had rested not only on a balance of power and the rights of the victor countries, but "on the fact that its 'founding fathers' had respect for each other and did not try to put a squeeze on others, but attempted to reach agreements."[5]

According to him the loss of those values was the main cause of the current crisis.

Putin did not speak at the Valdai Club meeting as a scholar but as a political leader, and he reflected on the situation as he saw it from Moscow at a time when his country was under great pressure and was at least partially isolated. However, I think that he provided a rather accurate analysis of the international situation and in spite of all the personal attacks on him, he expressed his readiness to talk and to search for common ground with Western leaders.

Putin's real problem is not, as Western media and politicians suggest, his lack of goodwill, but his country's relative weakness in relation to the global Superpower and its allies. As long as the Western elites would like to believe that they are invincible and that Russia is, as President Obama indicated, easy to defeat, it is unlikely that even moderate and rational proposals from Moscow are going to be heard and taken seriously.[6] The West would probably respond with additional threats and political and economic pressure.

Being most likely aware of that, Putin still wants to preserve some hope and to gain more opportunities for understanding and better future relations

---

1 Robert D. Blackwell and Dimitri K. Simes, "Dealing with Putin," *The National Interest*, November 16, 2014.

2 "Putin speech to Valdai Club," http://eng.kremlin.ru/news/23137, October 24, 2014.

3 *Op. cit.*

4 *Op. cit.*

5 *Op. cit.* In fact, since the Viennese Congress in 1815 this relatively mild and respectful treatment of the defeated was seen in the European diplomatic tradition as a necessary precondition for a more stable settlement.

6 See for instance Nicolai Petro, "Why the Putin Peace Plan is Working," *The National Interest*, October 22, 2014 and the following 52 comments are of considerable interest.

with the Western powers. He knows that "Ukraine is essentially of no interest to Western leaders per se, only as an exceptionally powerful lever for influencing Russia"[1] and forcing it to accept Western domination. Asked about the way in which his Valdai speech was received in the West, he replied that "it takes time for someone to understand what I actually said."[2] Debate forums such as the Valdai Club are for open and even provocative talks, but it would be good "to return to the issue in the calm of offices and talk everything over."[3]

It would be difficult to deny that "the global political system is destabilized and has entered a period of transition with a growing vacuum of power and institutions," as Professor Tsygankov has remarked.[4] A number of other Western scholars have admitted the same. The US remains the leading power but it has became mired in national debt now amounting to over $17 trillion and rising. Such a debt would be almost impossible to pay back. At the same time, the country has to face the declining value of the dollar — with all the domestic and international implications, including the erosion of social confidence and trust in the world at large. Both the emergence of new economic power centers among the former Third World nations and the tensions in the Middle East, which the Americans are either unable or unwilling to control, now represent major challenges to the only remaining Superpower. Although Europe has lost its role as "the world's geopolitical center of gravity"[5] and today's European leaders are quite submissive to American wishes, their own populations (including the European business class) are more critical and reluctant to follow the Washington policy.

As the two American security experts argue, "The US should take these international realities especially seriously when dealing with Russia that has a powerful strategic nuclear arsenal, a global presence that includes regional superiority in key areas along its frontlines, and an acute sense that its own existential national interests are at risk in the Ukraine crisis."[6]

In this crisis and the new cold war against Russia, the US wants to demonstrate its might and its dominant global position. Most American

1 Mikhail Rosthavskiy, "In the Wake of G20 Summit. It is Time to Try to Reach Agreement with the Russian Bear," *Moskovskiy Komsomoletz*, November 18, 2014.
2 "Russian President Putin says it would be useless to initiate discussion of anti-Russian sanctions at the G20 summit in Australia and denies cooling in relations with German Federal Chancellor Angele Merkel," *Interfax*, November 14, 2014.
3 *Op. cit.*
4 Andrei Tsygankov, "Will Russia be able to build a functioning state?" *Russia Direct*, November 17, 2014.
5 Luis Simon, "A post European world? American-Russian Relations in Perspective," http:www.eurostrategy.org, April 20, 2014.
6 Robert D. Blackwill and Dimitri Simes, "Dealing with Putin," *The National Interest*, November 16, 2014.

politicians apparently do not believe in, and probably reject, the concept of a multipolar world order and the other nations' right to have their own ways of developing. Because of the memory of the previous Cold War confrontation, some of them are also suspicious that Moscow would be inclined to take America's place as the world hegemon,[1] despite the fact that that is not presently Russia's intention and would be completely impossible for a number of reasons.

I have already argued that the Russian Federation cannot be considered to be a new Soviet Union or even the Tsarist Empire as it stood before World War I and the Bolshevik revolution. It has neither the economic nor demographic basis for that, and its military might is much diminished and, compared with the Western powers, relatively modest. Its political and economic elites are divided and Moscow does not have sufficient soft power, or popular attraction, at its disposal. Russia also has in its own vicinity the real and growing Chinese power which even the Americans have to respect.

Putin and his team are a pretty realistic group of people. In his Valdai speech and numerous other statements the Russian president has always stressed that his country has no aspirations to global leadership and does not want to follow the Soviet example to represent a kind of 'savior to the world.' That has already cost too much and it did not prove to be effective. His political doctrine is to call for a multipolar world order and "every nation being sovereign."[2]

Putin's use of the Siberian bear as a symbol was intended to send a similar message. Talking about the relations between the Western powers and Russia, he recalled the ancient Roman proverb, "Whatever Jupiter may be entitled to, the ox is not."[3] However, his comment was that "we cannot agree with such an approach. The ox might not be allowed something, but the bear does not even ask permission. Here we consider it the master of the taiga, and I know for sure that it does not intend to move to any other climatic zones; it would not be comfortable there. However, it will not let anyone have its taiga either. I believe this is clear."[4]

Unfortunately his message seems not to be either clear or acceptable to the leaders of the West. The problem is not their lack of intellectual comprehension but their will to preserve their global domination.

In spite of all the challenges they currently face, most of the American political and academic elites still believe that for the foreseeable future their

---

1 "An overview from Sharon Tennison," in "Now is the time to find a way out of the East-West Confrontation: Will Europe or Washington lead the way?" www.us-russia.org, *November 23, 2014, 17.00*

2 "Meeting of Valdai International Discussion Club," President of Russia, www. kremlin.ru, October 24, 2014.

3 *Op. cit.*

4 *Op. cit.*

country will continue to preserve the status of a global hegemon and they are not ready to accept Russia and other non-Western nations as equal partners.[1] The only possible exception here might be in China, but even this case is highly controversial in the US. This kind of ideological approach and psychological attitude may not correspond to the real situation, but they might persist for several decades and lead to the most dangerous developments since the end of World War II in 1945.[2] Russia, which unlike China is perceived as a weak but prickly nation and generally treated with scorn and mistrust, seems to be in a particularly difficult situation.[3] However, Russia is neither as weak as some Western leaders believe nor as strong as some of their Kremlin counterparts might dream. As Henry Kissinger reminded us all, "Russia is still an important part of the international system and therefore, useful in solving all sorts of other crises, for example in the agreement on nuclear proliferation with Iran or over Syria."[4] According to him, "this has to [take precedence] over a tactical escalation in a specific case."[5]

The Ukraine crisis initiated by the West might not bring it the expected results.[6] Russia is just across the border and considers what happens in Ukraine to be a matter of existential interest. The West is acting mostly for ideological reasons and out of its neo-imperial impulses. However, after launching this project, the subsequent level of involvement and readiness to pay for it are quite different. Kissinger believes that "nobody [in the West] is willing to fight over eastern Ukraine. That is fact of life,"[7] and "NATO has no winning strategy and has admitted as much at the Wales summit in September 2014 by failing to develop a coherent response to Russia."[8] Economic measures are too limited to isolate a huge country from the global market and the society's reactions to the sanctions, at least so far, have been quite different than the West expected. As Professor Tsygankov writes, "the more Western governments try to squeeze the Kremlin, the more nationalist and anti-Western the Russian public becomes."[9] And as the American

1 Andrei Tsygankov, Otlozhennye Politsentrismu, http://www.globalaffairs.ru/ number/Otlozhennyi-policentrism–16924

2 Robert D. Blackwill and Dimitri Simes, "Dealing with Putin," *Op. cit.* As they indicate "the stage is being set for an even more dramatic confrontation between the West and Russia over Ukraine. Obama must recognize the danger to US national interests that crisis might create and act accordingly."

3 Andrei Tsygankov, *Op. cit.*

4 "Do We Achieve World Order Through Chaos or Insight?" *Der Spiegel*, November 13, 2014.

5 Henry A. Kissinger, "To settle the Ukraine crisis, starts at the end," *Washington Post*, March 5, 2014.

6 Andrei Tsygankov, "Pressure on Russia Will Not Benefit the West," *European Leadership Network*, November 17, 2014.

7 "Do We Achieve World Order Through Chaos or Insight?" *Op. cit.*

8 Andrei Tsygankov, *Op. cit.*

9 *Op. cit.*

scholars note, "Western sanctions are the most important mechanism for the mass mobilization of Russian public opinion against the United States and Europe."[1] That is quite a typical reaction in a traditional ethno-national society, which the post-modern individualistic West apparently failed to foresee. In addition most non-Western countries are not willing to follow the Western sanctions and their companies are profiting from them. Russia has also been able to capitalize on Moscow's image as a force ready to resist US global hegemony and willing to assist those seeking to improve their position in the world.[2] China and most of the other non-Western nations consider the Kremlin's policies on Ukraine as defensive and understandable, even if of dubious legality.

According to Henry Kissinger, who is probably the most knowledgeable expert on international relations, "For the greatest part of history until really the very recent time, world order was regional order. This is the first time that different parts of the world can interact with every part of the world. This makes a new order for the globalized world necessary. But there are no universally accepted rules. There is the Chinese view, the Islamic view, the Western view and, to some extent, the Russian view. And they really are not always compatible."[3]

The Ukraine crisis might be the most recent and probably the most dangerous example. In the fall of 2013 the EU, while negotiating its association agreement with Ukraine, did not want to take into account Russia's economic and security interests and its more than 1000-year links with this country. It goes without saying that Moscow has to accept that, as Putin admitted, Ukraine has become a separate and independent (even though deeply divided) nation, but as Kissinger stresses, "the West must understand that, to Russia, Ukraine can never be just a foreign country. Russian history began in what was called Kievan Rus. The Russian religion spread from there. Ukraine has been part of Russia for centuries, and their histories were intertwined before then. Even such famed dissidents as Aleksandr Solzhenitsyn and Joseph Brodsky insisted that Ukraine was an integral part of Russian history and indeed of Russia.[4] Also now the Black Sea Fleet — Russia's means of projecting power in the Mediterranean — is based in Sevastopol, in Crimea. Kissinger argues that Russia's annexation of Crimea, following the anti-Russian coup d'état in Kiev, "was not a move toward global conquest."[5] In his view Putin acted out of strategic weakness masked as tactical strength, not to be compared to "Hitler moving into

---

1 Robert D. Blackwill and Dimitri K. Simes, *Op. cit.*
2 Andrei Tsygankov, *Op. cit.*
3 "Do We Achieve World Order Through Chaos or Insight?" *Op. cit.*
4 Henry A. Kissinger, *Op. cit.*
5 "Do We Achieve World Order Through Chaos or Insight?" *Op. cit.*

Czechoslovakia."[1] Almost all the circumstances were quite different and an analogy like that would be both spurious and dangerous. The renewal of a full scale Cold War and the possible outbreak of a hot one would be possible outcomes and an enormous tragedy for the whole world. A compromise solution is possible and necessary but as Dimitri K. Simes, the President of the Center for National Interest, and his colleagues indicate, "A realistic and lasting solution would have to reflect the national interests and protect the dignity of both sides, including President Putin."[2]

According to Dmitri Trenin, "Ukraine is not a cause, but a symbol for the serious and deepening crisis between the US and Russia."[3] In his view, "Essentially, Russia, in dealing with [the coup d'état in Kiev and the Western take-over of] Ukraine, has broken out of the US-dominated international system. Moreover, it has materially challenged the global order that the US strives to uphold."[4] Representing here the American ideology of the unipolar world order, Trenin seems to be correct. At the same time he is still willing to admit that, "for both sides, the stakes are exceedingly high. For Moscow it is the survival of the Russian state. For Washington it is the continuity and credibility of the US hegemony."[5] Consequently, "a compromise is virtually impossible,"[6] because any compromise, by its very nature, would require the recognition of at least some of the Russian claims, a nonstarter for the US. Trenin, Director of the Moscow Carnegie Center, has to represent the American line and yet he still calls for building a European "relationship with Russia on a new foundation of realism and pragmatism, without the sweet illusions and false expectations of the past."[7]

However, he does not provide any indication as to how to find a way out of the present stalemate. It sounds a bit like the 'Sunday preaching' he himself has ridiculed in some other cases, devoid of any word about the possible role played by the West which initiated the conflict and now controls most of Ukraine.

Some other scholars and politicians, mostly retired, including Edward Lozansky and Mikhail Gorbachev, asked this question,[8] and although it is obvious that none of them is able to now find a plausible solution acceptable

---

1 "Do We Achieve World Order Through Chaos or Insight?" *Op. cit.*
2 Robert D. Blackwill and Dimitri K. Simes, *Op. cit.*
3 Dmitri Trenin, "West and Russia now in permanent crisis," *Global Times (China)*, November 4, 2014.
4 *Op. cit.*
5 *Op. cit.*
6 *Op. cit.*
7 *Op. cit.*
8 "Now is the time to find a way out of the East-West confrontation: will Europe or Washington lead the way?" Expert Panel http://us-russia.org/2807-now-is-the-time-to-find-a-way-out-of-the-east-west-confrontation-will-europe-or-washington-lead-the-way.html, November 23, 2014. See also a recent poll of the

to both sides, they nevertheless initiated a serious debate which will have to be continued in order to prevent some of the more dramatic potential outcomes, including a full scale World War III with the use of nuclear weapons.

Following the Gorbachev essay, a panel discussion was held at the American University in Moscow where the following questions were asked:

1. Where do we in fact look first for the solution to the present global confrontation, to Washington or to Brussels?

2. Will Europe back down on sanctions first, due to the harm they are causing its own economy and political fragility after six years of austerity? Will Washington be able to go it alone in containing Russia?

3. Given the Foreign Affairs poll results, is there some basis for expecting the Washington political elites to crack on the Russia question even without reference to Europe?[1]

Having been a Panel member myself, I would like to provide here a summary of my replies and add some of my historical reflections on Western–Russia relations and the possible future alternatives.

I do not think that Brussels itself would be able to take any major game-changing initiative. It is too bureaucratic, corrupted in a subtle way, and — what is probably most decisive — too dependent on Washington. Brussels does not have sufficient support from the European population.

Some traditional European powers, such as France, Germany and perhaps Italy, might play a more active role. According to many analysts Germany's chancellor Angela Merkel put an end to German Ostpolitik and to the good relations between Berlin and Moscow established by the previous chancellors Willy Brandt and Helmut Schmidt.[2] Her new strong criticism of Putin and Russia might have had a negative impact on Russian–German relations, but she is unlikely to lose her influence on Kiev–Moscow relations and the developments in Ukraine. She represents a major European power with long lasting and well-established links

---

29-man "Brain Trust" by *Foreign Affairs* magazine published online November 11, 2014.

1 Expert Panel, http://us-russia.org/2807-now-is-the-time-to-find-a-way-out-of-the-east-west-confrontation-will-europe-or-washington-lead-the-way.html, November 23, 2014, *Op. cit.*

2 Natalie Nougarede, "Why Angela Merkel is saying farewell to Ostpolitik?" *The Guardian*, November 26, 2014. See also Andreas Rinke, "How Putin Lost Berlin Moscow's annexation of Crimea has transformed Germany's Russia policy," *German Council of Foreign Relations*, September 29, 2014 and Catherine Blinova "Merkel chooses the dark side and abandons Germany's pro-Russian Ostpolitik," *Sputnik News*, November 27, 2014. For the scholarly analysis see Professor James Petres, "The Rise of German Imperialism and the Phony Russian Threat," www.thepeoplevoice.org, December 7, 2014.

with Russia and Ukraine.[1] In addition it would be understandable that as Chancellor of Germany she needs to tread a very fine line and to take American wishes into account.Her influence might seem diminished sometimes, but it certainly has not vanished. French President François Hollande, who stopped in Moscow in December 2014 to meet his Russian counterpart, Vladimir Putin,[2] is apparently also willing to talk with the Russian leader and to understand his situation. However, he is not in a secure enough position to take a strong political stance, and the Italian leaders have even less strength at their disposal.[3] Because of the old continent's present weakness, the European nations would be probably either rather passive or, as in the case of Poland and Baltic nations, would play a very negative role as the instruments of the most hawkish parts of the American establishment.[4]

Washington has many means at its disposal not only to contain, but also to undermine the present Russian "regime" and even to destroy that nation. However, it would be still a risky and probably very costly operation, and I do not believe that the US would be willing to go it alone to do that. It wants to use further economic sanctions and information warfare and at a same stage even military means, making the Europeans its tools and potential cannon fodder. At present it is the EU which has to bear practically all the burden of the anti-Russia sanctions. In the case of an eventual military intervention, the Americans would need to use the Eastern European nations such as Western Ukraine, Poland,

---

1 For her further interests in the Ukrainian developments see: "Better Implementation of the Minsk Agreements," https://www.bundesregierung. de/Content/EN/Artikel/2015/08_en/2015-08-24-ukraine-treffen-merkel-poroschenko-hollande.html, April 25, 2015, and: "We are committed to the peace process says Merkel," http://www.bundesregierung.de/Content/EN/Artikel/2015/08_en/2015-08-31-sommer-pk-ukraine_en.html, August 31, 2015.
2 "Will meeting with Putin and Nazarbaev help Hollande grow a spine?," http://www.sott.net/article/289902-Will-meetings-with-Putin-and-Nazarbaev-help-Hollande-grow-a-spine, December 7, 2014.
3 However, this year Italy's former Foreign Minister Federica Mogherini replaced Catherine Ashton as the EU's European High Representative for Foreign Affairs. "Italy's Federica Mogherini appointed as new EU High Representative," http://www.eeas.europa.eu/top_stories/2014/300814_federica-mogherini-appointed_en.htm, August 30, 2014. Hawks that were concerned that she would be too soft in her dealings with Moscow opposed Mogherini's appointment as the Chief of EU Foreign Policy. In fact, on November 17, 2014 she stated that, "Russia is for sure a part of the problem, but is also for sure part of the solution," Mark Adomanis, "Did the EU just blink?" *Business New Europe*, November 20, 2014.
4 In the difference with the Middle East and the Latin America's the West does not need to use direct military pressure to subordinate the Eastern and Central European political elites. Their obedience is mostly based on a skillful use of number of their internal historical and socio-economic factors including sometimes blackmail and bribery of their leaders. Those of them who used to be previously involved in the communist state apparatus were particularly vulnerable to be targeted.

the Baltic States, and even Germany. In all these countries the political leadership, though not necessary the population and the business class, are very pro-American and would probably follow almost any decision by Washington. The reasons for that are complex and would require a special analysis.

At least at this moment I do not see any reason why the Washington political elite would be willing to crack on the Russia question, even without reference to Europe and a search for compromise. The 2014 House legislation H. Res. 758 ("Strongly condemning the actions of the Russian Federation, under President Vladimir Putin, which has carried out a policy of aggression against neighboring countries aimed at political and economic domination") and almost all of the administration's statements and political actions indicate quite the opposite. Although there are a number of experts and respected people in the US who opposed that, they do not seem to represent a sufficient counterbalance. They do not have direct access to the levers of power and the mass media (MSM), which are now under other people's control.

The situation is thus difficult, but there is still some basis for a more optimistic outlook. First of all, unlike Russia and some European nations, none of America's vital interests are at stake. Ukraine might be a handy lever to press Russia with, but on its own it holds, for the West, only modest geopolitical and geo-economic importance.[1] In addition one can argue that because of the uncertain situation in the Islamic world, the rising power of China and numerous other challenges, a long confrontation with Russia might not serve American interests. In the 19th century, the famous French writer Ernest Renan commented that "Russia is never as strong as it appears; Russia is never as weak as it appears. Its diplomacy is always relentless." It might be more difficult to defeat than some Western elites anticipate, and even such a victory might bring more problems than benefits, creating (among other things) a great and dangerous power vacuum in Eurasia which the US would not be able to control.

As quite a few security experts have already observed, the general contours of a settlement of the crisis in Ukraine can be imagined[2] and, with some diplomatic effort, be put into practice.[3] However, as President of the Center for National Interest Dmitri K. Simes and some of his

---

1 Mark Adomanis, "Whatever Happen to Ukraine The West Won't Collapse," *Forbes International*, September 5, 2014.

2 Robert D. Blackwill and Dimitri K. Simes, "Dealing with Putin," *The National Interest*, November 16, 2014.

3 Michael Brenner, "Washington Post-Cold War Containment Strategy Obama, Putin and Ukraine," *Counterpunch*, December 1, 2014.

experienced colleagues have stressed: "A realistic and lasting solution would have to reflect national interests and protect the dignity of both sides, including President Putin, yet most in Washington want to treat Putin as if he were Slobodan Milosevic, Saddam Hussein or Muammar Gaddafi."[1] In their view "it should be clear that this cannot succeed"[2] and that "under the circumstances, there is no sensible alternative to open a private channel to Putin trying to end the US–Russia confrontation on Ukraine."[3] There are similar suggestions from other scholars and politicians such as Professor Michael Brenner[4] and even Henry Kissinger himself.[5]

All the present political tension notwithstanding, their opinions could have some influence and the threat of a major hot war could be avoided. However, even if the more optimistic scenario became reality, it would not necessarily mean that peace will prevail and that international harmony will flourish.

For more than a year Washington was playing out a game designed to: 1) reassert US control over Europe by blocking or at least hampering EU trade with Russia, 2) bankrupt Russia, and 3) get rid of Vladimir Putin and his team of independent nationalists and to replace them with people like Yeltsin who would be subservient to American interests.[6]

Although Russia's role in Syria and Iran may have inspired the new anti-Russian reaction in America, the main issue at stake was Russia's economic relations with Europe. Prosperous, with a market economy but politically independent and economically integrated with Europe, Russia would be a real anathema for Washington and, perhaps, a far worse perceived threat than the former Soviet Union. In such a situation the US might lose the political and economic control of Europe that it won after World War II, and perhaps its global hegemonic status. Even a capitalist, strong and independent Russia would remain the second most important nation and it would not be able to count on the friendship and benevolence of the dominant power.

Even if the world removes itself from the Ukraine crisis, Western–Russian relations will likely remain a problem and a long-lasting challenge for both sides. In all its previous history, even in the 19th

---

1 Robert D. Blackwill and Dimitri K. Simes, *Op. cit.*
2 *Op. cit.*
3 *Op. cit.*
4 Michael Brenner, *Op. cit.*
5 Henry A. Kissinger, "To settle the Ukraine crisis, start at the end," *Washington Post*, March 5, 2014 and his more recent interview, "Do We Achieve World Order Through Chaos or Insight?" *Der Spiegel*, November 13, 2014.
6 Diane Johnstone, "Washington Frozen War Against Russia," *Counterpunch*, December 9, 2014.

century, Russia was never seen as a part of the West. Under the present circumstances of American domination and the decline of Europe, Russia has even less chance than before of being accepted and integrated. In fact, at present, absorption into the West might amount to an enormous disaster, destroying the country's national independence and threatening both its traditional culture and the wellbeing of the majority of the population. The best thing which Moscow can do is to follow its own course, restructuring its economy and protecting its culture and national security. This is the way of China and some other BRICS nations, but for a number of reasons it might be for Russia much more difficult. One of the major obstacles here is the internal split in the Russian elites and their well-established Western orientation. Although some conflicts might be difficult to avoid, this would still probably be an optimal solution to the perennial "Russian Problem."

Unfortunately, such a balance, though perhaps not quite a satisfactory solution for part of the Russian elite,[1] would not be easy to be achieved. Since the US and its European allies backed the coup d'état in Kiev in February 2014, helping to overthrow the elected government and enabling a hostile anti-Russian regime to come to power, the Western powers and their media have been persistently demonizing Russia. They accuse it of subversion, annexation and all possible crimes against humanity. At least until now, no one in the current American establishment seems to understand that such violent and often highly abusive criticism directed at Russia as a result of the crisis in Ukraine is exaggerated, at least, and frankly harmful to both Russia and the US. As Professor John Mearsheimer (University of Chicago) says, "The United States and its European allies share most of the responsibility for the crisis. The taproot of the trouble is NATO enlargement, the central element of a larger

---

1 Medvedev: "Russia is part of Europe but also eyeing Asia," *Interfax*, December 10, 2014. As he said "There is no doubt that Russia is part of Europe and European civilization and there is nothing to add here. I have always said so and Vladimir Vladimirovich Putin has said so too." However, not all Russian intellectuals and politicians are exactly of the some opinion. It is true that as the prominent representatives of the German elite have recently reminded, "Even since the Congress of Vienna in 1814 Russia has been recognized as one of the global players in Europe. All who tried to violently change that have failed bloodily." "Prominent German Signatures – Open Letter: Another War in Europe? Not in our name!" *Die Zeit* (Germany), December 5, 2014. However, I believe that Western-Russian relations might be somewhat comparable with the Western European relations with the Byzantine Empire. In spite of its impeccable Greek-Roman traditions and its splendid cultural achievements it had always been seen in the West as an alien body and either destroyed as in 1204 or left without help from the Ottoman final assault in 1453. In 988 Kievian Rus was converted to the Eastern Orthodox form of Christianity and thus inherited the Byzantinian culture.

strategy to move Ukraine out of Russia's orbit and integrate it into the West."[1]

It would be easy to question the Russian annexation of Crimea, but how else might Moscow have reacted to a perceived existential threat to its own national security and to those of Russian citizens? As Henry Kissinger recalled, the very birthplace of "Rus," the Russian cultural identity, was Kiev, centuries before Moscow was founded, and "there is no historical relationship for the United States with any other country that comes even close to that of Russia and Ukraine."[2]

The whole crisis would not be understandable without knowledge of the previous background of American–Russian relations, which had a great impact not only on the views of Washington's elites but, because of the power of American media and the continent's isolation from the rest of the world, have shaped the widespread social clichés and opinions of most Americans.

The American scholar who had studied American images of post-Soviet Russia in Historical Perspective concluded that "in view of the long history of distorted representations of Russia by even the best US newspaper, it seems likely that American journalists will continue to try to get the story of Russia to justify their assumptions about the United States and its role in the world."[3] The failure to achieve an acceptable post-Cold War settlement, discussed by Gorbachev and Trenin, led to the emergence of the new arc of instability in the very heart of Europe, running from the Baltic to the Balkans and the Black Sea.[4] If the Ukraine problem is not solved, the continent will need to be ready for a military buildup and a new arms race with all the associated negative economic and social consequences.

There is still a chance to avoid that, and whatever decision Washington takes will be decisive. While the Russian political and social elites are divided, their American "partners," members of the political class in the United States, are certainly much more coherent and united.

1 John Mearsheimer, "Why the Ukraine crisis is the West Fault, The Liberal Delusions That Provoked Putin," *Foreign Affairs*, September/October 2014.

2 David C. Speedy, "Needs Work: A Troubled US-Russia Relationship," *Carnegie Council for Ethics in International Affairs*, October 14, 2014.

3 David Fogelson, Professor of History, Rutgers University, San Antonio, Texas, November 2014, *Dark Pictures are Easy to Paint: Journalist and American Images of Post-Soviet Russia in Historical Perspective*, Association for Slavic, East European, and Eurasian Studies Convention. See also "Campaign to End Cold or Hot War with Russia," http://www.russiaotherpointsofview.com/2014/12/campaign-to-end-cold-or-hot-war-with-russia.html, December 8, 2014.

4 These are almost identical conclusions of the researchers by the two leading European think-tank: European Council on Foreign Relations in London (UK) and Friedrich Ebert Stiftung in Berlin, Germany.

However, even the American elite is divided between various kinds of global interventionists and the more moderate "realists." As of December 2014, the imperial interventionists still seemed to dominate the American scene and the realists, though outspoken, were in retreat. Consequently, as Professor Immanuel Wallerstein wrote at the time, "The forces in the US and Europe who are seeking to avoid military folly risk being overtaken by what can only be called a war party."[1]

However, in 2015 the relationship between the interventionists and realists has become more complex and subject to fluctuations. Because of developments in Syria, the general situation has also become more difficult to determine, but I do not think that at present the realists are in retreat. Henry Kissinger writes that, "The US has already acquiesced in a Russian military role. Painful as this is to architects of the 1973 system [including himself], attention in the Middle East must remain focused on essentials...it is preferable for ISIS held territory to be re-conquered either by moderate Sunni forces or by outside powers than by Iranian jihadists or imperial forces. For Russia, limiting its military role to the anti-ISIS campaign may avoid a return to Cold War conditions with the US."[2] Going even further, Jeffrey White, a defense fellow at the Washington Institute for Near East Policy, argues that the new situation "bolsters the argument that there can be no solution to the conflict without Moscow's involvement.[3]

---

1 Immanuel Wallerstein, "NATO: Danger to World Peace," http://www. iwallerstein.com/nato-danger-to-world-peace/, November 15, 2014.

2 Henry Kissinger, "A Path Out of the Middle East Collapse: With Russia in Syria, a geopolitical structure that lasted four decades is in shambles. The US needs a new strategy and priorities," *Wall Street Journal*, October 16, 2015.

3 Patrick Martin, "Russia's move into Syria: A game changer," *The Globe and Mail*, September 18, 2015.

CHAPTER 4. THE NEW COLD WAR AND ITS DANGERS

The Ukrainian problem is not the special focus of my monograph, however, the events which began in 2013 and are still unfolding force me to include a brief description of them in relation to the framework of analysis of Russia's place in the world and its struggle for survival in the international system that is now changing shape.

The whole crisis in Ukraine was instigated by the ruling elite of the US in reaction to Moscow's involvement in the Middle East[1] and in order to prevent Russia from regaining its status as a great power.[2] Another specific reason was

---

1 As the well known American political scientist George Friedman who is also the founder and the head of Stratfor, the private analytical and intelligence agency which is often referred to in the US as a "shadow CIA," admitted, "Russia had begun to take certain steps that the United States considered unacceptable. Primarily in Syria. It was there that Russians demonstrated to the Americans that they are capable of influencing processes in the Middle East. Russians intervened in the process in the Middle East, among other reasons, because they hoped to get leverage to influence US policy in other areas. But they miscalculated. The United States thought that it was Russia's intent to harm them. It is in this context that we should be evaluating the events in Ukraine. The Russians, apparently, simply have not calculated how seriously the US side might perceive their actions or the extent to which they can easily find countermeasures. It was in this situation that the US took a look at Russia and thought about what it wants to see happen least of all: instability in Ukraine." "Stratfor Chief's 'Most Blatant Coup in History,'" Elena Chanenko, *Kommersant* (Moscow), January 20, 2015. I do personally admire the sincerity of the leading American intelligence expert, but I am still astonished that the Americans were able to consider as a serious threat the Syrian chemical disarmament and the subsequent lack of pretext for more military intervention in the region.

2 In his interview to the Russian newspaper *Kommersant* Friedman has also stressed that, "no American president can afford to sit by idly if Russia is becoming more and more influential. About three years ago, in one of my books, I predicted that as soon as Russia starts to increase its power and demonstrate it, a crisis would

Washington's wish to disrupt Europe's economic relations with Russia and to prevent the establishment of any kind of 'Greater Europe' from the Atlantic to the Pacific, something that people had started to talk about.[1] The outbreak of the Ukrainian crisis was very timely for that reason and made the American pet project of the Transatlantic Trade and Investment Partnership (TTIP) in Europe more acceptable. As one Russian liberal commentator remarked, "If adopted, [it] will pin the Old World in the wake of the New."[2] In my opinion, the TTIP is likely to bring more profit to US businesses, but it almost certainly will destroy the European welfare state which has already been greatly undermined. In its political implications the TTIP and the similar Trans-Pacific Partnership free trade negotiations (TPP) with some other nations would mean further expansion of the global architecture of financial, defense and other neo-liberal institutions that Washington created at the start of the Cold War and which later became the economic and social basis of its power.[3]

The disruption of good relations with Russia, the new Cold War, and even more so, the possible new hot war, can only harm any rational European interests. With the exception of the UK and a few former Soviet dependencies such as Poland and the Baltic states, where public opinions are divided or silenced, almost all European nations, including not only France, Germany, Greece, and Italy, but also the Czech Republic and Hungary, are opposing and trying to avoid that. However, because of America's superior strength it is by no means certain that their voices are going to be heard taken into account.

The present developments are in fact logical consequences of Paul Wolfowitz's doctrine of neoconservative ideology based on American global hegemony and full spectrum dominance, which might represent a great threat to the Old World.[4]

The tragic outcomes of both World Wars (1914–1945) brought to an end more than four centuries of Europe's worldwide centrality and economic

occur in Ukraine," *Op. cit.* As I have already indicated the US intelligentsia has considered Ukraine as the soft spot of Russia. See Peter Zeihan, "Russia After Ukraine," www.stratfor.com, December 12, 2004.

1 See for instance Heinrich Bonnenberg, "Europe is More than the EU," www.atlantic-community.org, February 5, 2010.

2 Fedor Lukyanov, "Russian pundit sees Ukraine conflict as aftermath of Cold War," *Rossiyskaye Gazeta*, February 25, 2015.

3 As the Princeton Professor G. John Ikenberry admits the purpose of global architecture of financial, defense and social neoliberal institutions that they (US) established after World War II was to manage geopolitics in order to maintain and expand the American empires, G. John Ikenberrry, "The Illusion of Geopolitics. The Enduring Power of the Liberal Order," *Foreign Affairs*, May/June 2014.

4 Paul Craig Roberts, "The Neoconservative Threat to World Order," www.paulcraigroberts.org/2015/02/26

and political leadership. European great powers such as France and the UK may have preserved their traditional honorary position, but neither their former power nor their influence. Germany was utterly destroyed, divided and humiliated and a similar — though for various reasons not as drastic — punishment was inflicted on the great Asian power, Japan. As China was at that time still torn apart by its civil war, and its future rise was estimated to require several generations, there were only two real great powers left to coexist and compete for global leadership: the US and the Soviet Union, which though painfully affected by the last war itself, and with a weak and shaky economy, was nevertheless the real military victor of Nazi Germany and controlled crucial parts of Central Eurasia. Although until 1949 the USSR did not have nuclear weapons, its geopolitical position and its prevailing worldwide prestige forced the Americans to take a more cautious Cold War policy (1947–1989) without direct military confrontation and, compared with the present day, a relatively mild information war.

The Cold War period from 1947 to the late 1980s was a time when millions of people lived under the potential threat of a nuclear war and destruction. At the same time it was also a period of relative stability and predictability in international relations which, especially in Europe, were based on a balance of power between Washington and Moscow. As Dr. Mark Galeotti and Professor Stephen Cohen have both indicated, "despite its adversarial nature the Cold War was governed by a set of unwritten rules worn smooth by use, which prevented the war ever getting hot."[1] In 1962, in an effort to provide security insurance for Fidel Castro's socialist government in Havana, Moscow sent some of its nuclear weapons to Cuba. However, after the US issued a strong protest, it withdrew them rather quickly and Washington instead provided security guarantees for the Cuban regime. At that time the Kennedy administration was diplomatic enough to provide Moscow with a face-saver by withdrawing its own missiles from Turkey. However, I do not think that this had any real impact on the balance of power that was then in place. In fact the American military already considered the Jupiter missiles deployed in Turkey as obsolete and wanted to replace them with the more modern and effective Polaris submarine ballistic missiles, which Turkey did not wish to accept.[2] As the new missiles were located on submarines and not on the land, this did not create any obstacles to the further, and in fact increased, presence of US ballistic missiles in the region.[3] Prior to that, the

---

1 Ben Aris, "It is time for a new post-European security treaty," *Business New Europe*, www.bne.eu, January 13, 2015.
2 "Turkey's Nuclear Missiles: An Important Player in the Cuban Missile Crisis," *Turkey Wonk: Nuclear and Political Musing in Turkey and Beyond*, November 4, 2012.
3 *Op. cit.* America offered Ankara to "give" 5 Polaris submarines to NATO and the permanent stationing of at least one nuclear submarine in the Eastern Mediterranean. However, the Polaris submarines were not going to be

US had stood by and did not intervene during the anti-Communist uprising of 1953 in East Germany and the Hungarian anti-Soviet revolution in the fall of 1956 (from 23 October until 10 November). At that time, both East Germany and Hungary were seen as parts of the Soviet bloc.

The system that was then in place was neither just nor moral, but it was still able to provide the necessary preconditions for a relatively peaceful coexistence of various cultures and political regimes. In addition, because of the nature of the bipolar international system, both superpowers had for a long time rather limited chances to intervene outside their direct zones of influence. Communist-led movements won the wars in China and Vietnam, but during the 1967 Six-Days War, and in the 1973 Yom Kippur War, Moscow did not provide any real military support for the radical Arab regimes in Egypt and Syria in their wars with Israel, which have always been supported by the Americans.

The disintegration of the Soviet Union changed the world. As Paul Craig Roberts, former Assistant Secretary of the Treasury for Economic Policy (in Reagan's administration) admitted: "The collapse of the Soviet Union removed the only constraint on Washington's power to act unilaterally abroad...Suddenly the US found itself to be the Uni-power, the world's only superpower."[1] The ideology for it was soon created by the Neoconservatives, who started to proclaim 'the end of history,' by which they meant the final end of competition between various socio-political and economic systems. Consequently, if history had chosen "American Democratic Capitalism," Washington might now have claimed the right and duty to shape the rest of the world in accordance with its own models and principles.

In fact, for about two decades the United States did enjoy almost complete power to impose its will on the rest of the world. As Ben Aris, the Editor in Chief of *Business New Europe*, noted, "Russia was on its knees in the 1990s and helpless to prevent the West from doing anything it wanted to, such as expanding NATO eastward."[2] However, since the end of the last century, partly because of the high natural gas and oil prices, but I think even more likely because more rational leaders rose to power who were less subservient to Western interests, Russia started to get on its feet again and push back to protect what the majority of its population sees as the country's economic

---

constantly present on the Turkish territory and Turkey did not want to be compared with Cuba – a non-Warsaw pact country and a small client of the Soviet Union. Turkey considered itself a strong nation and an equal member of the NATO alliance. In addition the territorial borders between the two major blocs had been quite stable. No side wanted to endanger itself to the risk of nuclear attack.

1 Paul Craig Roberts, "The Neoconservative Threat to World Order," www. paulcraigroberts.org, 26 February 2015.
2 Ben Aris, *Op. cit.*

and strategic interests — especially in Ukraine, but also in the Caucasus and some parts of the Middle East and Asia.

On February 10, 2007, Russian President Vladimir Putin, in his speech at the Munich Conference on Security, had enough courage to say that, "One state, and of course, first and foremost the United States, had overstepped its natural borders in every way. This is visible in the economic, political, cultural and educational policies it imposes on other nations."[1] As a result of that, according to him, "today we are witnessing almost uncontained hyper use of force — military force — in international relations, force that is plunging the world into an abyss of permanent conflict. Finding a political settlement also becomes impossible. We are seeing a greater and greater disdain for the principles of international law, and independent legal norms are, as a matter of fact, coming increasingly closer to one state's legal system."[2]

President Putin's Munich speech was the first openly stated critical assessment of the Post Cold War period by the head of what was still a major power. It is no wonder that the reactions of the Western media and politicians were so strong and negative.

However, in practical terms the speech was negligible in effect. All hopes raised by the Obama administration's accession to the White House in January 2009 and the "reset" of 2009–2011, which was welcomed by the Russians, proved to be short lived or just futile. The reset brought Washington some desired concessions from Moscow concerning Afghanistan, Libya, and Iran, but Russia did not get anything in exchange; the US policy of ABM deployment in Europe and further expansion of NATO, for instance, continued unabated. The situation soon became even more tense because of the civil war in Syria and the outbreak of the Ukrainian crisis. As I believe, President Obama might have had some new ideas about US relations with the Middle Eastern countries and Russia, but he was later unable, or unwilling, to change the predominant mindset of the American power elite and the established directions of the Superpower's foreign policy.

At present Russia as a nation probably has to face the greatest challenge in all of its long history. More than 20 years since the disintegration of the Soviet Union, NATO (under American leadership) wants not only to humiliate Russia but actually to destroy it as a sovereign state. Russia has

---

1 Speech by Russian President Vladimir Putin at the 43rd Munich Conference on Security Policy, www.securityconference.de/en, February 10, 2007. Between 1997-2005 as a frequent visiting professor to Polish universities and travelling in some other Eastern European countries I had a chance to see how the imposition of the American programs almost destroyed the Polish educational system and greatly undermined all inherited national culture. The Communist Rule had also done some harm but not nearly as much as what was going to happen after the American and EU enforced "reforms."

2 Speech by Russian President Vladimir Putin, *Op. cit.*

proved to be uniquely willing and able to oppose the Western elites' imperial expansion and the wars of domination they instigated in Ukraine, Syria, Libya, Iraq, Afghanistan and a number of other places. Consequently, Dmitri Trenin, talking at a symposium hosted by Tufts University (near Boston, Massachusetts) commented that "the thing fundamental for the US is that Russia is challenging the US leadership, essentially the world order that the US leads. No major things can go unpunished if they go against the grain of the people here."[1] At the same symposium, during the follow-up discussion, Columbia University Professor Robert Legvold noted, "Throughout much of the post-Cold War period, there was a tendency on both sides to operate with a 'useful ambiguity.' That is, we didn't know whether the other side was friend or foe."[2] Unfortunately, as he pointed out, now the situation has changed. "Each country has defined the other side as an adversary. This is determining our policies more than anything else in the past and will affect the way in which we [the Americans] redesign NATO to deal with Russia as a threat."[3]

Since the beginning of the Ukraine conflict Trenin has indicated several times that, in stark contrast to Cold War I, the present confrontation is very asymmetrical. He said recently, "The bad thing about this confrontation is that it's held very much on the Russian side. I do not think the US believes that this is a confrontation with Russia. For a lot of people Russia is a threat but not a big one. As Obama said, something between Ebola and ISIS. The stakes are very different for Washington and Moscow. This injects a very important aspect of asymmetry into the situation. This confrontation could be more dangerous; it could get out of hand. It could push us in a direction that people do not anticipate."[4]

In fact some American analysts and politicians, including Zbigniew Brzezinski and George Friedman, not only want Russia to disintegrate into a number of smaller states and statelets, but they anticipate that it will happen in the near future. Their main concern now is the fate of the "post-Russian" nuclear weapons and a potential threat of their getting into the hands of some criminal forces, or ones hostile to Western interests. In a geopolitical forecast published in March 2015, Statfor predicted that loose nuclear weapons in Russia would be "the greatest crisis in the next decade."[5]

---

1 Legvold and Trenin, "How to fix the US-Russian relationship," www.russia-direct.org, March 7, 2015.

2 *Op. cit.* This kind of a "useful ambiguity" was also reflected in the title of my book: *Russia in the Middle East: Friend or Foe?* Westport: Praeger Security International, 2007.

3 *Op. cit.*

4 *Op. cit.*

5 Armin Rosen, "Stratfor predicts loose nukes in Russia will be the greatest crisis of the next decade," www.businessinsider.com, March 10, 2015.

In December 2014, during his visit to Moscow George Friedman (Statfor founder and CEO) became persuaded that the source of "Russian strength is that they can endure things that would break other nations"[1] and that the people there "tend to support the government regardless of competence when Russia feels threatened."[2] His conclusion was that, "If this is so, then the Americans and Europeans are deluding themselves on the effects of sanctions…Sanctions reflect European and American thresholds of pain. Applied to others, the effects may vary."[3] He had also admitted that, "the most important lesson I might have learned in Russia is that Russians don't respond to economic pressure as Westerners do, and that the idea made famous in a presidential [Bill Clinton] campaign slogan, 'it is economy, stupid,' may not apply the same way in Russia."[4] He has even expressed misgivings that "Russia has military and political power that could begin to impinge on Europe."[5] However, he did not believe that would happen. While in Moscow, Friedman seemed to understand the Russian geopolitical situation. As he wrote at the time, "The West has the resources to deal with multiple crises. Russia needs to contain this crisis in Ukraine, which is for her of fundamental strategic importance."[6] Even in his earlier writings Friedman indicated the role and existential importance of Ukraine as a buffer in Russian history. His last conclusion was interesting: "History is about power, and the West is using its power to press Russia hard. But obviously, nothing is more dangerous than wounding a bear. Killing him is better, but killing Russia has not proven easy."[7]

During the following three months Stratfor's analysts apparently changed their opinion. The Stratfor "Decade Forecast: 2015–2025" report published on February 26, 2015, argues that the Russian Federation will not survive the decade within its present borders. In combination, international sanctions, plunging oil prices, and the declining value of the ruble are anticipated to cause a terminal crisis for the nation. Moscow, they predict, will lose its ability to support the national infrastructure, which would result in the fragmentation of the large country into a number of impoverished and small entities which would be hostile to each other and outside of any Kremlin control.[8] The dream of the US political elites might thus come true, but as mentioned, then Russia's nuclear weapons would probably become a serious

1 George Friedman, "Viewing Russia From Inside," *Geopolitical Weekly*, December 16, 2014, https://www.stratfor.com/weekly/viewing-russia-inside
2 *Op. cit.*
3 *Op. cit.*
4 *Op. cit.*
5 *Op. cit.*
6 *Op. cit.*
7 *Op. cit.*
8 "Decade Forecast: 2015-2025 Report," www.stratfor.com, February 26, 2015.

concern. According to Stratfor, "The decline of Moscow's power will open the question of who controls those missiles and how their non-use can be guaranteed."[1] Stratfor's analysts suggest that US Special Forces could take fissile material out of the country and thus resolve the issue, but such an intervention would certainly raise tensions with whatever authority still survives in Moscow. Any possible Russian leadership would likely consider such US or allied military action to be an act of aggression. However, that might not matter. A disintegrated Russia would have no chance of regaining its strength and unity, and Stratfor predicts a major power vacuum to emerge there in the near future.[2]

Although Stratfor, the Austin-based think tank, is officially just a private company and its forecasts do not necessarily reflect Washington's policy, it is an influential American organization which is often called "the Shadow CIA" and its analyses generally correspond to the projects and wishes of the US political establishment. The hardening of Stratfor's vision is thus not insignificant and might signify a more hawkish US policy and a more bellicose mood among the ruling elite. Its political philosophy and strategic goals have not changed, but the actual tactics might become even more brutish and open.

In his interview with the *Kommersant*, Friedman admitted that the US was behind the February unrest in Kiev, which according to him "was the most overt coup in history"[3] and he seemed to be well aware of Ukraine's existential importance for Russia. As he wrote, "Russian history is a tale of buffers. Buffer states save Russia from Western invaders. Russia wants an arrangement that leaves Ukraine at least neutral."[4] However, at the same time he argued, though, that "the United States and Europe have trouble understanding Russia's fears. Russia has trouble particularly understanding American fears."[5] What he means by that is the fact that, "For the United States any rising power in Europe triggers an automatic response born of a century of history."[6] He was even more precise about that in his more recent presentation at the Chicago Council on Foreign Affairs when he said, "The primordial interest of the United States, over which for centuries we have fought wars — the First, the Second and Cold Wars — has been the relations between Germany and Russia, because united there, they're the only force

---

1 *Op. cit.*
2 *Op. cit.*
3 "Stratfor Chief's 'Most Blatant Coup in History,'" Elena Chanenko, *Kommersant*, Moscow, January 20, 2015.
4 G. Friedman, "Viewing Russia From Inside," *Op. cit.*
5 *Op. cit.*
6 *Op. cit.*

that could threaten us [Americans]. And to make sure that doesn't happen."[1] Although Friedman is, like Zbigniew Brzezinski, originally from Europe, he is now an American analyst and spokesman for American imperialism. He is decent enough to acknowledge Russia's existential defensive interest in Ukraine and he no doubt is well aware of the strong economic and cultural links between Russia and Europe, but because, as he noted, "history is rarely decided by moral principles,"[2] he maintains that Russian defensive interests in Ukraine and US imperial interests and its quest for global domination are equally legitimate.[3] Consequently, his agency predicts that in addition to Russia's disintegration as it weakens, territories traditionally in the Russian sphere of influence and pieces of Russia itself will join other nations. In the near future Ukraine and Belarus, they project, will be brought under the domination of Poland, Hungary, and Romania, while Karelia will "return" to Finland. Russian influence over the North Caucasus will evaporate, Central Asia will fall into anarchy, and the former Russian Far East will become dependent on China, Japan or even directly on the United States.

As even a superficial search of the mass media and last year's statements by American political leaders seem to suggest, Washington has already decided to kill the "bear" and to destroy the Russian Federation. There are numerous signs of that, ranging from the unprecedented demonization of Russian leaders[4] and their country to the increasing deployment of US and NATO armed forces on Russia's borders and the unlimited support for the ultra-nationalist Ukrainian government which was brought to power because of the US-supported coup d'état on February 22, 2013.

Although George Friedman has argued that a Russian invasion of the Baltic states is unlikely,[5] thousands of American troops and hundreds of tanks have already entered Estonia, Latvia and Lithuania as part of the "Atlantic Resolve" operation and there is a constantly growing US and NATO

---

1 "George Friedman at the Chicago Council on Foreign Affairs," "Europe: Destined for Conflict," February 4, 2015, https://www.youtube.com/watch?v=QeLu_yyz3tc

2 George Friedman, "Viewing Russia From Inside."

3 Op. cit.

4 As a professor at Princeton and New York University, and one of the most respected authorities on Russia, Stephen Cohen has recently reminded the public, "no Soviet leader in the past has been so personally attacked and demonized as the present non-Communist Russian President." Round Table on "Defining a new security architecture for Europe that brings Russia in from the Cold," which was held in Brussels on March 2, 2015. As I am older than Professor Cohen and having in the past observed the events from Poland, the Soviet Union, Israel, Western Europe and for the last 42 years, North America, I think that he is absolutely right. The Soviet Union was too powerful of nation for that to be possible.

5 "Viewing Russia From the Inside," Geopolitical Weekly, www.stratfor.com, December 16, 2014.

presence in Poland and Romania. Quite recently, even the Czech Republic, which has been more cautious than some of its neighbors, allowed a new American convoy to pass through its territory.

Together with the continuing war in Ukraine and the deployment of the US and NATO navies in the Baltic and Black Seas, Russia has been surrounded on all its European borders by hostile forces. The US is also making additional efforts to cause more problems for Moscow on its Asian and southern borders in Armenia, Kyrgyzstan and Uzbekistan.[1]

Anti-Russian and anti-Putin information warfare has also been quite successful. According to a Gallup Poll in March 2014, some 68% of Americans view Russia as unfriendly or as an enemy and the Russian President's "favorable" rating dropped to 9%, down 1% in one month.[2] One year later the situation was even worse. Eighteen percent of the 837 Americans polled between 8–11 February 2015 believed that Russia is America's greatest enemy.[3] The quoted statistics are much higher and the hostility expressed is much more intense than it is in relation to other traditional American scapegoats such as North Korea (12%), China (9%), and Iran (8%).[4]

Most Americans have probably already been prepared to accept and maybe even to follow the US Congress to support a new war in Europe. The Europeans themselves, such as France and Germany, who would be the most affected, have at least until now been cautiously reluctant,[5] but they are still unable to oppose US policy. In some Eastern European countries such as Poland and even more so the Baltic nations, traditional fears of Russia and therefore their phobias, which are now skillfully manipulated, have even generated a certain level of support for NATO's intervention.

---

1 Paul Craig Roberts, "Russia Under Attack. Russia faces the renewal of conflict in Ukraine simultaneously with three more Ukraine-type situations along its Asian border," www.infowars.com, March 21, 2015.
2 http://www.gallup.com/poll/168110/record-view-russia-unfriendly-enemy.aspx?utm_source=record%20view%20russia%20unfriendly&utm_medium=search&utm_campaign=tiles, March 27, 2014.
3 "Americans Believe Russia is Greatest Enemy of US-Gallup Poll," *The Independent* (UK), February 17, 2015.
4 *Op. cit.*
5 *Der Spiegel*, "Germany Had Enough with US Neocons: Berlin Stunned At US Desire For War In Ukraine," www.zerohedge.com, submitted by Tyler Durdan on 03.08.2015. Concerning France see statement by the leader of the French National Front Party Marine Le Pen to the Polish weekly, "*Do Rzcaczy*," February 16, 2015 that France should recognize Crimea as Russia territory. Le Pen who is a popular but politically controversial figure made her statement a week after France's former President Nicolas Sarkozy said that Crimea could not be blamed for joining the Russian Federation. Even the present French President François Hollande called for "quite strong autonomy for Ukraine's eastern regions of Donetsk and Lugansk, arguing that" it will be difficult to make them share a common life [with Kiev], "French President Hollande Calls for broader autonomy for Ukraine," www.rt.com, February 7, 2015.

At the same time the Ukrainian government, with the full support of Washington, is working to undermine the Minsk-2 Agreement. In addition to numerous military skirmishes whose origins might be disputed, the most important challenge by Kiev's government was its violation of the Minsk-1 and Minsk-2 Agreements and its refusal to negotiate with the representatives of the Donetsk and Lugansk Republics. While both Minsk agreements called for granting them special status and autonomous rule, legislation recently adopted by Kiev designated them as "temporarily occupied territories." This not only runs against the letter and spirit of the Minsk-2 Agreement, but it also represents a great insult to both the Republics and to Moscow. Almost immediately after the Ukrainian decision, US Vice President Joe Biden "welcomed the adoption of implementing measures relating the law of special status for certain areas of eastern Ukraine."[1]

All of Washington's reactions might seem rather puzzling and neither the case of Crimea nor the Ukrainian conflict seems to provide a rational explanation. Similarly, for Moscow the civil war in Syria was not just about Syria, but about the international system in general, while for Washington the Ukrainian conflict is not just about Ukraine. From the American power elite's perspective, other issues are at stake that are crucial to its present and future global dominance.

The Russian Federation is not the Soviet Union, which was more or less equal in power to the American Superpower. As I have already indicated several times, it is much smaller and weaker than its Soviet predecessor both in military power and its social and economic resources. It also lacks the ideological weapons of socialist or communist appeal, and it cannot represent any existential threat either to the US or to the capitalist system as such. In fact, Putin started out as a very pro-Western leader. He really wanted partnership with the West and at one time even intended that his country would join NATO. As Professor Cohen (Princeton and NYU) has repeated, he "provided a helping hand after 9/11 and saved many American lives in Afghanistan."[2]

The West's approaches to the Ukraine crisis are complicated by at least two major factors:

- There are rather cautiously articulated but still readily seen differences in the interests and approaches of the US and some of its European partners such as Germany, France, Italy and even

---

1 "US Combat Forces and CIA in Ukraine, Vice President Biden Congratulates Poroshenko for violating Minsk Peace Agreement," posted by *Unruly Hearts* on March 20, 2015.

2 Stephen Cohen, "War between NATO and Russia is a Real Possibility," at the Round Table on "Defining a new security architecture for Europe that brings Russia in from the cold" which was organized by the American committee for East-West Accord and held in Brussels on March 2, 2015.

some smaller nations such as Austria, the Czech Republic, and Christian Orthodox Greece which has been traditionally friendly to Russia.

- In the US, some respected groups of people who are now out of power oppose the hawkish policy of the War Party and want to avoid a major confrontation with Moscow, which might result in the use of nuclear weapons.[1] Though President Obama in his public statements and interviews has often used harsh anti-Russian and anti-Putin rhetoric, his general policy actions, at least until now, have been more moderate than those demanded by Congress[2] and even by some leading members of his own administration.[3]

While most Europeans first of all want to avoid a new major war and need to renew their economic links with Russia, the US power elite looks at the Ukrainian crisis as an instrument to weaken and probably even destroy the Russian Federation. Another, less openly articulated but probably no less important goal, is to further weaken Germany and the rest of Europe, economically and politically, by disrupting their trade and other economic cooperation with Russia and making them submit to American interests. As both George Friedman and Professor John Mearsheimer state, "For the US, the primordial fear is German capital and technology and Russian natural resources and manpower. This combination for centuries has scared the United States."[4] Consequently, "The primordial interest of the United States for centuries has been to stop a coalition between Germany and Russia."[5] Achieving those two goals would presumably strengthen Washington's position in relation to China and shore up its global hegemony.

The Minsk-2 Agreement between Kiev's government and rebels in Eastern Ukraine dated February 16, 2015 (which was sponsored by Germany, France and Russia), could not have been seen as corresponding to those American interests. Although France and Germany guaranteed the re-establishment

---

1 It is noteworthy that even Zbigniew Brzezinski, the man who had always been very hostile to Russia, has said recently that: "It is not necessary that Ukraine found itself in NATO. It might be even harmful. Making Kiev a close US ally would be a great insult for Russia and an unnecessary escalation of conflict." "Zbigniew Brzezinski: Polska powinna sie zbroic," *Dziennik Gazeta Prawna*, March 25, 2015.

2 Daniel McAdams, "Congress Demands War in Ukraine," *Ron Paul Institute For Peace and Security*, March 23, 2015.

3 James Garden, "Reckless: Obama Advisors Go Rogue on Ukraine," *The National Interest*, March 20, 2015.

4 John Mearsheimer, "The West Blew It Big Time and Irreversibly Endangered European Security," Round Table on "Defining a new security architecture for Europe that brings Russia in from the cold," *Op. cit.*, See also George Friedman, "Europe Destined for Conflict," The Chicago Council on Global Affairs, February 4, 2015.

5 George Friedman, *Op. cit.*

of the Donbass banking system and promised to reach an agreement with Moscow concerning a free trade zone between the EU, Russia and Ukraine, while taking into account the special status of Donbass,[1] the US and its close allies Britain and Poland, took a skeptical or even outwardly hostile attitude from the very beginning.[2]

Almost immediately after the agreement was signed, at a time when the situation in Debaltsevo was still unclear, US Secretary of State John Kerry announced that "Washington is considering further sanctions [against Russia]."[3] Just a little more than a month later, the bloodshed in Ukraine had been greatly reduced thanks to that Minsk-2 Agreement. Nonetheless, on March 23, 2015, the US House of Representatives adopted its Resolution (Res.) 162 demanding that President Obama send lethal military equipment to the US-backed Ukrainian government, making it clear that the weapons were to be used to take military action to return Crimea and parts of eastern Ukraine to Kiev's rule.[4] As an American analyst noted: "The Congress is giving Kiev the green light to begin a war with Russia with the implicit guarantee of US backing."[5] In the same resolution Congress declared that the US and its allies needed a "long term strategy to expose and challenge Vladimir Putin's corruption and repression at home and his aggression abroad."[6] It was in fact an open call for regime change in Moscow, something unprecedented in American–Russian history.

Though this resolution is not binding and President Obama can ignore its recommendations, it is nevertheless an important political statement. Not a single Member of Congress opposed its adoption and some Obama advisors seem to share the same views.[7]

According to the well-respected US investigative reporter Robert Parry, the Kiev government's maneuver, supported by US Vice President Joe Biden, challenging the Minsk-2 Agreement with a requirement for a rebel surrender

1 "Declaration by the President of the Russian Federation, the President of Ukraine, the President of French Republic and the Chancellor of the Federal Republic of Germany in support of the "Package of Measures for Implementation of the Minsk Agreement" adopted on February 12, 2015 in Minsk," *Current Concerns*, February 22, 2015.

2 Frances Coppola, "The Minsk Ceasefire Has Failed. What Now For Ukraine," *Forbes*, February 22, 2015.

3 *Op. cit.*

4 Daniel McAdams, *Op. cit.*

5 *Op. cit.*

6 Alex Christoforou, "The House of Representatives Openly Calls for Regime Change in Moscow," *Russia Insider*, March 25, 2015.

7 James Garden, "Reckless: Obama Advisors Go Rogue On Ukraine," *The National Interest*, March 20, 2015.

"is likely to drive the country [Ukraine] back to a full scale civil war and push the US and Russia closer to nuclear showdown."[1]

Although I hope Mr. Parry's opinion that Res. H162 "should make clear that the political leadership of the US will accept nothing short of war with Russia"[2] is exaggerated, a number of serious American, European and Russian scholars and political experts consider war between NATO and Russia a real possibility. According to Professor Cohen: "The possibility of premeditated war with Russia is real; this was never a possibility during Soviet times."[3]

These misgivings about the threat of a NATO–Russia nuclear war have also been discussed by the President of the Academy of Geopolitical Problems in Moscow, Colonel General Leonid Ivashov.[4] In his view, though still unlikely, "the impossible is possible."[5] Some of the preconditions necessary for such an event have already been established. Because of the last 25 years of Russia's decline and its military/technical retreat, the Americans can use their by-now highly developed offensive weapons and ABM systems to put pressure on Moscow and either destroy or submit Russia to obedience. Russia does not have sufficient ABM safeguards, so that if America launched its nuclear warheads at Russia, practically all of them would probably reach their targets. At the same time any possible use of Russian nuclear missiles would be limited. The US, with the European part of their missile defense system, can cover Russia up to the Ural Mountains. According to General Ivashov, "Even in the boost phase of our [Russian] ballistic missiles they will be able to intercept them."[6]

One of the main reasons for the Americans' expansion to Ukraine is their need to deploy the US ABM system there, to cover the Russian territory beyond the Urals. It is thus a dangerous situation, but Ivashov is

---

1 Robert Parry, "Ukraine's Poison Pill for Peace Talk," www.consortiumnews. com, March 19, 2015.
2 Daniel McAdams, *Op. cit.*
3 Professor Stephen Cohen, "This is the worst international crisis since the Cuban Missile Crisis," Round Table, *Op. cit.*
4 Leonid Ivashov, "US nuclear conflict: The impossible is possible," www.pravda. ru, March 23, 2015.
5 *Op. cit.*
6 *Op. cit.* General Ivashov apparently somewhat exaggerated that Russia does not have any real ABM safeguards. In fact, since 1995 there is a Russian military complex deployed around Moscow to counter enemy missiles targeting the city or its surroundings. The Russian experts are also working on a new weapons system or other defensive equipment. However, because of the great size of the country and US technological superiority, from the view of the Russian General, there are still many reasons to be concerned. One needs to keep in mind that US military bases are located in very close proximity to the Russian borders including Poland, and missiles fired from US submarines deployed in the Baltic Sea can reach St. Petersburg and Moscow in less than 30 minutes. I doubt if the existing Russian ABMs would be able to protect the cities sufficiently.

still unwilling to believe that war could start now. As he said, "No matter how strong and large the US missile system might be, Russian nuclear warheads will reach the territory of the US."[1] Although Russia would suffer enormously, the Americans might also pay a heavy price. The future thus depends on both political events and technological advances. The last leader of the USSR, Mikhail Gorbachev, the man who is lauded in the West as the one who helped to end the first Cold War, commented on the stance taken by the US and NATO, saying, "I cannot be sure that the [new] Cold War will not bring about a 'hot' one. I am afraid they might take the risk."[2]

Though the future is unpredictable, there are now more than enough reasons to be concerned. "The overall number of nuclear warheads in the world has significantly decreased since the end of the Cold War (with the fall of the Berlin Wall in November 1989), [but] the spectrum of risk and perils arising from nuclear weapons has actually expanded."[3] The US is seeking Congressional approval for $3.5 billion for the further modernization of its nuclear arsenal[4] and according to the London-based *Economist*, "A quarter of a century after the end of the Cold War, the world faces a grievous threat of nuclear conflict."[5] What are the causes of that? Why did the apparently bright prospects for international peace and security after the end of the Soviet–American confrontation turn so sour?

Because of all my previous studies and long life experience I am in full agreement with Professor Cohen that the present problem "did not begin in November 2013 [when the Ukrainian Crisis began] or in 2008 [with the Georgian Republic–Russia War]; this problem began in the 1990s when the Clinton administration adopted a 'winner takes all' policy towards post-Soviet Russia. Next to NATO expansion, the US adopted a form of negotiation policy called 'selective cooperation' — Russia gives; the US takes."[6]

The American scholar is also right that every president and every US Congress from President Clinton to President Obama has pursued this policy, and there is not a single example of any serious concession or reciprocal

1 *Op. cit.*
2 "Gorbachev: US dragging Russia into new Cold War, which might grow into armed conflict," RT, January 29, 2015.
3 Thalif Deen, "Nuclear Threat Escalating Beyond Rhetoric," InterPress Service (IPS), March 28, 2015.
4 *Op. cit.*
5 *Op. cit.*
6 Professor Stephen Cohen, "This is the worst international crisis since the Cuban Missile Crisis," Round Table, *Op. cit.* See also his more in depth analysis in *Soviet Fates and Lost Alternatives. From Stalinism to The New Cold War*, New York: Columbia University Press, 2011, pp. 162–198.

agreement that Washington offered to Moscow in return for what it has received since Gorbachev's time.[1]

For the reasons which Thomas Graham noted,[2] and which I discussed earlier, Washington would not have been willing to accept Russia as a major political and economic center in Eurasia. Consequently, the latent and sometimes even open tensions between Washington and Moscow also persisted during Yeltsin's presidency, and Putin's rise to power was welcomed by some American analysts as a possible start of a new, a better era in American–Russian relations. In fact, the new leader sought to ally his country with the EU and NATO and was even willing to recognize America's overarching global hegemony. According to Professor Sakwa, "[in] 2000, Putin sought engagement and accommodation with the West, through the policy of 'new realism,' and was perhaps the most pro-European leader Russia has ever had."[3] Though he intended to protect some of Moscow's interests and influences in the former Soviet territories, and autonomy in its foreign policy, he did not want to antagonize the West and did not perceive Russia as the core of an alternative geopolitical bloc.[4] According to various sources he wanted to follow the example of French leader Charles de Gaulle who, while remaining a part of the West, was still able to take an independent position. Unfortunately, his presidency was ended by the first "color revolution" in history in 1967, and with very few exceptions, such as the USSR during World War II or, at least until now, China, the Americans do not want to tolerate any independent-minded allies. While Washington considers the whole world as its own zone of security and influence, Moscow was not allowed to protect its interests even in Georgia and Ukraine, and in spite of all its efforts, for more than 20 years it was excluded from the European security system.

Worse was yet to come, under President George W. Bush's presidency. Violating previous verbal assurances, the wave of accessions to NATO in 2004 included not only the Central and Eastern European nations of Poland, Hungary, Czech Republic, Slovakia, and Slovenia, but also the former Soviet republics of Estonia, Latvia, and Lithuania. In 2007 Bulgaria and Romania and in 2011 Croatia were also added to the US-led alliance. The admission to both NATO and the EU of a number of former Communist countries (which in the case of Poland and the Baltic states are now ruled by elites very hostile to Moscow) strengthened American influence over all their allies in NATO

---

1 *Op. cit.*

2 Thomas Graham, "Managing Russian Unsettled Borders," *Nezavisimaya Gazeta*, April 18, 2011.

3 Richard Sakwa, *Frontline Ukraine. Crisis in the Borderlands*, London: I. B. Tauris, 2015, p. 30.

4 *Op. cit.*

and brought the spirit of a previously unknown primitive Russophobia to the EU. According to Professor Richard Sakwa (University of Kent), even more important "was the gradual breakdown of an inclusive pan-European security system in which Russia could act as an autonomous yet cooperative partner."[1] Though this system was never legally formalized and it was in practice far from perfect, Professor Mearsheimer argues that, "1990–2008 was the golden period for Europe with no serious possibility of conflict between Russia and the West."[2]

I do not quite agree with Dr. Sakwa and Mearsheimer's views that at least until 2008 NATO did not represent any threat to Russia.[3] The first NATO Secretary General Lord Ismay (1952–57) stated the organization's goal was "to keep Russians out, the Americans in and the Germans down." Though in a different way and to different degrees, the organization he led has always been faithful to these guidelines, only expanding its field of operations, using more sophisticated tactics, and acquiring new members and resources. However, I agree that until 2008, NATO did not represent any direct threat to the Russian Federation, and peaceful co-existence, and even limited cooperation, were still possible.

It is true; but one should not forget that at that time, after 1990 while Russia was on its knees, American and NATO actions leading to the destruction of the Socialist Federal Republic of Yugoslavia and after that the bombardment and partition of Serbia, represented a heavy political and moral challenge for Moscow. Those events, because they violated international law and even more because of the long historical and cultural links between Serbians and Russians, caused great indignation and strong popular reaction among the Russian people including President Yeltsin himself. And yet all these Western actions in the Balkan Peninsula did not directly affect the former Russian (post-Soviet) zone of influence or the direct Russian neighborhood. Even during Soviet times, at least since 1947–1948, Yugoslavia had not been a military ally of Moscow and it always conducted its own independent and military policy. From the formal standpoint Moscow had neither an interest in nor any obligation to Belgrade.

Unfortunately, since 2008 this "golden period" for Europe and to some extent for the global international system has come to an unprecedented crisis. Throughout the two years in which this book was written, we have been facing the frightening possibility of a major war in Europe or even World War III.

---

1 *Op. cit.*, p. 31.
2 "Leading American Scholar John Mearsheimer: The West Blew It Big Time and Irreversibly Endangered European Security," *Round Table, Op. cit.*
3 *Op. cit.* See also Sakwa, p. 37.

If Europe lost its central and dominant global position because of World War I and its political and economic independence because of World War II, this time it might be completely destroyed. As Professor Sakwa declared, although the EU was able to implement its peace project in Western Europe before 1989, it "spectacularly failed" to heal the post-Cold War divisions and to unite the old continent. Instead of doing that, "it has become little more than the civilian wing of the Atlantic security alliance. Atlanticism is becoming increasingly ramified, while Russia is increasingly left in the Cold."[1] It is more and more difficult to preserve peace and stability, and the prospects for sustainable development are waning.

Why is that? Was it inevitable after the collapse of the Berlin Wall and the Soviet Union's disintegration, or was it rather the result of some other and perhaps even originally unpredictable developments?

In my opinion although the post-Cold War international system had, since its very beginning, contained the seeds of major challenges, its further decline and the present critical situation have also been caused by other factors, not all of which have originated from the system itself.

The 18-year golden period of relative peace and stability in Europe after the Cold War, praised by Professor Mearsheimer, with all its global international implications, had always been based on precarious foundations. As the Cold War ended without any peace treaty being signed, that period never had any firm legal basis. Probably even more important, in the vacuum left after the Soviet collapse the balance of power was gone and that balance was what had provided stability among the states and political forces involved in the system.

Former US Secretary of State Madeleine Albright expressed the firm belief of the US power elite, averring that: "If we have to use force, it is because we are American. We see further into the future."[2] Consequently, Professor Mearsheimer admits that, "There is the sense in the US that it has the right and responsibility to run the world, and it also thinks that because it is incredibly powerful both economically and militarily, it has the leverage to push other states around and get what it wants."[3] Having this perception of international relations which, at least immediately after the Soviet Union's collapse, largely corresponded to the reality, Washington "since the end of the Cold War, has never been really interested in diplomacy because diplomacy involves compromise, and the US is not compromising these days."[4]

---

1 *Op. cit.*
2 "Madeleine Albright Quotes," *Brainy Quote*
3 "Interview with John Mearsheimer," RT, March 12, 2015.
4 *Op. cit.*

This was essentially the real structure of the post-Cold War international system since the late 1980s, especially in Europe, making possible not only the destruction of Yugoslavia and war in Iraq but also NATO expansion in Europe into the former Moscow satellites and even parts of the Soviet Union. None of these developments was recognized at the time as causing a serious international crisis, and occasional voices of protests were mostly soft spoken and easily put to silence.[1]

The present situation is different. In the cases of both Syria and Ukraine, the international system does not operate exactly the same way as before, and some new factors have begun to have an impact on the course of events.

1. The first and most visible is the resurgence of post- Soviet Russia as an active political player and its major open conflict with the American Superpower. Many observers did not anticipate this. In the 1990s and even in the early 2000s, Russia was so weak that the US started to take it for granted and to think that the United States could always impose its will on them. For some years after the Soviet Union's collapse, Washington's policy toward Moscow was not openly aggressive and, some provocations notwithstanding, did not seem to represent a major threat to the Russia's existential interests. That could have been caused in part by complacency and perhaps also the memories of Russia's earlier power and importance which remained clear in the minds of older members of the American elite.

The (first) Orange Revolution in Ukraine, from late November 2004 to January 2005, might be seen as a partial exception, but it was not actually decisive and in the end was unsuccessful.

During the Obama Presidency, in 2013–2014, a decisive change was seen. Reacting to the role Russia played in Syria and Iran, and with the Russian Federation apparently recovering from the post-Soviet crisis, Washington making use of the EU (which was by then almost completely under its political control), decided to "peel Ukraine out of Russia's orbit and make Ukraine a part of the West."[2]

As Dr. Dmitri Efremenko has noted, "The Eastern Partnership policy, which has been conceived by its proponents [Poland and Sweden] as dislodging Russian influence in the Western part of the post-Soviet

---

1 The possible partial exception was strong protests against the war in Iraq in the late winter and spring of 2003, which for a while united France, Germany, and Russia in the common opposition to the American invasion. However, Washington and the "coalition of the willing" including the UK and Poland organized by it invaded and conquered Iraq and the French, German and Russian leaders had to accept the situation created by that.

2 "Interview with John Mearsheimer," *Op. cit.*

landscape, inevitably drew the EU into a competitive geopolitical conflict."[1] The conflict has been severe for reasons beyond any importance Ukraine might hold, and the stakes involved are high.[2]

In spite of the inclusion of some Eastern European countries hostile to Russia, which the American hawks called the "New Europe," EU relations with Moscow remained relatively cooperative until then and reflected the quickly developing European–Russian trade exchange. However, with its policy of Eastern Partnership the EU for the first time stepped into a geopolitical rivalry that it had never experienced before. That contributed to confusion in the EU structures that were responsible for developing its foreign policy and facilitated the Americans forcing the Europeans to impose sanctions on Russia.

While it is part of the Atlantic community, the EU is not a coherent and homogenous body and the motivations of the European leaders and their policies towards Russia and Ukraine might be disputed.[3] As for Washington, which in a more stealthy and indirect way was deeply involved in the origins of the Ukraine crisis, its long term goals and strategy were established long ago. Ukraine was intended to become the eastern anchor of the American-led West[4] and perhaps even a gateway to Moscow.[5] Although these plans and projects were originally nourished by the hawkish wing of the American

---

1 Dmitri Efremenko, "Russia, 'American Mars' and 'European Venus': Ukraine's Future," http://www.russia-direct.org, July 8, 2014.

2 Dmitri Efremenko, "Rossiya v avangarde peresmotra Mirovogo Poryadka," *Rossiya v Globalnoi Politike,* June 2, 2014.

3 For instance as Dr. Efremenko says: "The new Europe is now noticeably different from the one that existed a decade ago. Poland, the Baltic States and Romania are willing to actively participate in organization of the cordon sanitaire. For various reasons, Bulgaria, Hungary, Slovakia, and the Czech Republic are showing less enthusiasm." Dmitri Efremenko, "Russia, 'American Mars' and 'European Venus': Ukraine Future," http://www.russia-direct.org, July 8, 2014.

4 As early as 1997 Zbigniew Brzezinski wrote: "Although that will take time, it is not too early for the West—while further enhancing its economic and security ties with Kiev—to begin pointing to the decade 2005-2015 as a reasonable time frame for the invitation of Ukraine's progressive inclusion, thereby reducing the risk that the Ukrainians may fear that Europe's expansion will halt on the Polish-Ukrainian border," Zbigniew Brzezinski, *The Grand Chessboard, American Primacy and Its Geostrategic Imperatives,* Basic Books, 1957, p. 121. Brzezinski had realized that: "Russia, despite its protestations, [was] likely to acquiesce in the expansion of NATO in the 1990s to include several Central European countries," but that "By contrast, Russia finds it incomparably harder to acquiesce in Ukraine's accession to NATO, for to do so would be to acknowledge that Ukraine's destiny is no longer organically linked to Russia," *Op. cit.*

5 In his view Russia's acceptance of Ukraine's integration with the West would then define Russia's own decision to be also truly part of Europe. Russia's refusal would be tantamount to rejection of Europe in favor of a solitary "Eurasian identity and existence," *Op. cit.,* p. 122.

---

elite and disputed by some more dovish people, the Obama administration decided to put them into practice.

Given the way the Ukraine crisis developed, the goal of a unified European foreign policy has not been achieved and a European–Russian rapprochement is, at least for now, not in the offing. For Washington it was a great political success.

2. The second, though not so visible, new factor of the post-Cold War era was a relative weakening of America's global hegemony due to economic problems in the US, the rise of new developing countries, and the not-quite-successful military operations in Afghanistan and Iraq. Consequently, the US started to perceive the expansion of European–Russian economic ties as a threat to their leadership. The economic links might have created the premises for a political rapprochement, and Washington never forgot the unpleasant memory of the 2003 joint French–German–Russian opposition to the invasion of Iraq.

Since the very beginning of the Ukrainian crisis, Washington has been Moscow's main opponent, seeing this not only as a chance to cut the resurgent Russia down to size but also to increase its control over Europe and to breathe new strength into its worldwide leadership. Although the annexation of Crimea by the Russian Federation was just a minor challenge and could not present any real threat to American power, the possibility of territorial change not authorized by Washington might present a challenge to the world order it controls. This provided a chance to mobilize allies to contain Putin's Russia. As Russia remains many times weaker than the US and its allies, mobilization was far more important than the containment itself. It gave new meaning to the actions of the Americans leading their political and military allies. The EU has to accept a long term American military presence in Europe and agree to the creation of a new military infrastructure on the European–Russia border. According to Dr. Efremenko: "New Europe is becoming a *cordon sanitaire* that in the near future may be bolstered at the expense of Ukraine (at least its western and central regions) and Moldova (excluding Transdnistria and probably Gagauzia)."[1]

As an outcome of the Ukrainian crisis, America's position in Europe has become stronger than ever before, and it not only enables Washington to punish Moscow for its involvement in Syria and the Middle East, but also has greatly increased US control over Western and Central Europe.

In the past, even at the peak of the Cold War, the US had to give more serious consideration to the interests of its major European allies than it does

---

1 Dmitri Efremenko, "Russia 'American Mars' and 'European Venus': Ukraine's Future," *Op. cit.*

now,[1] and the fathers of the European Union wanted to see their nations as the American's allies (while safeguarding their traditional cultural and political identities and political and economic interests). Although in my view the much-discussed threat of Soviet military aggression was never likely, the balance of power that existed in those days in central Eurasia, and what was probably more important, the European middle classes' fears of domestic upheaval and revolutionary attempts, persuaded them to accept the American protectorate,[2] which at that time also provided some economic advantages.

The present situation is quite different. For more than 25 years there has been no "red threat" around. The Soviet Union and all it represented by its social experiment belong to history, and the Western and Central European societies have become much more conformist and Americanized. Almost all the former Soviet satellites and even some former Soviet Union republics have now become part of a "New Europe," members of the EU and NATO, the most obedient American allies, and providers of cheap labor to the more advanced Western nations. Because of the disintegration of the Soviet Union and the ensuing socio-economic crisis, deprived of its previous strength and vigor the neo-capitalist Russian Federation cannot be a real threat to Old Europe (the Western one); and its occasional tensions with its Eastern European neighbors have mainly been caused by the provocative actions of the local elites that are politically hostile to Russia.

According to a number of scholars and analysts' views the economic and political interests of the Western and perhaps also Central European nations, with the possible exception of the UK, are now not only different but, as the developments in Ukraine seem to indicate, even contradictory to the American Empire. Although the era of European greatness and global superiority belongs to history, the leading nations of the old continent still represent a substantial economic and political power and have splendid cultural and civilizational historical achievements. Their role in a multipolar world might be by no means negligible and according to my argument, one of the main and perhaps crucial reasons for the Ukraine crisis was Washington's desire to put them back under its more strict overall control

---

1 There were at that time a number of exceptions, such as the humiliation of France and Britain during the Suez Crisis in 1956 and what some European analysts, including the prominent Polish economist and politician Jerzy Zdziechowski who called it an "imperial tax" because of the dollar domination in relation to the European currencies.

2 In the late 1990s Zbigniew Brzezinski admitted: "The brutal fact is that Western Europe and increasingly also Central Europe, remains largely an American protectorate, with its allied states reminiscent of ancient vassals and tributaries." Zbigniew Brzezinski, *The Grand Chessboard American Primacy and Its Geostrategic Imperatives*, Basic Books, 1997, p. 59.

and to destroy their economic relations with the hated Russia which was still feared by American elites.

Without the domination of Europe, the American role as global hegemon might be far more problematic if it were even possible at all. With his usual acumen Zbigniew Brzezinski rightly perceived that "Europe is America's essential geopolitical bridgehead on the Eurasian continent...without close transatlantic ties, American primacy in Eurasia promptly fades away. US control over the Atlantic Ocean and the ability to project influence and power deeper in Eurasia would be seriously circumscribed."[1]

The need for domination over Europe, or at least its western parts, is the necessary precondition for the domination of Eurasia, and as Brzezinski fully appreciates, the hegemony of Eurasia is decisive for the present and future of America's worldwide hegemony. He observed that, "how America 'manages' Eurasia is critical, Eurasia is the globe's largest continent and is geopolitically axial. A power that dominates Eurasia would control two of the world's three most advanced and economically productive regions...control over Eurasia would almost automatically entail Africa's subordination, rendering the Western Hemisphere [including North America] and Oceania geopolitically peripheral to the world's central continent."[2]

A realistic thinker, Brzezinski has also expressed his concerns. He has said that, "All potential political and economic challenges to American primacy are Eurasian. Cumulatively Eurasia's power vastly overshadows America. Fortunately for America, Eurasia is too big to be politically one."[3]

At least until now I have never heard of any project for the political association of all Europe and Asia. However, there have already been numerous theoretical projects and even practical efforts aimed at the association or even federalization of Europe, or at least its Western nations.

Professor Sakwa discerns two of major models:

- Wider Europe. This has already been partly put into practice by the development of the European Union "focused on Brussels, with concentric rings emanating from the Western European

---

1 Ibid.
2 *Op. cit.* p. 31.
3 Ibid. Brzezinski's observation was probably one of the main sources of Paul Wolfowitz's doctrine, whose main goal is to prevent any threat to unipolar and exclusive US global dominance. According to Professor Anatol Lieven: "something very like Wolfowitz's vision became the standard operating procedure not only of the second Bush administration, but of the intervening Clinton administration and of sections of the Obama administration too. To judge by the stances she has taken in the past, it will be the desired approach of Hilary Clinton if she wins the presidency in 2016." Anatol Lieven, "The spectre of Wolfowitz," *American Opinion-American Review-Global Perspectives on America*, April 15, 2015.

heartlands of European integration."[1] This highly bureaucratized and neoliberal organization is entirely subordinated to the Atlantic security alliance,[2] and its policy has alienated Russia more and more from the rest of the old continent.

- A Greater Europe. This model proposes a more pluralistic and multipolar concept for the European space. It would be based on the long European traditions and does not impose one single ideological flavor.

This more open and differential concept has been supported by some French leaders, such as Charles de Gaulle and Nicolas Sarkozy,[3] and by every Russian leader from Mikhail Gorbachev to Vladimir Putin. According to President Yeltsin, "Europe without Russia is not Europe at all. Only with Russia can it be a Greater Europe, with no possible equal anywhere in the globe."[4]

The concept of a Greater Europe, more faithful to its traditions and in some ways engaging Moscow, has for a long time had some social and intellectual support in Europe.[5] The well known French scholar Emmanuel Todd perceived the weakness of post-Soviet Russia as an asset in European–Russian relations.[6] During the last two decades before the outbreak of the Ukrainian crisis, this political orientation has also acquired a strong and promising economic component. According to Dmitri Trenin, "In 2013, the EU accounted for about 50% of Russia's foreign trade — some $417 billion. Europe was also dependent on Russia for about 30% of its energy supplies."[7] Trenin put particular stress on German–Russian economic relations, which included some 600 German companies doing business in Russia,[8] and he notes that "the economic and political links between Russia and Germany could potentially have formed an axis of what Putin called a 'Greater Europe,'

---

1 Sakwa, p. 27.

2 *Op. cit.*, p. 227.

3 Nicolas Sarkozy, "Déclaration de M. Nicolas Sarkozy, Président de la République, sur l'action de la France en faveur de la construction européenne, à Nîmes le 5 mai 2009," Available at http://discours.vie-publique.fr/notices/097001329.html

4 Cited by Leonid Berzhidsky, "No Illusion left. I am leaving Russia," *Moscow Times*, June 19, 2014.

5 See for instance: Marc Rousset, *Paris-Berlin-Moscow. Le continent paneuropèen face au choc des civilizations*, Godefrey de Buillon, Paris, 2009, pp. 195-2004. A similar approach was argued in Poland by the Polish scholar Leszek Sykulski: "*Ku Nowej Europie-Perspectywa Zvigrku Unů Europejskiej I Rosji* [Journals a New Europe – The perspective of Association the EU and Russia], Instytut Geopolityki Alfa 24, Czestochowa, 2011.

6 Emmanuel Todd, *Après L'Empire: Essai sur la decomposition du système americain*, Gallimard, Paris, pp. 191–193.

7 Dmitri Trenin, "From Greater Europe to Greater Asia? The Sino-Russian Entente," Carnegie Moscow Center, April 9, 2015, http://carnegie.ru/2015/04/09/from-greater-europe-to-greater-asia-sino-russian-entente/i64a

8 *Op. cit.*

an economic, cultural and security space from Lisbon to Vladivostok. In that scheme Russian natural resources would have been linked to European industries and technologies, with Russia providing the EU a geopolitical and strategic channel to Asia and the Pacific."[1]

However, the implementation of this great project, beneficial for all parties involved, would mean exactly the realization of the Americans' worst nightmare, described by George Friedman. In order to avoid this, they fought World War I, World War II and the (first) Cold War. It might lead to the end of their economic superiority and global political domination. Washington cannot tolerate that, and for that very reason the Ukrainian crisis became difficult to avoid.

As one major consequence, "a quarter century of Russian–Western post-Cold War cooperation has been unravelling."[2]

In the Western part of Eurasia, two major possible threats to US primacy have thus been avoided. Russia has again been greatly weakened and more than ever before demonized and isolated. What was probably even more important, the Americans succeeded in making certain that they would not have to face any kind of Greater Europe, based on Russian–German cooperation, which would be, according to Friedman, "the only force that could threaten us [Americans]."[3] At least at the Atlantic geopolitical front, the further decline of the empire has been avoided. However, the situation on its Pacific front and in eastern parts of Eurasia is far more complex and has had an impact on American–Russian relations and perhaps even the rest of the world.

3. The third new factor of the post-Cold War period, although not directly related to the Ukrainian crisis, was the unanticipated quick rise of China back to the rank of great power, and in the foreseeable future, the peer and rival of the USA. Because of its demographic size, geopolitical location and the historical traditions of its dominant position in Asia, the sudden renaissance of China was far more important than the rise of Japan more than 100 years earlier,

---

1 *Op. cit.*
2 *Op. cit.*
3 As George Friedman emphasized, "Our main task is to prevent the union of Russia and Germany, because together, they represent the only real and dangerous threat to the US." He also talked about the idea of a "*cordon sanitaire*" (mentioned above) in the area between the Baltic and Black Seas, to be a pro-American buffer zone between Russia and Germany. According to him, this zone will include Poland, Czech Republic, Slovakia, Hungary, Romania, Bulgaria and the Baltic States. In his opinion it is too early to include Ukraine in this zone. About Germany, Friedman thinks that "it is a major economic power, but is very weak geopolitically." "George Friedman at the Chicago Council on Foreign Affairs," "Europe: Destined for Conflict," February 4, 2015, https://www.youtube.com/watch?v=QeLu_yyz3tc

during the Meiji Restoration and Modernization period (1868–1912). I believe it was probably the most important development of the Post-Cold War period with growing impact on the whole international political and economic systems, including American–Russian relations and even the present Ukraine crisis. It was largely because of the moderating influence and relative neutrality of China that, as Professor Richard Legvold noted, the Ukrainian crisis "will not be universal, it won't incorporate the entire international political system, it would be Russia and the West [but] it is going to affect virtually every aspect of the international political system."[1]

An in-depth detailed analysis of Chinese issues would be out of place here, but I have to include some comments on their influence on Russia and the whole international political system, which after Beijing's rise has visibly changed its size and ways of operating.

If, until the middle of the 20th century, the international community was almost exclusively Western or Western dominated, and during the Cold War period it was mainly focused on the American dominated West and Soviet rivalry, the post-Cold War international system has become truly global, largely because of the rise and potential of China, plus a number of other rising non-Western powers and civilizations.

At the same time both the nature and scale of Western input into all aspects of international life have been submitted to great changes. The role of Europe, which was pluralistic in its languages and old cultural traditions, was replaced by American primacy based on different methods and principles. In spite of some earlier hopes and expectations, the European Union proved unable to create any original self-made alternative to Washington's direction and "finally" it has become little more than the civilian façade of NATO.[2] Although this historic shift of geopolitical and geocultural power made Moscow's situation much more difficult than ever before in its previous history, it also gave Beijing, with its original culture, strong statehood and flourishing economy, more opportunities to play a role as an alternative great power center.

At the same time, making use of its secure and favorable geopolitical location and following its late leader Deng Xiaoping's modified doctrine that China should not attract attention but "lie low," avoiding confrontation in foreign affairs to keep the nation focused on domestic affairs, Beijing's foreign policy has for a long time remained extremely cautious and reluctant

---

1 Robert Legvold, " 'Protracted Conflict' How the Crisis in Ukraine Became the New Cold War," *The Newsletter of The National Fellowship*, Woodrow Wilson Foundation, Fall 2014, p. 9.
2 Sakwa, p. 227.

to undertake any foreign engagement. In recent years, while no longer keeping a low profile, the Chinese still speak very diplomatically and are "very careful not to antagonize the US, the reigning superpower."[1]

Although in 2013 Beijing, together with Moscow, stopped the US military intervention in Syria, and has always cultivated good relations with Teheran, in the last two years since the beginning of the Ukrainian crisis and the Washington–Moscow conflict, Beijing has wanted to show its neutrality, and its behavior has been quite diplomatic. After Crimea's annexation by Russia and the Western–Russian conflict that was aggravated by that, China at first stayed in the background. On March 19, 2014, the Chinese foreign ministry issued a statement that the Crimea crisis should be resolved politically and that all parties involved should restrain themselves to avoid escalation.[2] This apparently cautious, neutral and often ambiguous approach has been often for Chinese diplomats.

In the words of Chinese foreign ministry spokesman Hong Li, "the international community ought to play a constructive role in ameliorating the present situation,"[3] and similar conciliatory and peacemaking appeals have been repeated since then by other Chinese leaders and diplomats, including Premier Li Kequang.[4] However, at the same time both the Chinese Premier and a number of Chinese analysts admitted that there was a "strong public show of understanding from China of the Russian position."[5] The Chinese spokesman, while saying that they are sticking to the basic norms

1 Pepe Escobar, "Eurasia As We (and the US) Know It Is Dead," *Asia Times*, April 20, 2015.

2 The 3Ds Blog, Mark Collins, "Russia/Ukraine and That Great 'International Community,'" March 19, 2014.

3 *Op. cit.*

4 At his annual press conference on March 15, 2015, the Chinese Premier said that China hopes to see a political settlement though dialogue. According to him, "We [Chinese leaders] hope there will be harmonious coexistence between neighbors, and what we hope to see is that there will be pursuit of common development and win-win outcomes between European countries and between all countries in the world." "Chinese Premier Won't Say If Crimea's Annexation Was Illegal," Radio Free Europe Radio Liberty, March 15, 2015.

5 *Op. cit.* See also Lyle J. Goldstein, "What Does China Really Think about the Ukraine Crisis?" *The National Interest*, September 4, 2014. Goldstein quotes a fascinating, in his view, analogy by the prominent Chinese military expert Senior Colonel Fang Bing between Russian and Chinese strategic geography. As he asserts, "For Russians the loss of Ukraine would be even more serious than if China were to lose Taiwan. This would be more akin to China losing the Yellow River Valley, or to losing Shaanxi Province – such a well-spring of culture." Colonel Fang Bing also stresses that the process of NATO expansion that took place after the collapse of the Soviet Union had been a "bitter pill" for Russia to swallow since its "strategic space was contracting." *Op. cit.*

governing international relations, also emphasized the complexity of the situation and the historical factors of the Ukrainian issue.[1]

The international importance of the Chinese position might have been more visible because of the fact that on March 5, 2015, Russian President Putin, and five days later US President Obama, called Chinese President Xi Jinping to discuss Ukraine.[2] It seems that although a Chinese scholar called it "a groundless speculation,"[3] few of the recent decade's international events have benefited China as much as the Ukrainian crisis.

This issue took much of Washington's attention and thus eased the pressure on China in the East and greatly increased Beijing's prestige as a mediator and an important factor in the other great powers' disputes and tensions. Even a short time ago few Europeans might have anticipated that China would play such a role.

Because of the problems of Taiwan, and to a point, Xingiang and Tibet, Beijing could not accept the legitimacy of the Crimean referendum or the separatist tendencies in Eastern Ukraine. At the same time China has repeatedly opposed sanctions against Russia and at the crucial moment in the Crimean annexation, in March 2015, Chinese Foreign Minister Wang Yi told the Chinese Parliament that Russian–Chinese relations were going through "their best period"[4] and that China would continue to make efforts to develop the strategic partnership. In spite of strong diplomatic pressure from the West, Beijing refused to join the anti-Russian coalition led by Washington. Because of its fear and dislike of color revolutions, it was by no means pleased by the overthrow of Ukrainian President Yanukovych by a coup d'état in Kiev in February 2014, and according to a Russian scholar "a fall of the current Russian regime under Western pressure would be regarded [by China] as a highly undesirable situation, which might result in a strategic encirclement of China."[5] The Chinese made the strongest supporting statement for Moscow on February 26, 2015, by Qu Xing, China's ambassador to Brussels. As he said, the "nature and root cause" of the crisis was the 'game' between Russia and Western powers, including the US and the EU. The crisis was accelerated by external intervention, and Moscow would feel it was being treated unfairly if the West did not change

---

1 Yu Sui, "China's Stance on Ukraine Issue and the Role It Can Play," China Center for Contemporary World Studies, April 2, 2015.
2 *Op. cit.*
3 *Op. cit.*
4 Dr. Vassily Kashin, "Propitious Balance," http://eng.globalaffairs.ru/number/ Propitious-Balance–16711, June, 2014.
5 *Op. cit.*

its approach. According to him: "The West should abandon the zero-sum mentality, and take the real security concerns of Russia into consideration."[1]

All their difficult and even bloody past confrontations notwithstanding, Russian–Chinese relations seem far more stable and, for both sides, beneficial than almost all Western analysts had predicted.

According to Dmitri Trenin, "What was originally Moscow's 'marriage of convenience' with Beijing has turned into a much closer partnership. Putin's vision of a 'Greater Europe' from Lisbon to Vladivostok, made up of the European Union and the Russian-led Eurasian Economic Union, is being replaced by a 'Greater Asia,' from Shanghai to St. Petersburg."[2]

Trenin is right that "The Ukrainian crisis shifted Moscow's foreign policy from the Euro-Atlantic to the Asia-Pacific"[3] and that China, rather than Europe and Germany, is emerging as Moscow's principal foreign partner.[4] However, he also indicates that Russia began pivoting towards Asia even before Ukraine.[5] In his view the main reason for that was the Kremlin's plan to modernize the underdeveloped regions of Siberia and Russia's Far East, which neighbors the rising economies of East Asia. This economic factor certainly played a role and it later became even more important. However, I think the turn to China and general pivot to Asia started earlier and was not caused by economic needs but more by geopolitical and foreign policy considerations.

It has been the dream of all post-Communist Kremlin leaders from Gorbachev to Putin to integrate their country as an equal member into a 'Greater Europe,' but because of Russian cultural traditions which can be traced back at least to the 17th century or even earlier, relations with Beijing and even some other Asian nations have been seen as equally important.

Many people overlook the fact that very large parts of Russia are located in Asia and that Moscow's history and present interests are strictly interrelated with those of the Asian nations. I think that after the disintegration of the Soviet Union and the ideological and socio-political transformations in China led by Deng Xiaoping, the rapprochement of the two regional Eurasian powers became a geopolitical requirement.

---

1 "Chinese diplomat tells West to consider Russia's security concern over Ukraine," Reuters, February 27, 2015.

2 Dmitri Trenin, "From Greater Europe to Greater Asia? The Sino-Russian Entente," Carnegie Moscow Center, http://carnegie.ru/2015/04/09/from-greater-europe-to-greater-asia-sino-russian-entente/i64a, April 9, 2015.

3 Dmitri Trenin, "Russia's Pivot to Asia – A Sino-Russian Entente?," *Carnegie Moscow Center*, http://carnegie.ru/2015/04/15/russia-s-pivot-to-asia-sino-russian-entente/i7bx, April 15, 2015.

4 *Op. cit.*

5 *Op. cit.*

The Russian Federation, unlike the powerful Soviet Union, as a relatively weak political and economic entity could not represent a threat to its stronger neighbor, China. Under Deng Xiaoping's leadership, China started to rebuild itself from the shambles of the Maoist Cultural Revolution and had to deal with many other complicated socio-political and economic challenges. Although, by then, both Russia and China had either completely rejected or modified their ideological premises and revolutionary aspirations, both still needed to deal with the American Superpower and its global imperial aspirations. Neoconservative in its ideology, America was unchanged ideologically and more powerful than ever. Russian and Chinese leaders were aware of the new existing balance of power and its political consequences. Their mutual rapprochement began to seem inevitable and was slowly put into practice.

On December 23, 1992, even the most pro-American Russian President, Boris Yeltsin, went to Beijing for his first official visit. He and China's leaders discussed bilateral issues and international relations in general. It was neither quick nor easy to reach a mutual understanding. Chinese Premier Li Peng had to visit Moscow at least six times, until in December 1998 both countries issued a joint communiqué pledging to build an "equal and reliable partnership."[1] The long-persisting memories of Mao Zedong's and Nikita Khrushchev's animosity and their infighting over the correct interpretation of Marxist-Leninist theory, now repudiated by both nations, and the leadership of the now defunct socialist bloc countries, were finally overcome and some other historical and territorial issues, which divided both countries, were put on the back burner. The then achieved understanding was at that time perceived as a visible and formal expression of the now prevailing "Sino-Russian view that the United States was their main competitor in the global political scene."[2]

The Ukrainian crisis has accelerated the process which had started a long time before and was caused by both economic needs and even more by Washington's aspirations for full spectrum domination, and its unwillingness to respect the interests of the regional powers of Eurasia.

Moscow has been moving towards Beijing because of political and economic pressure from the United States and Europe. Ever since the Soviet Union's disintegration, Moscow's "Western partners have never articulated their vision of Russian relations with the West and especially the United States."[3] In fact, as I have already indicated, quite a few voices have urged the complete disintegration of Russia and the destruction of the Russian nation.

---

1 "Sino-Russian relations since 1991," Wikipedia.
2 *Op. cit.*
3 Andranik Migranyan, "Washington's Creation: A Russian-China Alliance?" *The National Interest*, July 10, 2014.

Although China has never faced a threat like that, many American scholars and politicians consider China a main competitor and future rival in the struggle for global priority.[1] In all local conflicts the US has always expressed its support for China's opponents, and the Obama administration's 'pivot to Asia' has, as its primary objective, to contain a rising China.[2]

Because of US hostility, which has a long tradition and which got a new lease on life during the second term of President Obama's administration,[3] and the West's unprecedented anti-Russian political, economic and media campaign, Moscow had no choice but to join Beijing. According to Dmitri Trenin: "Russia has reverted to its traditional position as a Eurasian power between East and West, and it is tilting toward China in the face of political and economic pressure from the United States and Europe."[4] Consequently, it "is now more likely to back China in the steadily growing competition between Beijing and Washington."[5] This may be very beneficial for China, which is now emerging as a much greater power in all Eurasia and not just East Asia. Closer relations with Moscow also provide Beijing with "not just an absolutely safe rear in the north but also an enormous strategic depth. If and when this position becomes solidified, China will have made a major step in its slow but steady rise to continental pre-eminence.[6]

China is now gaining almost unlimited access to the abundant and much needed Russian natural resources, from hydrocarbons to fresh water, and potentially would be able to get to "Europe via Central Asia as well as across Russia and the Arctic."[7]

All those Chinese achievements and actual business profits notwithstanding, I believe that the closer relations with Beijing are no less, but probably even more, politically advantageous for Moscow. Dmitri Trenin acknowledges that, "Thanks to the backing from China, the world premier rising power, Russia should not fear isolation at the hands of the US and its allies."[8] The Chinese do not want Russia to be defeated by the Americans and "they wish it to stay united internally which fully conforms

---

1 See for instance John J. Mearsheimer, "China's Unpeaceful Rise," *Current History*, April 2006.
2 "Pivot to Pacific? The Obama Administration's 'Rebalancing' Toward Asia," *Congressional Research Service*, March 28, 2012.
3 As Professor Sakwa notices, in 2013, "it was clear that the US had moved to become Russia's main opponent. The September 2013 G20 summit in St. Petersburg was marked by a bitter chill in relations between the two countries, exacerbated by attempts in Washington to lead a boycott of the Sochi Olympics, scheduled for February 2014," Sakwa, *Frontline Ukraine. Crisis in the Borderlands*, I.B. Tauris, 2015, pp. 79-80.
4 Trenin, "From Greater Europe to Greater Asia? The Sino-Russian Entente."
5 *Op. cit.*
6 *Op. cit.*, p. 16
7 *Op. cit.*
8 *Op. cit.*

to their [own] national interests."[1] The disintegration and increased internal political upheavals sought by some Americans might represent a threat to China's own security, and Beijing "has no geopolitical, economic, or security interest in seeing Moscow's will broken by Washington, or Russia itself broken and falling apart."[2] In fact both countries are very concerned about a threat of 'color revolutions' which they consider to be the instruments of Western domination and interference in their domestic affairs.

Although both nations have very different cultural traditions and, in contrast to the situation in the 1950s and 1960s, the People's Republic of China is much stronger and internationally influential than the Russian Federation, China and Russia share not only a number of vital interests but also in some ways similar goals and opinions. According to them, the most important one is a strong national state that enjoys freedom from foreign interference and control.[3]

In terms of the world order, though both the Russians and Chinese anticipate that at least in the near future the US will remain the most powerful state in the world, since the 1990s they have believed that multipolarity is the optimal structure for the international community. They expect that such a system would give China more prominence and Russia more security and freedom of action.

Its present economic and demographic superiority notwithstanding, I don't think China would be able or willing to dominate Russia. (Perhaps only the Americans with their culture, which is easily assimilated and devoid of major historical traditions, would be able to do that.) As Trenin remarks, "Russia's sense of identity is very strong, and its civilization and culture are very distinct from China's, as the stark divide along the Sino–Russian border visibly demonstrates."[4]

Like all great and independent nations, China and Russia differ in their political style and approaches to a number of international issues. During the Ukrainian crisis Beijing did not want to support Moscow outwardly because that "would damage its central relationship with Washington,"[5] and "China and Russia will not form a bloc to oppose the West militarily."[6] Trenin describes their relationship as an "entente," a harmonious association of two

---

1 *Op. cit.*

2 *Op. cit.*

3 During my youth and studies in Europe (1950–1968) it was also the common belief and predominant concern of the majority of both Polish and French peoples. They considered their national states as their most precious value. It seems to me that traditional European and American approaches are quite different.

4 Trenin, "From Greater Europe to Greater Asia? The Sino-Russian Entente."

5 *Op. cit.*

6 *Op. cit.*

major powers based on the commonality of some key interests and mutual, but by no means equally, expressed resentment of the global hegemon. In sharp contrast to their relations with Russia, the Americans treat the Chinese far more kindly and pay due attention to their interests and political proposals.[1] Perhaps Chinese President Xi Jinping's proposal of "a new type of great-power relationship" could contribute to more peaceful and stable international relations and to the avoidance of a major violent confrontation.

The chances for that are by no means certain. According to the US Council on Foreign Relations Special Report published in March 2015, the further rise of China represents a threat for US influence in Asia and even to its global domination. Consequently, its authors suggest a number of political, economic and military measures in order to put China in its place. Although according to them, "these measures do not treat China as an enemy," in their final conclusions they have to admit that as their outcomes: "There is no real prospect of building fundamental trust, 'peaceful coexistence,' 'mutual understanding,' a strategic partnership or a 'new type of major country' relations between the US and China. Rather, the most that can be hoped for is caution and restrained predictability by the two sides as intense US–China strategic competition becomes the new normal, and even that will be not easy to achieve in the period ahead. The purpose of US diplomacy in these dangerous circumstances is to mitigate the severe inherent tensions between these two conflicting strategic paradigms, but it cannot hope to eliminate them."[2]

Though the authors of the report seem to represent a rather hawkish orientation and are openly critical of the Obama administration, which they blame for "a profoundly different and much more benign diagnosis of China's strategic objectives in Asia than we do,"[3] their opinions seem to prevail in Washington now. Both the publication of this report by the prestigious Council on Foreign Relations and the US pressure on countries around the world to stay away from the $50 billion Asian Infrastructure Investment Bank (AIIB) which had been just launched by China[4] seem to indicate that.

Interestingly, in spite of US opposition, the United Kingdom, Germany, France and Italy, together with more than 30 other nations[5] including the Russian Federation became founding members of the AIIB. It is a very important development for both economic and political reasons which might

---

1 See for instance Stephen Hadley and Paul Haenle, "The Catch-22 in US-Chinese Relations. The Future of Bilateral Ties," *Foreign Affairs*, February 22, 2015.
2 Robert D. Blackwill and Ashley J. Tellis, "Reversing US Grand Strategy Toward China," Council on Foregin Relations, *Special Report No. 72*, March 2015.
3 *Op. cit.*
4 Joseph E. Stiglitz, "Asia Multilateralism," *Project Sindicate: The World's Opinion Page*, April 13, 2015.
5 *Op. cit.*

indicate both the growing role of Beijing and the chance that a multipolar and peaceful future may yet be possible.

4. The fourth new factor of the post-Cold War period is the changing perception of nuclear weapons and their relevance to major international conflicts.

During the Cold War I (1947–1986) period, in spite of the outwardly hostile ideologies and contrasting interests of the two superpowers, there was no major military confrontation between them mainly because of the rough balance of nuclear weapons (parity) between the two sides which existed after 1949. According to the doctrine of mutual assured destruction (MAD), neither side could initiate war without expecting cataclysmic retaliation. At that time neither the US nor the USSR had the means to protect their territory from nuclear attack, and any effort in this direction was only in the very initial stages. In addition there was a massive pro-peace movement all over the world, including the US, and after Hiroshima and Nagasaki the eventual use of nuclear weapons might have been widely seen as an enormous crime against humanity.

The present situation is different and the world might perhaps be closer to nuclear war than at any time since the 1962 Cuban Missile Crisis. There are several reasons for that and the ongoing Ukrainian crisis might provide the mass media with an easy pretext and explanation.[1]

1. The first and most important reason is the fact that the Russian Federation is in its political, economic and military aspects incomparably weaker than the US and its allies. Moscow's military spending cannot exceed about 10% of the US expenditures and that without taking into account America's much more developed infrastructures and other technological facilities. The Russian Federation now lacks reliable allies, while NATO remains firmly under Washington's control.

2. As some analysts have already indicated and as should be obvious to any informed observer, I believe, since the beginning of the Ukrainian crisis if not earlier Washington and its European allies have been seeking to overthrow the Russian government by escalating the confrontation with Moscow up to the "threshold of thermonuclear war."[2]

---

1 Professor Sakwa notices that at the NATO summit in Newport, Wales, on 4-5 September 2014 "the rise of the Islamic State in the Levant served to divert attention from what ultimately at the international level was an artificial conflict over Ukraine," Sakwa, p. 221.
2 "Estulin Warns We are on the 'Threshold of A Thermonuclear War' with Russia," Susan Duclas, *All News Pipeline*, March 7, 2015.

3. According to Daniel Estulin, the US President "is attempting to topple Russian President Vladimir Putin, and the US and Britain have 'reactivated a policy of threatening tactical nuclear warfare against Russia and China to force them to submit to the crumbling transatlantic financial empire."[1]

The American public sees Russia's military power as "a critical threat to the US."[2] In view of this any pro-peace mass movement would probably be difficult to set in motion. The public opinion of the masses is now largely formatted by PR efforts, and for a number of reasons including the decline of the traditionally well-educated and politically involved middle class, the perfections of the means of social and political influence including a stringent control of the school and university curricula, have made it unlikely that a social movement could emerge along the lines of those of the 1950s and 1960s. The passive attitude or even an active acceptance gives the ruling elite almost unlimited freedom of action, and they believe that their long-term goals are now getting to be technically achievable.

The anti-Russian campaign run by the government and media is to a large extent caused by the belief in that America can win a war with Russia, a belief boosted by the ABM and DMS deployment in Europe and almost on Russia's border. Some analysts are prone to thinking that by a first preemptive strike the US could hit Russia so hard that it would be either unable or even unwilling to retaliate in fear of a second strike and total destruction.[3]

However, the Obama administration does not seem inclined toward the use of nuclear weapons in order to preserve American hegemony. The threat of Russian retaliation, still possible, and the resulting ecological damage, make its use far from attractive. In addition, I believe that because of the present unequal power relations, which are favorable for the West, the use of nuclear weapons could not correspond to the US strategic interest. The

---

1 *Op. cit.*

2 Jeffrey M. Jones, "Americans Increasingly See Russia as a Threat, Top U.S. Enemy," http://www.gallup.com/poll/181568/americans-increasingly-russia-threat-top-enemy.aspx?utm_source=americans%20increasingly%20see%20russia%20as%20a%20threat&utm_medium=search&utm_campaign=tiles, February 16, 2015. In March of the same year "in US, record 68% view Russia as unfriendly or and Enemy."

3 For the first time it was openly argued by Professors Keir A. Lieber and Daryl G. Press in their article "The End of MAD? The Nuclear Dimension of US Primacy," *Foreign Affairs*, March/April 2006. Their article was then reposted by Valery Yarynich and Steven Starr: "'Nuclear Primacy' is Fallacy," http://www.globalresearch.ca/nuclear-primacy-is-a-fallacy/4991, May 26, 2006, but the issue has still remained debatable. See for instance William Engdahl, "US missile shield: 'Russian Bear sleeping with one eye open,'" http://rt.com/op-edge/us-missile-shield-russia-361/, February 17, 2013 and Carol Osgood and Rachel Douglas, "US Moves Toward Nuclear First Capability," *Executive Intelligence Review*, March 15, 2013.

US and its allies now have at their disposal an overwhelming superiority in all types of their conventional forces over all possible opponents. Although the US was the first nation to build and use nuclear weapons, those weapons have now become the power equalizers, enabling relatively weak and small nations to deter the attack of their more powerful neighbors or even some major powers. The present situation is quite different than the one that existed in Europe after World War II in the 1940s and 1950s when the Americans might have justified their deployment of nuclear forces as a necessary countermeasure against the Soviet Union's large, battle-hardened conventional forces. The present Russian Army is but a poor shadow of its Soviet predecessor and I believe that when President Obama, in Prague on April 5, 2009, called for a world free of nuclear weapons, he expressed not so much humanitarian and ecological concerns but US strategic interests properly understood. At the same time I do not believe that anyone could completely abolish nuclear weapons now. There are too many political and economic interests involved and a number of states, including the Russian Federation and Israel, would strongly oppose it. The United States would probably continue to use its nuclear potential as a political pressure tool, but it will be rather cautious with its use for military purposes. It simply does not need to do that, especially in view of the development of the Prompt Global Strike (PGS) systems that can deliver a precision-guided conventional weapon airstrike anywhere in the world within one hour, similar to a nuclear Intercontinental Ballistic Missile (ICBM), and even to replace nuclear weapons.

The PGS systems are much more powerful and potentially destructive than the other conventional weapons, and the US is a pioneer and leader in its construction and further improvements. Their development has already increased US military options and offensive capacities. In September 2014 Russian President Vladimir Putin included PGS among a number of new threats Russia faced, along with the US Ground Based Midcourse Defense System in Europe and increased NATO presence in the Eastern European countries bordering Russia.

At present both Russia and China are trying to develop their own versions of hypersonic missiles like GPS, but they are probably still lagging behind. In the case of Russia all those efforts might now be more difficult because of the economic sanctions and other financial problems.

Since the end of World War II and in a more decisive way since the disintegration of the Soviet Union in 1991, the American power elite[1] has

---

1 For the concept of the American Power Elite see C. Wright Mills, *The Power Elite*, Oxford University Press, 1956. This prominent American scholar indicated the Power Elite interests in maintaining permanent war economy in order to protect US' capitalist economy from the boom and bust cycle and as

been seeking strategic primacy. Any states or other political forces which seem to represent even a potential threat are seen as targets to be cut down to a modest and obedient size or, if they do not want to surrender, to be destroyed.

During the Cold War I period, none of these goals might have been achievable. According to two American security experts: "By the mid-1960s, a truly effective nuclear counterforce strike by either side — that is a disarming blow by one superpower against the nuclear arsenal of the other — became impossible. The sheer number of targets that would have to be destroyed, combined with the limitations of contemporary guidance systems, virtually guaranteed that any disarming attack would fail, leaving the enemy with a number of surviving weapons with which to retaliate."[1] In addition they admit that any larger scale use of nuclear weapons "would have produced enormous quantities of lethal radioactive fallout and hence caused millions of civilian casualties."[2]

However, according to them and to the hawkish part of the American establishment, the situation has changed. As they argue: "Two fundamental 'truths' about nuclear weapons — they reliably produce stalemate and their use would necessarily create mass casualties, have been quietly overturned by changes in technology and dramatic force reduction."[3] They are certainly right that since the end of Cold War I, American military technology has made great progress which could be contrasted with the Russian military technical retreat during the same period.[4] However, their conclusions might be far-fetched.

Professors Leiber and Press consider it feasible and even necessary for the US to attempt to develop what they call "counter force capability" — to be able to attack and destroy the nuclear arsenal of its rival or rivals and to thus prevent their possible retaliation. According to them: "The counter force revolution means that nuclear exchange may not lead to mutual destruction; one party [presumably the US] may suffer far less or even be spared entirely."[5]

As I am not an expert on nuclear weapons and post-modern warfare in general, I cannot judge the realism and practicality of their arguments. They

manipulative use of media in order to preserve the existing social and political order. Of some interest might also be one of his last books, *The Causes of World War Three*, M.E. Sharpe, 1976, which although written almost 50 years ago might still be relevant today.

1 Keir A. Leiber, Daryl G. Press, "The New Era of Nuclear Weapons, Deterrence and Conflict," *Strategic Studies Quarterly*, Spring 2013, pp. 3-4.

2 *Op. cit.*

3 *Op. cit.*, p. 5.

4 "US–Russia nuclear conflict: The impossible is possible," Leonid Ivashov interviewed by Alyona Mirgorodskaya, http://english.pravda.ru/russia/politics/24-03-2015/130108-usa_russia_nuclear_conflict-0/, March 24, 2015.

5 Keir A. Leiber, Daryl G. Press, p. 11

are most likely controversial and they are challenged by a number of other American, European and Russian[1] experts. It would be rather difficult to make a successful surprise nuclear attack on Russia or China.

However, I believe the very much modernized and updated US nuclear forces are only one dimension of Washington's efforts to preserve its strategic primacy, which includes as its major new asset the ABM systems deployed in Europe, anti-submarine warfare, intelligence surveillance reconnaissance systems, cyber warfare, various PGS systems mentioned before and possibly some other super modern means of mass killing and destruction.[2]

In the last few years the government and the media's unusually harsh anti-Russian campaign is largely fostered by the conviction that America could win a nuclear war with Russia and that the US population would be relatively safe. This is a new and I think quite dangerous notion. Certainly not all Americans and even not all members of the US power elite share such a view, but there is now an influential group who do, and its role should not be underestimated.[3]

According to the French analyst and website editor Jean-Paul Basquiat, the American media has set up US citizens for nuclear war with Russia, but according to him the ensuing conflict will mark the end of both civilizations in the usual sense.[4]

Fortunately, awareness of that seems to be rising, and the unexpected meeting of US Secretary of State John Kerry with President Putin and the Russian Foreign Minister Lavrov in Sochi on May 12, 2015, according to the American TV channel CNN, "[broke] the ice, but there is still a long way to improve bilateral relations."[5]

1 See for instance opinions of the American nuclear arms experts Steven Starr and the Australian nuclear expert Helen Caldicott.

2 Carl Osgood and Rachel Douglas, "The US Moves Towards First Strike Capability," *Executive Intelligence Review*, March 15, 2013.

3 For the broader public and even for better-informed people, the existing threat and some of its causes are presented in an excellent 14-minute video "The Road to World War 3" by Aaron Hawkins.

4 Mediapart: Russian nuclear response will be devastating preventive strike, http://en.cyplive.com/ru/news/mediapart-rossiyskiy-yadernyy-otvet-budet-sokrushitelnee-preventivnogo-udara-ssha.html?selcat=7, May 15, 2015.

5 "Washington has refused calls to isolate Russia," *Cyplive*, May 13, 2015. See also, "Kerry holds talks with Putin during first visit to Russia in two years," *Guardian (UK)*, May 12, 2015.

Chapter 5. Prospects for a New 'Reset.' Is It real?

Especially since the coup d'état in Kiev in February 2013 and the ensuing annexation of Crimea by the Russian Federation, many analysts have suggested we have embarked on a new Cold War, though different from the first one in shape and scale. The present period started with the visit of US Secretary of State John Kerry to Sochi on May 11–12, 2015, which surprised many observers. his long meetings with Russian President Putin and Foreign Minister Lavrov seem to suggest a change in direction, while the continued harsh rhetoric and name-calling in the US media suggest more of the same. This period may be difficult to characterize, but apparently, In spite of outspoken opposition by some hawks,[1] the ice between Washington and Moscow has been broken and official contacts reinstated.

As the *New York Times* journalist and Moscow correspondent David Herszenhorn notes, for more than a year the American President "has worked aggressively to isolate Russia and its renegade [in the American understanding] president, Vladimir Putin, portraying him as a lawless bully atop an economically failing, increasingly irrelevant petro-state. Mr. Obama led the charge by the West to punish Mr. Putin for his intervention in Ukraine, booting Russia from

---

1 Mark Adomanis, "The US Must Keep Talking to Russia," *Moscow Times*, May 18, 2015. As he wrote, "despite the apparent [as he thinks] banality of the Putin-Kerry chat, some people managed to find fault with it. Leon Aron of the American Enterprise Institute and David Kramer of the McCain Institute for International Leadership both wrote angry editorials in which they denounced Kerry for his trip to Sochi in extremely harsh terms...Both Kramer and Aron were angry with Kerry for the mere act of speaking with Putin...both editorials made very similar arguments that by meeting with Putin, Kerry was affording him a legitimacy that he does not deserve."

the Group of Eight economic powers, imposing harsh sanctions on some of Mr. Putin's closest associates and delivering financial and military assistance to the new [and in spite of its radical nationalism, protected by the West] Ukrainian government."[1] However, as he has to admit, "Russia has not only weathered these attacks and levied painful countersanctions on America's European allies, but also proved stubbornly important on the world stage."[2] Consequently, most of the respected analysts came to the conclusion that "the policy of isolating Russia, economically and diplomatically, is failing."[3] Obama's administration's decision to send its envoys to Russia and to restart its contacts with Putin thus seems to reflect a pragmatic recognition of that. However, it does not necessarily mean any real concessions for Moscow or even less any change in its previous goals and political aspirations. I feel it is just an alternative and perhaps a more thoughtful tactic to achieve them. The "Battle for Russia" now is expanding into a battle for Eurasia and, because of its geopolitical and geo-economic importance, for the struggle for global domination and the new international system. Because of the contrasting interests of the parties involved, no compromise seems to be in the offing. What is now more likely instead is that the hegemonic power simply wants to temporarily relax some of its repressive measures in order to acquire Russia's cooperation in some areas vital for Washington — such as Syria, Iran, Afghanistan, and perhaps all of the Middle East. The US has used the same approach towards Moscow in the past. After the disintegration of the Soviet Union, it became almost typical for various presidential administrations in their relations with the Russian Federation.[4]

It is possible that American leaders are starting to act in a more realistic and pragmatic way than was the case a year ago, when according to Karaganov, they were essentially trying to battle Moscow.[5] However, there are still no signs that they have changed their goals and diminished their imperial aspirations.

The new Cold War, initiated by Washington against Moscow, certainly brought suffering to Russia, but from the American point of view it has not brought the expected results. Neither economic sanctions nor the unprecedented political and media campaigns made the expected impact

---

1 David Herszenhorn, "Diplomatic Victory, and Affirmation for Putin," *New York Times*, May 15, 2015.
2 *Op. cit.*
3 *Op. cit.*
4 Stephen Cohen, "US must address Moscow's grievances," *Washington Post*, February 14, 2013.
5 Sergey Karaganov, "Russia-USA relations may remain frozen at least through 2016," *Rossiyskaya Gazeta*, May 13, 2015.

on Moscow's behavior,[1] and, as a right wing American scholar admits, the predictions that the Russian political system verges on collapse "amount to the wish fathering the thought."[2] Despite the Western boycott of the May celebration of the Soviet victory over Nazi Germany, "Washington's mantra that Russia stands isolated internationally amounts to wishful thinking. India and China have refused to follow the West's lead on Russia, and so have a host of other Asian, African and Latin American countries."[3] In fact this year's (2015) celebration was more solemn than in previous years and caused a great outburst of popular enthusiasm and national support in Russia.[4]

The US, being overwhelmingly powerful, does not need to worry about its security, and even less its existential survival, as Russia does. However, as a result of Moscow's resilience, Washington needs to now think about some new problems.

Because of the global balance of power considerations, the most important of those problems is the emerging Russian–Chinese entente, which is an inevitable outcome of the Ukraine crisis and the ensuing Cold War and witch hunt against Moscow and its leader. Russia has no choice but to join

---

1 As Rajan Menon, the Anne and Bernard Spitzer Professor of Political Science at the Collin Powell School for Civic and Global Leadership at The City College of New York and a Senior Research Scholar at the Saltzman Institute of War and Peace at Columbia University, notes, "The bite of economic sanctions was supposed to bring him [Putin] around. But a year has passed since the penalties were imposed, and rather than extending an olive branch [to capitulate] he has boosted Russia's military role in Ukraine's east and stepped up air and submarine patrols...There isn't a scintilla of evidence that he plans to ditch the Donbas republics, let alone seek a compromise on Crimea, to ease the economic pressure on Russia." Rajan Menon, "Avoiding a New 'Cuban Missile Crisis' in Ukraine. Unlike in 1962, Russia has geography and national will on its side in Ukraine," *The National Interest*, May 22, 2015.

2 *Op. cit.*

3 *Op. cit.*

4 After the military parade, 500,000 Russians, including Putin who carried a picture of his father who lost his legs as a soldier defending Leningrad/St. Petersburg, marched in Moscow on May 9 carrying pictures of relatives who lost their lives in the war ("the immortal regiment"). Paul Robinson, "Self-Hating Russian," https://irrussianality.wordpress.com/2015/05/11/the-self-hating-russian/, May 11, 2015. Similar marches took place in a number of other Russian cities and gathered many thousands of participants who thus commemorated their country and their families. According to Dmitri Trenin, "May 9 is, for the Russian people more than Victory Day in the war that lasted almost four years and claimed 26-27 million [at least] men and women. It was the shared grueling experience that shaped and formed Russia's modern nation, and has helped keep it together, even after the fall of the Soviet Union. The memory of the war has become sacred, and for most people, according to a recent poll, May 9 is as important as their own birthday." Dmitri Trenin, "Russia's Victory Day Celebration: Much More Than Just a Parade. Five key takeaways from this year's show in Red Square," *The National Interest*, May 11, 2015.

Beijing, and the Chinese leaders have long been deeply convinced that their country is going to be the next victim, after Russia, of the American empire.

In Spring 2014 Andranik Migranyan warned that "Russian–Chinese relations are entering a qualitatively new stage. They are now more than merely partnership relations, but are not quite those of allies. However, it is entirely possible that increasing US sanctions on Russia and attempts to contain China will push the two countries into a full-blown alliance."[1] Even then, Dr. Migranyan had noted that the present situation in trilateral US–Chinese–Russian relations is at odds with the strategy postulated by Henry Kissinger during the Nixon presidency, according to which, "American relations with either Russia or China had to be substantially better than the bilateral relations between Russia and China themselves."[2] By that strategy Washington might always have been able to pit one country against the other, and preserve its dominance. It has become much more difficult now, but the American leaders certainly have not forgotten their traditional methods, and before the BRICS (Brazil, Russia, India, China, South Africa) Summit, held July 8–9, 2015, in Ufa, the capital of Russia's autonomous Bashkortostan republic, Konstantin Kosachyov, head of the International Affairs Committee of the State Duma, the lower house of the Russian parliament, warned that geopolitical rivals of BRICS would attempt to "artificially stir up trouble among the bloc's members.[3] This risk might have applied especially to Indian–Chinese relations, and Moscow has been quite pleased about the recent visit of the Indian Prime Minister, Narendra Modi, to China and the new prospects for the project of RIC (Russia–India–China) launched by Evgeniy Primakov at the end of the 1990s, which according to him could create a "triangle of survival" in the constantly changing and unstable world.[4]

Developments in the Middle East are no less important for Washington than the events in Ukraine and even the Moscow–Beijing entente. It is

---

1 Andranik Migranyan, "Washington's Creation: A Russian-China Alliance?" *The National Interest*, July 10, 2014.

2 *Op. cit.*

3 "Russia expects 2015 BRICS summit to help tackle global challenges," *Xinhua*, May 21, 2015, 18:15

4 Kamma Arora, "PM Narendra Modi in China, Day 2: As it happened," http://zeenews.india.com/news/india/pm-narendra-modis-beijing-leg-of-china-visit--live-updates_1595553.html, May 15, 2015. See also, "America's new nightmare: India, China plus Russia," May 15, 2015. Svobodnaya Pressa in *Russia & India Report*. However, as Professor Alexei Maslov, Director of the Center of Strategic Research on China at the Russian University of People's Friendship indicated, Primakov, who was then Prime Minister of Russia, "thought that Russia would play the leading role in the triangle...Now it is clear that China will play this role and this changes the entire situation." According to him, "At present Russia is the largest country that is supporting the expansionist policy of China. This reinforces our political and economic positions. On the other hand, a number of risks and conflicts can arise in the future, which [as he believes] can be resolved only if Russia will be able to equally engage with the West and the East."

obvious to all analysts that Moscow has always been and still remains an active player in this region, and that its importance there, especially in the cases of Syria and Iran, should not be underestimated. In the view of American scholar Galen Carpenter, a senior fellow at the Cato Institute, "It is unrealistic for Western officials to believe that they can adopt hostile measures in response to the Ukraine quarrel and related matters without paying a geopolitical price in the Middle East and other regions where the Kremlin is a relevant player."[1]

Last but not least, as a number of analysts including Henry Kissinger have already indicated, the West should keep in mind that Ukraine is vastly more important for Moscow than it is for Washington and its European allies. Russia would be able and willing to pay a much higher price for the future of this country than the West. Consequently, as quoted already, Professor Rajan Menon argues, "Given that sanctions have not worked and that renewed full-scale war is both probable and dangerous, the only sensible approach is shoring up Minsk II and working with Russia — and of course Kiev — on a formula that keeps Ukraine whole and addresses Russia's principal security concerns."[2] Professor Menon is certainly neither a dove nor a leftist, but in this case he presents a rational and realistic argument. Unfortunately, it is by no means certain that he will be listened to.

Not being a prophet, I cannot predict the coming events in the Ukraine crisis or the chances of avoiding a new large-scale war in Europe, which would be potentially tragic. However, I would like to briefly scrutinize the background of the existing situation and discuss the likelihood of various events.

First of all, I would like to stress that although the ancient Romans were absolutely right that "historia est magistra vitae" (history is life's teacher), history can hardly ever repeat itself in the same form again, and all historical analogies are useful only to a certain extent. In fact, the present situation in Ukraine and all of Europe is without any historical precedent and is certainly very different from the situation after World War II.[3] Comparisons with even earlier situations, such as the eve of World War I, might be even more misleading, overlooking a number of crucial developments, which changed the face of the world during the last 100 years.[4] As Dr. Monaghan

1 Ted Galen Carpenter, "Alienating Russia: How Washington's Middle East Policy May Suffer," *Real Clear Defense*, April 25, 2015.

2 Rajan Menon, *Op. cit.*

3 It was strongly stressed by Dmitri Trenin in his dialogue with Professor Legvold during the symposium hosted by Tufts University. Ekaterina Zabrovskaya, "Legvold and Trenin: How to Fix the US-Russia Relationship," *Russia Direct*, March 7, 2015.

4 The issues of abusing history and misunderstanding of Russia has been recently discussed in depth by the British scholar, Dr. Andrew Monaghan, in his Research Paper, "A New Cold War? Abusing History, Misunderstanding

indicates, "A new Cold War" narrative is not only misleading and leading to simplistic polemics but, in fact, prevents understanding of present day Russia. The British scholar is particularly critical of, as he writes, "the use of sensationalist historical analogies — such as comparing modern Russia's actions to those of Nazi Germany in the late 1930s [which] further detracts from the understanding of a complex international crisis."[1] According to him, "It is an abuse of history in which political myth and abstractions obscure informed arguments about Russia."[2] I would say that, even more, it in fact obscures much more than that — informed discussion about present day Europe or even the whole existing international system.

There are several major factors which make the present Russian–Western conflict, focused on Ukraine, quite different from all previous historically similar confrontations:

1. The first and probably the most important factor is the fact that the US, which wants to preserve its power as a global hegemon, is able to almost completely control both Western and Central (post-socialist) Europe, imposing not only its foreign policy directions but also shaping the political and economic domestic developments and cultural values of the old continent. One consequence of that is the clear decline of the old European powers and their lack of political initiative and independence.[3]

Writing on, as he called it, "The New World Disorder," the well-known Pakistani–British writer and social activist Tariq Ali has remarked that "We have seen the rise of a global empire of unprecedented power. The United States is now unchallengeable militarily and it dominates global politics, even the politics of the countries it treats as its enemies...There hasn't been such an empire before, and it is unlikely that there will be one again."[4]

Russia," Chatham House – The Royal Institute of International Affairs, March 2015.

1 *Op. cit.*

2 *Op. cit.*

3 In his interview with the French media (France 24) on December 16, 2014 Russian Foreign Minister Lavrov admitted that Moscow previously overestimated the independence of the EU from the US and cited as an example that Washington [US Vice President Biden] publically recognized that it had forced Brussels to impose sanctions on Russia. Going even further, former French Prime Minister Francois Fillon in his interview with Jean Jacques Bourdin on June 10, 2015 on BMFTV said that "The US is drawing us [the EU] into a crusade against Russia, which contradicts the interests of Europe" and pursues "extremely dangerous" policies in the Middle East that the EU and European states including France, have to agree with. In addition even in the European nations' domestic affairs the American justice system often interferes with the work of the European justice systems. He concluded that "Europe is not independent" and called for "a broad debate about how Europe can regain its independence."

4 Tariq Ali, "The New World Disorder," *London Review of Books*, Vol. 37, Nr. 7, 9 April 2015.

However, he has also commented, "Despite all its advances in capitalist technology, the internal political structure of the United States has barely changed for a hundred and fifty years. It may be militarily, economically and even culturally in command — its soft power dominates the world — but there is as yet no sign of political change from within."[1] Although that looks like a contradiction and apparently does not please him, Tariq Ali does not believe that the American empire is in decline and perceives all voices arguing that as "wishful thinking."[2] The US has suffered some setbacks but overall it "remains unassailable: it exerts its soft power all over the world, including the heartlands of its economic rivals, its hard power is still dominant, enabling it to occupy countries it sees as its enemies, and its ideological power is still overwhelming in Europe and beyond."[3]

In spite of being a radical left-winger, but perhaps also because of his East Indian origin, he rejects the idea that China might be able to replace America as a leading world power. The Americans were able to knock the British bourgeoisie out, but according to him the Chinese are still too backward to dream about challenging US primacy.[4]

Tariq Ali is not a professional scholar but his political analysis is often clear cut and convincing. In this case he did not follow his own Marxist-Trotskyist sympathies and went against many other left-wing analysts. I think that although he might exaggerate[5] the stability of the US, he has correctly indicated its present power and influence.

---

1 *Op. cit.* Tariq Ali, who is neither a historian nor a political scientist, seems to underestimate the impact of the tremendous socio-political and economic transformations which took place in US life during this period. Even if the political structure preserved its previous forms, they in fact probably work in quite different ways. However, it is true that as prominent American journalist and thinker William Pfaff indicated, the United States' geographical distance and cultural isolation from the eighteenth-century European Enlightenment and its consequences permanently influenced Americans' view of the world and its own nation. The radicalism of the French Revolution, the origins and development of Marxist socialism, the class struggle and social revolutions were remote and threatening events to Americans. William Pfaff, *The Irony of Manifest of Destiny: The Tragedy of American Foreign Policy*, New York: Walker and Company, 2010. Largely because of that the Americans have never had any real social revolution and have little if any understanding of the issue of ethnic nationalism, which is often blamed as just one more old world evil.

2 *Op. cit.*

3 *Op. cit.* However, there are now in Europe, including Poland, a growing number of ideological and political concepts and approaches critical of it.

4 The Chinese leaders have always denied any global hegemonic aspirations. Chinese Vice-Premier Wang Yang recently stated that the People's Republic of China "does not have any ideas or capabilities with which to challenge or displace America's global command," Jack A. Smith, "The Hegemonic Games': the US vs. PRC," *Global Research*, May 31, 2015.

5 Tariq Ali was born in the still British Indian Empire and has spent most of his life in the UK. His knowledge of both Russia and China is certainly rather superficial and his assessment of China by the national share of world

The American empire is certainly a unique historical phenomenon which cannot be easily compared with any previous ones, and at least at present it has no serious challenger. Other states and nations including both the Russian Federation and China are trying to protect themselves as best they can against its interference and even open aggression, but it is by no means certain that that they will be successful.

2. The second, and probably only a little less important, factor has to do with a number of historic breakdowns that led to the decline of Russia. The rise of the US to its present global domination was possible because of two major historical developments.

- The decline of the political, economic and even cultural might of Western Europe including the UK, France and Germany following World War I and World War II.
- The dramatic decline of Russia, which in contrast to the European decline, was not so easily predicted.

In 1831 the French scholar and traveller Alexis de Tocqueville, who sympathized with the new American Republic and did not like Tsarist Russia, which had one generation earlier defeated the French Napoleonic Empire, wrote in the conclusions of his famous book, *Democracy in America*, that:

> There are, at the present time, two great nations in the world which seem to tend towards the same end, although they started from different points...the Russians and the Americans...All other nations [Tocqueville included here only European or other broadly Western culture nations] seem to have nearly reached their natural limits,[1] and only to be charged with the maintenance of their power, but these are still in the act of growth,...Their starting point is different, and their

---

millionaire households (in 2012 9.4%) compared with 42.2% in the US is not convincing. Much depends on the social structure and distribution of income and the relevant figures for Germany and France are 2.7% and 1.9%. Also, he did not include in his argument Taiwan, with 2.3% of millionaire households. For a much more critical analysis of the US situation and its international prospects see Professor Michael Klare, "Superpower in Distress," *Tomgram*, May 28, 2015. Michael Klare is a Professor of Peace and World Security Studies at Hampshire College.

1 Tocqueville seemed to indicate the coming decline of Europe. Similar analyses have become repeated and even dramatized since the beginning of the 20th century and especially after the outbreak of World War I. See for instance the perhaps most famous example, Oswald Spengler, *The Decline of the West*. The decline was not then predicted, and even less the total breakdown of Russia. The West was rather concerned about the Russians' power and Russia's enormous potential.

courses are not the same, yet each of them seems to be marked out by the will of Heaven to sway the destinies of half the globe.[1]

In fact, in the 19th and at the beginning of the 20th century, Russia seemed not only to be very powerful but was a rising and promising nation. Its ensuing decline, present weakness and diminished international importance were not, as perhaps was the case of Western Europe, the outcomes of the *sui generis* natural historical or even genetic cycle. These were caused by a number of shocks and disasters, which were unpredictable and unprecedented, that started with the Russians' entrance into World War I, its ensuing military defeat, and the 1917 Revolution, which in its second phase brought to power the radical Communist Party of the Bolsheviks. As I have already discussed, all these events undermined the Russians' international legitimacy and internal stability, and though the new rulers later did much to rebuild and strengthen the country, World War II, which started there on June 22, 1941, with the German invasion of the Soviet Union, brought enormous human and material destruction. There were from 26 to 27–28 million military and civilian casualties, mainly young men, and the impact of that on the country's future was even more dramatic, permanently lowering Russia's potential population.[2] As an American researcher concludes, "Had the cataclysmic war with Germany not taken place, or had it not been so enormously costly, Russia would be a totally different country inhabited by many more (and very different) people than is actually the case."[3]

The Soviet victory over Nazi Germany, unappreciated in the West, cost an enormous price which could not be compared with the price paid by any other European nation, including even Germany. The US did not suffer the direct impact of the war on its own territory (with the exception of Pearl Harbor), and its military casualties, mainly in the war with Japan, amounted to 405,399, a number which though substantial was only a small fraction of the Russian casualties. Because of World War II, the US became much richer and more powerful than ever before, while Russia fell into great misery.

As I have already discussed, that was by no means the end of the Russian 'Via Dolorosa' (Path of Suffering). Still to come was the Cold War, imposed by the American superpower (that until the end of 1949 preserved a monopoly on nuclear weapons), and the ensuing arms race that was very costly for Russia. The next period, during and after the Perestroika pro-

---

1 Alexis de Tocqueville, *Democracy in America*, ed. P. J. Mayer, part 2, Conclusion, final paragraphs, pp. 412-413, (1969). Originally published in French in 1835, 1840.
2 "Russia is a Product of the Second World War, in Terms of Demography," by Mark Adomanis, http://readrussia.com/2015/05/01/russia-is-a-product-of-the-second-world-war-in-terms-of-demography/, May 1, 2015.
3 *Op. cit.*

capitalist transformations, was also very painful for most of the population and it culminated in the disintegration of the Soviet Union. All these events caused probably only a little fewer human deaths and slightly less material destruction in Russia than World War II, though at the same time it created the new Russian bourgeoisie and the multimillionaire oligarchs, who, the same as in the other capitalist nations, achieved a strong political influence. Their economic and social interests often contrasted with those of the majority, and the internal and often violent tension within the country persisted until Putin became president in 2000. He has been and is still trying to preserve a certain balance among the various social forces in Russia and to strengthen the Russian state as such. However, his political options are far more limited than the Western media want us to believe, and his efforts to rebuild Russia have never been acceptable to Washington. As Dmitri Trenin has stated, "one other [alongside the asymmetric nature] distinction between the situation today and the Cold War is that, as seen from this part of the world [the United States] no compromise is possible. In the Cold War you [the Americans] could compromise with Soviet leaders Stalin, Brezhnev and Khrushchev. Compromising with Putin is somehow not acceptable... This is clearly more than just about Ukraine. It's about two fundamental things. The fundamental thing for Russia is the ability to move around without any constraints and to do what the Russian leadership thinks is important for the Russian national interests. The fundamental thing for the US is that Russia is challenging US leadership, essentially the world order that the US leads."[1] The Ukrainian crisis in its present form was possible only because of Moscow's weakness. At the same time it is only one stage in the long battle for Russia.

3. The third factor that has acquired more visibility is the growing role and influence of China and some other non-Western, mainly Asian, powers on international developments also in Europe. I think that Moscow would not probably have been able to survive the confrontation with Washington and the EU without the political and economic support of Beijing and some other non-Western nations, especially the BRICS and Shanghai Cooperation Organization's members. This development created a new situation perhaps not even anticipated by the US, where more globalization and international connections might not work according to their wishes or interests. If the War Party within the Beltway were to prevail, the US response to that might be more aggressive interventions, such as naval conflict with China, which, according

---

1 Ekaterina Zabrovskaya, "Legvold and Trenin: How to fix the US-Russian relationship," *Russia Direct*, March 7, 2015.

to a Polish analyst, is "only a question of time"[1] as America will not be able to pay its enormous debts to that country. However, this is not necessarily true. In spite of occasional political tensions that have mostly been focused on matters in the South China Sea, there are still enough common economic interests and business connections to stabilize interstate relations. Largely because of that, Beijing's situation is different from that of Moscow. According to an American scholar, "Neither China nor the United States wants war, at least not in the near future."[2] The American elites consider China as an economically useful but overall semi-developed nation, and they do not have the same mixture of scorn and mistrust as they do towards Russia. On the Chinese side the People's Liberation Army is not ready to fight the US Army with its advanced technologies (PGR) and nuclear missiles. The recent visit of the US Secretary of State John Kerry to Beijing was characterized as "a trip in depth communication" and a "constructive visit."[3]

4. Probably a more likely place to attack would be a new front on the Russian Federation's border. In addition to the southern front in Ukraine, Washington might instigate a new violent conflict in the north involving Latvia, Estonia and Lithuania. In the American expert's view, "Latvia, Estonia and Lithuania form the Achilles heel of the NATO alliance."[4] According to a leading Polish expert, Dr. Mateusz Piskorski, the increasing American military presence in these countries and their military supplies there seem to confirm that.[5]

The official visit by US Secretary of State John Kerry to Sochi and Victoria Nuland's trip to Moscow to talk with Russian officials do not necessarily indicate real improvement in political relations or a prospect of a major deal between the two parties. In my opinion the situation is far more complicated and any real solution of the present crisis, if at all possible, might require all-Eurasian continental, if not global, transformations. At the same time it does not mean that a major hot war is in the offing.

---

1 Krakauer, "Konflikt z Chinami jest tylko kwestią czasu," *Observator Polityczny*, May 30, 2015.

2 Robert Farley, "3 Ways China and the US could go to War in the South China Sea," *The National Interest*, June 6, 2015. See also M.K. Bhadrakumar, "Hello G7, This is China Calling," *Indian Punchline*, June 10, 2015.

3 Jack A. Smith, "The Hegemonic Games: The US vs. PRC," *Global Research*, May 31, 2015.

4 Graham Allison and Dmitri K. Simes, "Russia and America: Stumbling to War," *The National Interest*, April 20, 2015.

5 Dr. Mateusz Piskorski, "Geopolityczna Ukraina," www.prisonPlanet.pl, April 8, 2015.

As an influential liberal Russian analyst has recently noted, "communication between nations is not necessarily about negotiating deals."[1] During the Cold War (1947–1985) the US and the Soviet Union established sophisticated systems of constant communication at high political and military levels of both nations. The main reason for that was not a search to "conclude agreements or to resolve specific issues."[2] Quite simply both sides "needed to know the logic and, if possible, the intentions of the other"[3] in order to avoid a possibly fateful misunderstanding.

In the post-Cold War period all those useful tools and customs lost their importance or were even discontinued. In view of Moscow's moral and political capitulation during the Gorbachev period and the following disintegration of the Soviet Union and general socio-economic breakdown under Yeltsin, there was apparently no need for them. Washington believed that with the help and cooperation of part of the former Soviet establishment, it had definitively won the Cold War and did not see any reason to listen to the defeated and impoverished Russia.[4]

Fyodor Lukyanov correctly indicates that "The real Cold War, such as it was over the span of four decades of the 20th century, will never be repeated. This is because its main distinguishing characteristic was not the confrontation between the Soviet Union and the United States, but the balance of their military-strategic capacities. The balance of power offered by nuclear-missile parity facilitated a stability in the global system that was unprecedented in the history of international relations."[5] However, when the balance of power came to an end, the post-Cold War international system became based on the US's unilateral hegemony and no opposition to it would have been tolerated. From the American power elite's point of view any criticism, or even more, opposition, such as for instance French–German opposition to the war in Iraq in 2003, was perceived as a kind of treason, which needed to be punished and strongly condemned. [6]

---

1 Fyodor Lukyanov, "Obama legacy and Russia: What future holds for Moscow and the US," *Russia Beyond the Headlines*, May 22, 2015.

2 *Op. cit.*

3 *Op. cit.*

4 When the German Chancellor, Helmut Kohl, suggested to President George H.W. Bush in 1990 that Moscow should get something in return for its acquiescence in the reunification of Germany, the American President responded, "To hell with that! We prevailed, they didn't. We can't let the Soviets clutch victory from the jaws of defeat." Leslie H. Gelb, "Russia and America: Toward a New Détente," *National Interest*, June 9, 2015.

5 Fyodor Lukyanov, "Russia not pursuing Cold War in Mideast over Ukraine," *Russia in Global Affairs*, April 28, 2014.

6 In the late winter and spring of 2003 American media and politicians anti-French campaign was not far behind the anti-Russian one of the last two years (2013-2015).

Since Putin's return to the Russian presidency in 2012, Moscow came to be viewed by the West with increased suspicion and growing hostility, which were demonstrated before and during the Sochi Olympic Games in the Spring of 2013. Other events of the period, such as Russia's effective prevention of an American bombardment of Syria, and Moscow's opposition to the Western-supported coup d'état in Kiev further aggravated Russian–Western relations, which led to the present crisis after the Russia's annexation of Crimea in March 2014.

The present Russian–Western conflict might be, but does not necessarily need to be, connected with the other major possible conflict of the era between the Peoples Republic of China and the West. Although, n 2014–2015 Beijing provided Moscow with some support and international protection, its foreign policy has always been very nuanced and its future direction difficult to predict. Much will depend on Washington's readiness to compromise with Beijing on what Beijing considers its essential national interests, and how the Americans are going to align that with their relations with China's close neighbors.[1] Beijing has been very pleased that the 2015 G7 summit voiced only concern about the tensions in the South China Sea but did not condemn any of the parties involved and did not perceive the situation there as a reason to impose sanctions against China.[2] This fact visibly demonstrated much more favorable Western recognition and acceptance of China than of Russia.

Writing in March 2014, shortly after the beginning of the Ukraine crisis, the former US Secretary of Defense Robert Gates clearly expressed his own and his Beltway colleagues' fears and views of the events. According to him, "Russia has encroached upon the outcomes of the Cold War, upon the world order that was established in 1991. This revisionism needs to be strangled in the cradle, otherwise, the position of the United States begins to crumble across the entire planet."[3]

In my view this kind of perception seemed rather strange and even puzzling. Why did this high-ranking American official so much exaggerate the importance of events in Ukraine, including even the Russian annexation of the Crimean Peninsula, territorially small and far away from US borders, populated mainly by Russians, but which also provides Moscow with, in practice, the only warm water port at its disposal? Did American officials really felt so uncertain of their country's power and worldwide leadership, or

1 Peter Ford, "A newly modest China? Official assurances raise eyebrows in US," *Christian Science Monitor*, January 7, 2015.
2 M.K. Bhadrakumar, "Hello G7, This is China calling," *Indian Punchline*, June 10, 2015.
3 Robert M. Gates, "Putin's Challenge to the West. Russia thrown gauntlet that is not limited to Crimea or even Ukraine," *Wall Street Journal*, March 25, 2014.

did they rather want to use remote events in order to increase their control over their own society and mobilize their reluctant European allies?

It would be impossible now to provide a clear cut and credible answer to these questions, but I think that both causes may have been involved. The American power elite certainly needs to discipline and mobilize both its own citizens and its foreign vassals. At the same time it cannot be completely excluded that the American leaders sitting at the top of the fragile world order pyramid might sometimes be concerned and uncertain of the future.

For all these reasons a new harsh anti-Russia political, economic and information campaign had to be started.

As the Chief of Stratfor, George Friedman, has openly admitted, "No American president can afford to sit idly by if Russia is becoming more and more influential. Russia's actions in the Middle East, or say, in the granting of asylum to Edward Snowden were perceived in the US as being directed against US interests."[1] He has also explained the reasons behind the anti-Russian sanctions. According to him, "The purpose of sanctions is to — with minimal damage to the US and with a somewhat larger damage to the EU — hurt Russia in order to make it capitulate to US demands. The sanctions demonstrate the power of the United States."[2]

Though John Kerry's May 11, 2015, visit to Russia and his long talks with Russian President Putin and foreign minister Lavrov were characterized as a sign of a "break in the ice," the ensuing events seem to confirm my opinion that the present American leaders would be either unwilling or perhaps even unable to change their country's imperial foreign strategy in Eurasia.

Former Indian Ambassador and international relations expert M.K. Bhadrakumar has recently written that, "Unless Russia is cut down to the stature of Portugal or Greece on the global stage, the US will not give up."[3] According to him, "the choice is clear for the Russian side: capitulate or face isolation."[4] However, he asks, "can a country of Russia's proud history capitulate?"[5]

Without suffering a total military defeat and the foreign occupation of its main centers, that might be uncertain or perhaps even unlikely. However, there is also another important question: can the US be able to impose its will and solve numerous global challenges just by itself and without any

---

1 ""In Ukraine, US interests are incompatible with the interests of Russian Federation," Stratfor Chief George Friedman on the root of the Ukrainian crisis," interview by Elena Chernenko and Alexander Gabuev, www.Komersant.ru, January 17, 2015. English translation on www.US-Russia.org
2 *Op. cit.*
3 M.K Bhadrakumar, "Kerry left Sochi laughing to himself," *Indian Punchline*, May 29, 2015.
4 *Op. cit.*
5 *Op. cit.*

kind of agreement and cooperation with Moscow and some other major regional powers?

In the past even the great empires, including the British one, have often looked for compromises and accommodations. The American Empire is apparently much stronger than all its historical predecessors, but I do not believe that it might be able to see itself as a kind of 'Almighty God' of the monotheistic religions. With all its power it is still a human-established entity and needs to adapt itself to the existing political and socio-economic circumstances.

Without assuring a truly Orwellian super-totalitarian global control, which would not be easy to establish and would be much more difficult to maintain, it would probably be impossible to eliminate the repeated confrontations of the numerous ethnic groups, cultures and daily interests. The imposition of the imperial will by the military forces, police controls or economic and diplomatic pressures is not only costly but often not effective. The use of soft power works overseas only under some auspicious circumstances, and even then has never been truly overwhelming on political issues. The peoples in Europe, Asia, the Middle East and probably Latin America and at least some parts of Africa are not easy to indoctrinate. They have their own national and cultural identities and generally do not want to accept foreign intrusion. In the case of a direct foreign threat, they are usually prone to support their own national government, even if previously it was unpopular and criticized.[1]

As I have already discussed in Chapter I, Western–Russian relations have hardly ever been cozy.[2] However, in the previous centuries neither Europeans nor Americans were able to treat it in the way they treated the other non-Western nations that were subjected to their rule, exploited and in some cases exterminated. Although, even in the times of its greatest

---

1 According to the public opinion polls conducted under sanctions, increased prices and uncertainty, and according to many Russian bloggers, the aggressive Western politics against Russia "produced exactly the opposite results. Instead of dividing the country, it pushed the "intelligent opposition" to consolidate with the Russian mainstream for a common goal to overcome the Western threat, while the grant eating opposition completely lost any legitimacy and respect." http://fortruss.blogspot.ca/2015/05/opinion-best-result-of-last-year-is.html, May 25, 2015, "Opinion: the best result of last year is consolidation of Russian elites before global challenges," Pavel Shippillin, translated and supplemented by Kristine Rus. As I have already written in one of the earlier parts of this monograph it would be rather an expected and typical response of the predominant ethnic and historically formed population. However, such a situation does not need to be stable, and after the Soviet disintegration Russian society has already been submitted to intensive Western propaganda and partly Americanized.

2 On this subject, see one of my previous articles: "Russian Problem: Russia's Place in the World – An Attempt at Historical and Geopolitical Analysis," *Polski Przeglad Stosunkow Miedzynorodowych*, February 2012, pp. 15-43.

achievements in the 19th and the first part of the 20th century, Russia, and between 1922–1991 the USSR, was only partly and perhaps superficially Westernized, it still almost always had enough military power and social resilience to defend itself against various foreign encroachment.

However, after the disintegration of the Soviet Union in 1991 and the following socio-economic crisis, for the first time in its long history, Russia, at least temporarily, became largely dependent on the West. Even earlier, since World War I, the West itself was submitted to major and far-reaching transformations which in fact have changed both its geopolitics and culture. Instead of a number of the old European powers with different and often clashing interests, which had well-established and long-lasting relations with Moscow or St. Petersburg, the West is now led and represented by the American Empire, which is neither a European nor an Asian nation and which is based on quite different political and cultural premises. Being isolated by two oceans from all of the world's major conflicts and being able at the same time to dominate the global economy, the USA was able to become the mightiest and most expansive power in all known human history.

In view of the present Western power and the real or alleged weakness of the Russian Federation, and the imbalance of power that creates at the regional and global levels, it is no wonder that "the most common refrain in Washington where the topic of Russia comes up is that 'Russia doesn't matter anymore'[1] and, consequently, "No one in the capital enjoys attempting to humiliate Putin more than President Barack Obama, who repeatedly includes Russia in his list of current scourges alongside the Islamic State and Ebola."[2]

The Ukrainian crisis which started in the fall and early spring of 2013–2014 is linked to events including developments Syria and Iraq. However, it was possible to create and inflate that crisis for two major reasons:

- Russian weakness, real or just imagined in the West, which followed the disintegration of the Soviet Union, the origins of which might be traced back to Brezhnev's "Era of Stagnation" 1964–1982.
- Western anxieties that Russia, which since 2000 started to develop better economically, might under Putin's leadership begin to regain at least some of its lost power and importance. Although the "march on Moscow" had already started earlier, it was additionally stimulated by, and culminated in the developments in Ukraine.

1 Graham Allison, Dmitri K. Simes, "Russia and America: Stumbling to War," *The National Interest*, April 20, 2015.
2 *Op. cit.*

As this book has not been conceived as a moralizing treatise, and even less as a political pamphlet, it is not my intention to blame America for its expansion in Eurasia or to search for a moral fault on the part of any other party. My attempt has been to provide the historical background and a realistic analysis of the recent events in order to look for some ways out of the present crisis.

If imperial expansion is the common behavior of powerful nations at some stages of their development, without the rational purposes associated with it and the realistic assessment of the existing situation, it might often cause more harm than advantage for the nation and even lead to a major human disaster. It is also necessary to preserve as much as possible a correct image of the other sides involved, both "friends" and real or alleged foes, in an effort to avoid being easily misled by the often widespread propaganda clichés. After a largely historical analysis of both previous and quite recent stages of Russia's national development, I want to focus now on some of its essential features which might enable a better understanding of the situation of this nation which has to fight for its survival against the often wrong perceptions and misleading strategies of the Western powers.

Both the idea of an autonomous Russian or Eurasian civilization and the Russian Federation's present foreign and defense policy are usually presented as challenges and threats to what are claimed to be universal Western values. The American effort to impose their political and cultural models on other nations is rather unique in history. The Roman Empire preserved and even protected the Hellenistic culture of its eastern provinces, which because of that were later transformed into the Byzantine Empire (AD 476–1453), and the British rulers of India were very proud of their preservation of the traditional Indian culture and institutions. The Russian culture or Eurasianism has no aspiration to universalism, but just to be accepted as a valuable form of civilization. Its religion, Christian Orthodoxy, has never promoted a Christian crusade and has always been capable of coexisting with other civilizations such as Islam. It has no concept of class conflict or social supremacy, and overall it is a rather passive ideology with little missionary zeal or tendency towards military and economic expansion.

It is quite unlikely that the Russian Federation might either now or in the foreseeable future represent any real security threat to the American or general Western interests. For Western (especially American and perhaps British and Polish) historians, it is not easy to accept that most Russian wars of the past were imposed by the other parties and were defensive in nature or were fought in the defense of their ethnic and religious relatives. In addition to the religious tradition, one important reason for that is the fact that apart from a few exceptional periods, Russia has always been weaker and more backward than the Western powers. It is even truer now. According to the figures which have been presented by British researchers on defense spending as a percent of world expenditure, in 2014 the USA spent 25.8%, the UK 2.4%, France 2.4% and other NATO countries 6.2%. Russian expenditures amounted to only 5.4%, almost 50% less than China with 9.8%.[1]

According to the International Institute for Strategic Studies, in 2014 the official American Defense budget amounted to $581 billion,[2] which did not include new expenditures on the modernization of nuclear missiles. The Russian Defense budget was equal to $70 billion,[3] below China ($129.4 billion),[4] and Saudi Arabia ($80.8 billion).[5]

Even without including the now somewhat less militarized but still strategically important American allies such as France, Germany and Japan, Western superiority is so overwhelming that any talk about a possible Russian threat to it seems out of the question by any real criteria.

While Washington and its allies believe in the ideology of liberal international interventionism in order to defend their type of political and economic institutions, and, if possible, to impose them worldwide,[6] a realistic political policy aims to preserve state interests — including not only its territory and material interests but also it national identity and inherited cultural traditions. In marked contrast to the Soviet Union, especially before Stalin, the foreign policy of the Russian Federation has been based on the realist tradition and on the traditional Westphalian concept of state sovereignty and non-interference in the affairs of other nations, without any urgent threat to its own state security. Both the annexation of Crimea and though in a different way, the limited support for the Eastern Ukrainian separatists (rebels) have been caused and still are caused by the Russian state's security concern about its access to its only warm water port (Sevastopol) and fears of a hostile pro-NATO Ukrainian state on its borders. Russia has already needed to accept NATO presence on its Northern borders and quite limited access to the Baltic Sea.

In his interview with the Italian newspaper *Il Corriere della Sera* on June 6, 2015, Vladimir Putin was probably right in saying that "only an insane person, and only in a dream, can imagine that Russia would suddenly attack

---

1 See Figure3, Defense Spending per cent of World Expenditure 2014 in *Military Balance*, London: Routledge, 2015, p. 22.
2 International Institute for Strategic Studies, *The Military Balance 2015*.
3 *Op. cit.*
4 *Op. cit.*
5 *Op. cit.*
6 The best example might be the involvement in the destruction of Yugoslavia and the establishment of Kosovo as an independent nation. Neither the US nor even its European allies had any direct interests involved there. An additional motive might have been a wish to destroy Yugoslavia as a socialist nation, though independent from Moscow.

NATO."[1] He was prone to believe, rather, that "some countries [presumably Poland and the Baltic states] are simply taking advantage of people's fears with regard to Russia"[2] in order to play the role of front-line nations and to receive more military, economic, financial and other kinds of assistance.[3] He called these fears "absolutely groundless,"[4] but he also implied that "some may be interested in fostering such fears," for instance the US, which "would like to maintain its leadership in the Atlantic community" and for that reason it might need "an external threat, an external enemy to ensure this leadership."[5] Such enemies would need to be big and scary enough to fit the bill. Neither Iran nor Islamic terrorism proved sufficient for that, and the Ukrainian crisis provided a chance to revive the specter of the former Cold War rival, Moscow.

Though Putin did not argue that this is exactly what happened, I think that he was partly right. Washington certainly wants to preserve its unique leadership, and in order to facilitate its international acceptance, especially in Europe, it needs to put stress on the external threats which might require its constant presence and protection. Because of its complex historical past, both as the Tsarist Empire and the Soviet Union, and the fact that even now Russia remains a very large and, at least potentially powerful country, it was relatively easy to perceive Moscow as a new danger, especially in the neighboring countries, some of which used to be part of the previous Russian empire.

However, the arguments about the Russian threat did not take into account the dramatic changes of the last century and the now firmly established unequal power relations, which favor the West. They also disregarded all efforts of post-Soviet Russian foreign policy and did not want to accept that this country has any legitimate interests and security needs.

Putin admitted that, when "suddenly this crisis unfolded in Ukraine, Russia [was] forced to respond. Perhaps, it was engineered on purpose, I don't know. But it was not our doing."[6] In fact Moscow had not the slightest

---

1 "Vladimir Putin interview to the Italian newspaper, "Il Corriere della Sera,""" on June 6, 2015, http://www.corriere.it/english/15_giugno_07/vladimir-putin-interview-to-the-italian-newspaper-corriere-sera-44c5a66c-0d12-11e5-8612-1eda5b996824.shtml

2 *Op. cit.*

3 *Op. cit.*

4 *Op. cit.*

5 *Op. cit.* Speaking at the St. Petersburg International Economic Forum Putin stressed again, "They [the Americans and their allies] should not have supported the anti-constitutionalists' armed coup that in the end led to a violent confrontation in Ukraine, a civil war in fact. We are not the cause of all those crisis events that Ukraine is experiencing." "West's support for state coup in Ukraine prime cause of crisis in Ukraine – Putin," St. Petersburg, *TASS*, June 19, 2015.

6 "Vladimir Putin interview to Italian newspaper Il Corriere della Sera," *Op. cit.*

---

interest in initiating the domestic Ukrainian developments and there are now no credible political forces in Russia which would be willing or even less able to restore the former Soviet Union.

All these facts, which could not have been unknown to Western elites, did not prevent the initiation of the large-scale information media and political campaign, with a brutality and harshness unprecedented even during the Cold War.

Putin assured the Italian journalists that "there is no need to fear Russia. The world has changed so drastically that people with some common sense cannot even imagine such a large-scale military conflict today."[1] It was an optimistic statement, which might have implied his faith in the rationality and basic goodwill of people, including even the top leaders. Such a faith has not always been supported by history, and though I think the Western nations including Poland have no good reason to be afraid of Moscow now, the "Battle for Russia" described by Trenin is still on, and the international system needs to be adjusted to be able to accommodate not only Russia but also a number of other rising powers and global transformations.

The events now unfolding could be briefly summarized as a well-premeditated Western effort to cut down to size or perhaps even to destroy the Russian Federation. The decline discussed in the previous chapters, including the disintegration of the Soviet Union, the Yeltsin period of economic breakdown, impoverishment of most of the population and semi-colonial dependency on the West, came to an end. Under Evgeniy Primakov and later Vladimir Putin's leadership, Russia started to recover and to get back onto its feet.

In 2013 both the socio-economic situation of the Russian population and Moscow's international strength and influence were much higher than in 1990–2000. The Russian Federation's role in Syria and, in spite of all Western efforts to prevent it, the successful Olympic Games in Sochi, seemed to introduce a new era of Russian prosperity and international prestige. However, Washington could not tolerate that, and the reaction in the form of the Ukrainian crisis was soon to come.

The Americans did not achieve all their goals during the last two years, and in May 2015 the John Kerry visited Sochi and held long talks with the Russian president, but the anti-Russian campaign did not come to an end. On June 7, 2015, during the G7 meeting in Schloss Elmau, south of Munich, the US President personally attacked the Russian leader and asked rhetorically, "Does he continue to wreck his country's economy and continue Russia's isolation in pursuit of a wrong-headed desire to recreate the glories of the Soviet empire? Or does he recognize that Russia's greatness does not depend

---

1 *Op. cit.*

on violating the international integrity and sovereignty of other countries?"[1] He has also warned that additional steps "would be taken if Russia were to double down on behavior in Ukraine."[2]

Obama blamed Moscow for the entire crisis in Ukraine which, according to him, was caused solely by Russian aggression, and he stated that although the US and its allies had expected that Russia would live up to the Minsk agreement, that has not happened.

Standing the truth on its head in this case, Obama seemed to overlook the fact that both Minsk agreements had been largely initiated by Putin and the German and French leaders, without American involvement and no real support. He also did not mention that the Ukrainian government in Kiev, supported by Washington, had almost completely ignored both Minsk agreements that it signed. His speech at the G7 meeting sounded like a war talk, and it stimulated a number of similar events.

On June 10, 2015, the European Parliament in Strasbourg adopted a resolution urging the European Union to reassess its relations with Moscow because of the Ukrainian crisis, as a result of which Russia "can no longer be treated or considered as a 'strategic partner.'"[3] The resolution was adopted by the majority (494–135 with 69 abstentions) and shortly after that the ambassadors of all of the EU members agreed to extend sanctions on Russia for the next six months. Even Greece did not oppose this.

Although those sanctions have been and still are quite harmful for the Russian economy, they seem to be less important now than a year ago. The St. Petersburg International Economic Forum (SPIEF) held in June 2015 attracted more participants than the Forum held a year before. At least 24 chief executives including 12 from US companies arrived, and according to Yuri Ushakov, an advisor to President Putin, in total 70 American company officers attended.[4]

Speaking at the Forum, the Russian President argued that though the country is going through hard times, no deep economic crisis which had been previously predicted has happened. As he stated, "we [the Russian leaders] have stabilized the situation and are confidently going through the obstacle course."[5] In his public speech he may have been too optimistic, but as I have already written, at least until now, both the Russian economy and

---

1 "Obama lambasts Putin: 'you're wrecking Russia to recreate Soviet empire,'" http://www.theguardian.com/world/2015/jun/08/g7-leaders-sanctions-russia-ukraine-conflict-obama, June 8, 2015.

2 *Op. cit.*

3 "Russia is no longer a strategic partner of the EU, say MEPs," *European Parliament News*, June 11, 2015.

4 Andrew E. Kramerst, "Despite Tensions US Companies Officials Attend Russian Economic Forum," *New York Times*, June 19, 2015

5 "Putin St. Petersburg," *TASS*, June 19, 2015

Russian society have proven to be far more resilient in the face of economic sanctions than Western experts had anticipated. Consequently, it seems to me that at present, for Russia the growing NATO military "defensive" deployment on its borders with the Baltic states and, also until now to some lesser degree, Poland is more threatening than the sanctions.[1] Both NATO and Washington itself present their moves as a way to "reassure European allies in the wake of the Russian annexation of Crimea in March 2014."[2]

The probability of Russian aggression is in fact nil. Even George Friedman has indicated that it would in any case be highly unlikely, because Russia has to be focused now on the Ukrainian crisis, and being weaker and poorer than the West cannot afford to deal with two crises at the same time. Until now no one was able to find any proof for, or even a sign of, a possible Russian push to the north. It is true that some substantial Russian minorities live in the Baltic states and in Latvia and Estonia they have for a long time been discriminated against and devoid of civil rights and citizenship. However, in the last few years before the beginning of the Ukrainian crisis, their situation started to improve, and successful Russian business groups have emerged in the Latvian capital Riga. These people have certainly no interest in a new war and destruction.

From the Kremlin's viewpoint a Russian attack on NATO state members would be simple suicide. The new deployment of American weapons and military units around Russian borders, just like the number of NATO military maneuvers in Poland and other Eastern European countries, look in fact more like a kind of provocation, or even preparation for a great invasion of the Russian Federation.

In response to the Canadian daily newspaper *The National Post* calling for "Boxing in Russia,"[3] one of the readers noted that "It won't be long before NATO and Russian forces will face each other a mere 100 metres apart. All it would take is some over-zealous commander, a nervous soldier or a Russian-hating Ukrainian fascist to pull the trigger, and that war would go nuclear in a heartbeat."[4]

This is not an impossible, but hopefully unlikely scenario of future events. In spite of the existing tensions I would still like to think that all of that is just an unusually brutish political campaign rather than the preparation for new full-scale war in Europe. However, the deployment of American forces at Russia's borders has by itself a substantial political and psychological

---

1 "Official: Pentagon may store heavy weapons in Baltics, Eastern Europe," *Al Jazeera and Reuter*, June 13, 2015.
2 *Op. cit.*
3 "Editorial: Boxing in Russia," *The National Post*, June 18, 2015.
4 "Letters: The dangers of poking the Russian bear," *The National Post*, June 19, 2015.

role and importance, and can have an impact on the future of the region. For these nations it might mean not so much security against the unlikely Russian threat but rather more domestic and inter-state conflicts in the near future.[1] All of that might provide Washington and its allies with increased chances to intervene there and to keep Russia under constant pressure and insecurity.

Although "there has been not a single feasible indication yet that Putin has any interest in the annexation of the Baltic states"[2] and he is well aware that "there are American submarines on permanent alert off the coast of Norway, equipped with missiles that could reach Moscow within 17 minutes,"[3] Western propaganda still runs an intensive fear-mongering campaign warning of forthcoming Russian aggression.

The constantly repeated warnings and accusations against Russia are probably intended to nourish the fear and hatred of it among its bordering nations and to make them more readily accept American protection. All these goals have already been, at least at the level of the ruling elites, quite successful.[4] If the US is now willing to alleviate its previous hostilities with

1 Danielle Ryan, "Fear Mongering in Baltic Does More Harm than Imagined Russian Threat," http://russia-insider.com/en/fear-mongering-baltics-does-more-damage-imagined-russian-threat/ri7898

2 None of the Baltic States (Estonia, Lithuania and Latvia) can be compared with Crimea which had and still has enormous strategic importance (Sevastopol) for Russia and is inhabited by an overwhelmingly Russian population. In the case of annexation of any of the Baltic nations, Moscow would need to face the hostile majority of the local population and an even stronger Western reaction including military attack. In addition, I do not think that the occupation of any of these nations might provide Moscow with much strategic or economic advantages. All of them are mostly poor countries, and the Baltic Sea, which is in fact controlled by NATO, does not now represent such strategic importance as the Black Sea, which provides a way to the Mediterranean and the Middle East. Last but not least, Russia already has the Baltic enclave, Kaliningrad. The Baltic states were part of the Russian Empire for a long time, but I do not see any real interest in Moscow in encroaching on their territories. We are not in the times of Peter the Great, more than 300 years ago, when the Baltic Sea might have been considered the "Russian window onto Europe."

3 Vladimir Putin interview to the Italian newspaper, *Il Corriere della Sera*, June 6, 2015.

4 This issue in relation to Poland has been discussed by Professor Ziemba, the head of the Institute of History and Theory of International Relations at the University of Warsaw (Poland). In his interview by Anna Leszkowska, "Ryszad Ziemba, "Polska Polityka," http://www.geopolityka.org/komentarze/wywiady/ryszard-zieba-polska-polityka, June 17, 2015. According to him, Polish elites had and still have a superiority complex towards Russian and other Eastern European peoples that prevents them from formulating a foreign policy based on realist premises. In addition, after the late 1980s socio-political transformations among the political ruling class, previous knowledge of the Russian language, which was intentionally eliminated from public spaces, disappeared. There is now a lack of knowledge and understanding of the Eastern European neighbors. I think Professor Ziemba is right but I believe the Russophobic elements would not get to power without strong American political and financial support.

former "enemies" such as China, Cuba, and even Iran, the Russian Federation has been chosen as the whipping boy in order to show the rest of the world the USA's might and potential for control. As Russian Prime Minister Medvedev has correctly indicated, "It was not us who started these sanctions [and the whole Ukrainian crisis] confrontation, and in order to end it, joint efforts are needed," but Russia does not see the West making any attempt to overcome the confrontation.[1] In fact, any of Moscow's attempts to show its readiness on self-defense, such as the military maneuvers on its own borders, have only increased the outburst of insults and predictions of its aggressive intentions.

Although during the first years of the present century — between 2001–2014 — military spending in the world increased by 58.5% to $1.76 trillion, and half of that or $880 billion (in fact probably much more) is accounted for by NATO members, the call is going out now to further increase it by 7–10%; that means $60–90 billion a year.[2] US Secretary of Defense Ash Carter recently visited in Europe, and his declarations that NATO must stand together against Russian aggression[3] and that "Russia must not be allowed to turn back the clock"[4] might have expressed the predominant Beltway opinion, though at the same time Carter stated that "we do not seek a cold, let alone a hot, war with Russia."[5]

A few days later, in June 2015, former US ambassador to Russia Michael McFaul tweeted, in the same vein, that "NATO will never invade Russia"[6] and that "Russia should also relax about NATO defensive weapons near Russian borders since it tells us it has no plans to invade NATO countries."[7]

However, the facts on the ground are more convincing than those empty words. At the NATO defense ministers' meeting on June 24, 2015, in Brussels, they accepted Carter's directive to triple the number of troops in the Response Force to 40,000 soldiers. The troops and heavy armaments are going to be stationed across Europe's eastern borders including Bulgaria, Estonia, Latvia, Lithuania, Poland and Romania.[8] It seems that the US and

---

Mass-scale propaganda developed by them nourished the negative image and hostility towards Russia among a large part of the population in the country.

1 "Russia does not see West attempts to overcome confrontation," Moscow, June 25, 2015, TASS.

2 Vladislav Inozemtsev, "Western attempts to use military to pressure Russia 'futile,'" www.gazeta.ru, June 11, 2015. Professor Inozemtsev is a Moscow based Russian liberal who is strongly critical of Putin's policy and also works for the Center for Strategic International Studies (CSIS) in Washington, D.C.

3 "Carter: NATO Must Stand Together against Russian Aggression," Associated Press, June 22, 2015.

4 *Op. cit.*

5 *Op. cit.*

6 "NATO will never invade Russia – McFaul," Interfax, June 28, 2015.

7 *Op. cit.*

8 James Garden, "NATO Ups the Ante in the Ukraine Crisis," *The Nation*, June 26, 2015.

NATO are waging a game of nerves, or a game of chicken, with Moscow, and the issue at stake is, does Putin blink first?

One should not exaggerate the political importance of the Russian president. Although his role is an important one, he also depends on many other people and social forces, and he cannot run counter to the major trends in his society. He might be a leader, but he needs to have followers. Until now the majority of Russians don't want to capitulate, but for how long are they going to persist?

This might be a moot issue. A majority of Russians (86%, up from 77% in June 2013) think that the US is using Russia's current difficulties to turn it into a second rate country and a "raw materials appendage" of the West.[1] According to another Levada poll, 89% of the respondents believe that Russia must strengthen its ties with other countries to counter the growing influence of the US (6% disagreed and 6% could not say) and most of them (70%) believe that Russia should continue its policy irrespective of the sanctions, though 20% suggest searching for compromises in order to be exempted from the sanctions.[2] Just as in January 2015, 10% of the respondents were not only ready to accept that compromises should be found, but that the attitude towards Crimea's accession to Russia should be revised. As I have already indicated, in Russia there is a group of well-established people, relatively small in number but politically vocal and still influential, who have almost always supported a pro-Western orientation and recently even the present Ukrainian government in Kiev. Those pro-Western liberals' role in Russian politics is now at a low ebb but has by no means disappeared.

However, according to a prominent foreign policy expert, Dr. Andranik Migranyan, "Russia is not going to yield anything...[it] has its interests, which are very clearly formulated."[3] He argued that the Ukraine crisis was not the only and not even the original cause of the tensions between Russia and the West.[4] The real reason behind them started after the Soviet Union's disintegration and the still ongoing West-to-East expansion, which was perceived in Moscow as threatening to the vital political and economic interests of Russia. What was at stake here was not only the disputed "Soviet heritage," but the historical socio-economic basis of the Russian nation and its external security. The country was not militarily defeated and occupied, like Germany and Japan, and yet American officials after the Soviet Union's collapse "have tended to see Russia as a country that can be written off and ignored."[5] He stressed that, "there [in Moscow] was no desire [and even less

---

1 www.levada.ru, June 26, 2015.
2 Interfax, June 29, 2015.
3 "This is What Russia Really Wants," *The National Interest*, June 24, 2015.
4 *Op. cit.*
5 *Op. cit.*

capability] to restore the Soviet Union or put NATO's Article 5 collective defense guarantees to the test in places like the Baltic states or Poland."[1] According to him, Russia "just wants to be treated as a great power and even a partner, and this entails Russian concerns being taken seriously," which he said, "'never ever' happened since the fall of the Soviet Union."[2] Migranyan argued that the long-standing Russian ambition is a dream of "a new security partnership in Europe, with NATO as one pillar and Russia as another,"[3] but in his opinion, "Unfortunately, Washington treats nobody as a partner."[4]

Migranyan's presentation of the origins of the present crisis and the European situation is largely in accordance with "The New Atlanticism" recently put online by British professor Richard Sakwa.[5] As he commented, although at the time of German reunification "there was no written commitment, it was clearly understood by all the participants that NATO's enlargement in the former Soviet bloc territory was simply inconceivable. The moral intent was clear, and thus [by that enlargement] the West reneged the spirit if not the letter of the terms on which the Cold War was deemed to have ended."[6] Probably the most negative outcome of that was that, "By design, Russia was left on the periphery of a post-Cold War Europe."[7] Simultaneously with the Russian internal crisis in 1991–2000, it became almost inevitable that "a negative dynamics" was going to set in and in the end contribute to the breakdown of the post-Cold-War order.

The New Atlanticism which is not only the security bloc but rather a hermetic and comprehensive neo-liberal ideological community, "sought to achieve the impossible: to retain its original Atlantic character by ensuring the predominance of the US in the expanding [to the East] security alliance, and to bring Russia in as a security partner."[8] Professor Sakwa rightly says that, "without the institutional transformation of NATO [which I feel was out of the question], the proclaimed partnership with Russia was unable to transcend the growing security dilemma"[9] and in fact caused the present consequences which became the Ukraine crisis.

---

1 *Op. cit.*

2 *Op. cit.* In spite of all the darker side of its system most people in Russia regretted the end of the Soviet Union, which brought them socio-economic deprivation and decreased international importance. Vladimir Putin expressed this opinion, saying, "He who did not mourn the passing of the Soviet Union had no heart, but anyone who tried to re-establish it had no head."

3 "This is What Russia Really Wants," *Op. cit.*

4 *Op. cit.*

5 Richard Sakwa, "The New Atlanticism," Valdai Papers, #17, May 17, 2015.

6 Mary Elise Saratte, "A Broken Promise? What the West Really Told Moscow about NATO Expansion," *Foreign Affairs*, vol. 93, Nr. 5, September-October 2014, pp. 90-97.

7 Sakwa, *Op. cit.*

8 *Op. cit.*

9 *Op. cit.*

In addition three major factors aggravated the situation and contributed to the coming crisis:

1. The first one was also indicated by Professor Sakwa: the fact that new Atlanticism became "increasingly unable to reflect critically on the geopolitical and power implications of its own actions, a type of geopolitical nihilism that in the end provoked the Ukraine crisis."[1] Being originally, at least in theory, a defensive alliance established to resist Soviet expansion, the New Atlanticism is now far more expansive and culturally aggressive, setting up a model of civilizational achievement. Consequently, it is "unable to accept the geopolitical pluralism of Europe"[2] and as an inevitable outcome of that, the exclusion of the greatest power and the largest state in Europe mean that it is unable to avoid the new confrontation which might remind people of World War I or the Cold War. Such a situation might be just a way towards a new Cold War or, if things were not kept under proper control, even a hot war, which certainly needs to be avoided.

2. The second factor in my view was an unfortunate change in the nature of, and the political failure of, the EU, which though it was brought into being in order to preserve peace and reconciliation in Europe has now become a "civilian wing" of NATO and the instrument of its further expansion. It has been correctly indicated that "It is pure hypocrisy to argue that the EU is little more than an extended trading bloc, after Lisbon, it was institutionally a core part of the Atlantic security community, and had thus become geopolitical."[3] All new members are now obligated to align their defense and security policies with those of NATO and that was probably one more important cause of the political tension around the Association Agreement between the EU and Ukraine, which led to the overthrow of President Yanukovich and the ensuing Ukrainian and international crises.[4]

---

1 *Op. cit.*
2 *Op. cit.*
3 Richard Sakwa, *Frontline Ukraine: Crisis in the Borderland*, London: I.B. Tauris, 2015, p. 255.
4 This issue has been thoroughly discussed by Professor Sakwa in his book: *Frontline Ukraine: Crisis in The Borderland*, I.B. Tauris, 2015, especially in Chapter II "Two Europes" pp. 26-49 and in his recent paper "The New Atlanticism," Valdai Papers, #17, May 17, 2015. On the implications of that for the Ukraine EU Association Agreement see also the article by Eric Draitser, "EU Association Agreements – NATO Expansion by other means," *New Eastern Outlook*, March 12, 2015, http://journal-neo.org/2015/03/12/eu-association-agreements-nato-expansion-by-other-means/ and Bruno Adrie, "The EU-Ukraine Association Agreement and the Upcoming War," *Global Research*, August 3, 2015. See

3. The third and perhaps most directly threatening development was the major and quite negative change in American political life. Since the end of the Cold War and especially after 1990, Russia began to be seen as a defeated enemy and an unimportant nation which does not deserve any particular attention and even less respect. Partly reborn in the late 1990s and after 2000, Russia has come to be perceived as a revanchist state compared with Nazi Germany in the 1930s. If during the Cold War the hawkish and Russophobic party was always offset to some extent by the political realists or some other more moderate political forces in the West, there is now no effective political counterbalance to them in Congress and the media. As I have already mentioned, Professor Immanuel Wallerstein and other prominent Americans are concerned about that. Their concerted efforts would be required to avoid further tension and unnecessary but potentially tragic consequences.[1]

Russia and Western Public Opinion

Both in the US and Europe there are now quite a few knowledgeable and prominent people who, though of different ethnic and social backgrounds and of various political orientations, are calling for an end to the present crisis and a new détente. Although to various degrees (and for often different reasons), they are all concerned about the threat of a new major military conflict in Europe. They seem to agree that such a war would be senseless and harmful to all parties involved. Whatever their motivations might be, at least in my opinion they are right and in this aspect I do not see any analogies with the outcomes of World War I or World War II. It is highly unlikely that in this case, there could be any real winner, and if both the Russian Federation and the West suffered unacceptable and perhaps, especially in the case of Europe, irreparable damages, only China and/or some other Asian nations would be able to increase their global role and importance.

Jean Pierre Chévènement, who was France's defense minister (1988–91) and interior minister (1997–2000), provides an independent European analysis of the origins and later stages of the conflict and appeals for an increased European role in its solution.[2] As he indicates, some of the causes of the present Ukrainian crisis need to be traced back to the circumstances of the breakup of the Soviet Union in 1991 when the then largest country

---

also "NATO-EU: a strategic partnership," *NATO-OTAN North Atlantic Treaty Organization*, Last Update: 4 December 2014.

1 That was the real reason for the recent creation (re-establishment) of the American Committee for East-West Accord.

2 Jean-Pierre Chévènement, "EU and Russia antagonistic by accident, No need for this Cold War," *Le Monde diplomatique*, July 2015.

in the world was divided among its previous 15 federal republics, and the administrative division lines became the state borders. As a result, 26 million ethnic Russians were left outside their country and overnight became the subjects (not always citizens) of the newly founded, and often (as in Latvia and Estonia) strongly nationalist political entities.

The Soviet Union used to be an enormous but highly complex country with, according to the last census (in 1989) 286 million citizens. Although it had always been divided into a number of federal republics and autonomous administrative units, borders among them had often been arbitrary and included ethnically diverse populations. When all of them were included in one overarching political entity, this may not necessarily have created major problems, but it became a source of tensions when the former administrative units were transformed into sovereign nations.

The Ukrainian state, as it emerged in 1991, was the result of the Soviet break-up and had almost no recent historical background.[1] The multiethnic population, who have substantial historical and cultural differences, particularly between the strongly nationalist Western Ukraine which for many centuries was part of Poland or the Habsburg empire, and Eastern Ukraine, whose population was largely Russian-speaking and belonged to the Eastern Orthodox Church. Their mutual relations had never been easy and preservation of the unity of the country, which in addition included hundreds of thousands of individuals belonging to other minorities such as Hungarians, Poles, Romanians, Greeks and Tartars and which was very economically dependent on Russia, had always been a delicate matter. However, some Western politicians believed that Ukraine's inclusion in NATO and cutting off its links with Russia "is inseparable from the reconfiguration at the European and global level."[2] Consequently, the EU, while preparing the Association Agreement with Ukraine, refused any discussion of its content with its major economic partner, Moscow. Brussels did not want to take into account any Russian and joint Russian–Ukrainian

---

1 As I have already written in Chapter 1, the part of present Ukraine around Kiev was the cradle of Russia, Belarus, and part of Ukraine, but since the 13th century it was dominated by foreign powers. The Ukrainian state, though much smaller in size, had only been made independent by Imperial Germany in 1917, but, being torn apart by civil wars and foreign invasions, soon became divided by the Treaty of Riga, signed March 18, 1921, between Poland and Soviet Russia (also acting on behalf of Soviet Belarus) and Soviet Ukraine, which in 1922 became a member of the Union of Soviet Socialist Republics (the USSR).

2 As early as 1997 Zbigniew Brzezinski argued that "the only way to prevent Russia from becoming a great power again was to remove Ukraine from its sphere of influence." *The Grand Chessboard: American Primacy and its Geostrategic Imperatives*, New York: Basic Books, 1998.

economic interests, and its economic and political conditions "presented Kiev with an impossible choice between Russia and Europe."[1]

Being in a difficult position, Ukraine's President Victor Yanukovych asked for a delay in the signing of the association agreement scheduled for November 13, 2013, but his request provoked the "pro-European" Maidan demonstrations supported by Western politicians, which led to Yanukovych losing his position and the ascent to power of the far right nationalist and anti-Russian elements.[2]

Chévènement accepts that "Russia's decision to annex Crimea was a disproportionate reaction [to the developments described above], and ran counter to the principle of territorial integrity of other states, constantly asserted by Russia, notably when it was flouted by Kosovo's exit from Yugoslavia."[3] However, he thinks, "the annexation of Crimea was not planned."[4] In February 2013 Putin attended the closing ceremony of the Sochi Winter Olympics, which were intended to be a showcase for Russia's rebirth and the new era, but "he then overreacted to an event that the EU had not planned but encouraged through carelessness."[5]

Chévènement probably cannot say more, but he admits that, in the case of Crimea, "Putin put Russia's strategic interests in the Black Sea first, probably fearing that the new Ukrainian government would not respect the leasing agreement that gave Russia use of Sevastopol until 2042."[6]

A French politician has reminded readers that in the present conflict Putin has mostly played a moderate role favoring compromise. "He encouraged Ukraine's Russian-speaking regions to seek a solution to their problems within the country,"[7] and, when "on May 25 [2014] Peter Poroshenko had been elected Ukrainian president, Moscow recognized him immediately."[8] Putin also negotiated and signed both Minsk agreements from September 5, 2014 and February 12, 2015. Unfortunately, the present Ukrainian regime either has not implemented their political provisions or they have even in theory been greatly distorted.

Chévènement concludes that "The pursuit of this conflict may turn Ukraine into a lasting source of conflict between the EU and Russia. Through a widely echoed ideological crusade, the US is attempting both to isolate Russia and to tighten its control over the rest of Europe. Prophets of a new cold war refer to Russia as a dictatorship fundamentally hostile to universal

---

1 Jean-Pierre Chévènement, *Op. cit.*
2 *Op. cit.*
3 *Op. cit.*
4 *Op. cit.*
5 *Op. cit.*
6 *Op. cit.*
7 *Op. cit.*
8 *Op. cit.*

values, that wants to rebuild the USSR."[1] In his view, "The real issue in the Ukrainian crisis is whether Europe can assert itself as an independent actor in a multipolar world or will it take a permanently subordinate role to the US...It is up to France to represent Europe's best interests, through the Normandy format"[2] and "Germany must convince its European partners that it is not just the US' proxy in Europe."[3] He believes that "It is time for a "European Europe" to show itself. It could start by trying to convince the US that its true interests are not served by driving Russia out of the West, but in participation in redefining mutually acceptable rules of the game that can restore reasonable confidence."[4]

If the former French defense and interior minister has voiced the view of a European who is concerned about the fate of his continent, Leslie H. Gelb, president emeritus of the (American) Council on Foreign Relations and a former senior State and Defense Department official, has expressed an American imperialistic and yet sober and knowledgeable warning against the excessively hawkish policy and proposed a new way to make Russia useful and willing to cooperate with the superpower.

Gelb does not seem to be concerned about the fate of Europe or about any humanitarian goals and principles. His focus is rather on the pragmatic interests of a more effective and less costly American success. At the same time, he certainly dislikes the American hawks and considers the military activities and policy they support as harmful and potentially dangerous for the US.

Being a member of the American political elite and a former high-ranking official, he does not seem to have any compunction about violating the Minsk agreements or any other binding Washington obligation to the other nations, and Russia in particular. His main concern is that, as he perceives it, "Russia has military superiority on its borders with the Baltic States and Ukraine"[5] and that "Nothing the US or its European partners can do (or are likely to try) will change this fact...Certainly, NATO has clear military superiority beyond Russia's borders, but it is on those borders that the problem lies."[6] Because of that, he approvingly quotes the opinion of Supreme NATO Commander Philip Breedlove that to the present conflict, "there has to be a diplomatic and political solution."[7] According to him neither General Breedlove nor

---

1 *Op. cit.*
2 *Op. cit.*
3 *Op. cit.*
4 *Op. cit.*
5 Leslie H. Gelb, "Russia and America Toward a New Détente," *National Interest*, June 9, 2015 and Leslie H. Gelb, "America's Losing Strategy," www.dailybeast.com, July 5, 2015.
6 Leslie H. Gelb, "America's Losing Strategy."
7 *Op. cit.*

the other NATO commanders "think that direct NATO intervention makes any sense. They most certainly do not want to make Ukraine an American war."[1] Gelb's presentation of post-Cold War Russian history is overall quite in line with the official American narrative of blaming Moscow. It seems to me that this certainly well-informed man has done that on purpose in order to make his lengthy article more acceptable to the American establishment and perhaps help them to be more open to some of his other observations and suggestions.

In contrast to most other American analysts, Gelb recognizes that "It is totally unrealistic...to think that the West can gain the desired Russian restraint and cooperation without dealing with Moscow as a great power that possesses real and legitimate interests."[2] His suggestion of a Détente Plus "would not treat Russia as an enemy, but as a combination of adversary and partner," and going beyond the arms control issues which used to be central, would focus instead on the most pressing "first-rank political matters in Europe and worldwide." Gelb believes that the two nations have many common and overlapping interests and he thinks that "For the foreseeable future, Russia's and America's interests coincide more with one another's than with China's." He calls his proposed approach "mountaintop diplomacy" and expects that "the world would be watching as the two powers devised common solutions to common problems."

Doing that, Washington could achieve two of its major goals: to make Russia less assertive and more restrained on its western borders, and to increase joint cooperation on other critical fronts, such as terrorism, Syria, Iran and nuclear proliferation.[3] Gelb regrets that, as he writes, "Today's pervasive atmosphere of hostility and mistrust obscures these promising possibilities," and he believes that his proposed strategy deserves a trial. Gelb has been one of America's top foreign relations experts; he concludes that there are "serious conflicts on Russia's western border" and that "Russia has [perhaps regrettably for him] clear military superiority there." As Moscow can cause "a real turmoil in Europe," both parties have to understand that the solution lies in diplomacy and compromise rather than military means and pressures. He is even ready to admit that "the present mutual hostility imperils the interests of both sides." But he does not seem to recognize any moral rights and justice on the side of his "geopolitical opponents" and simply considers that since Russia is now stronger than it was just after the Soviet Union's breakup, diplomatic means and compromise would be less costly for Washington and could bring better results.

---

1 L.H. Gleb, "Russia and America Towards a New Détente."
2 *Op. cit.*
3 *Op. cit.*

One commentator seems to have more empathy and understanding for the predicament of the Russian-speaking population in Ukraine. A former vice-chairman of the National Intelligence Council at the CIA and recently an adjunct professor of history at Simon Fraser University in Vancouver (Canada), Graham Fuller, who is also a prolific writer and scholar with great knowledge and personal experience in the Middle East, even more than Gelb.

He emphasizes Russia's major role in diplomatic arrangements in this region and considers it an overall positive factor. In his opinion, "It is essential that Russia's role [in international relations] be accepted and integrated rather than seen as a mere projection of some neo-Cold War global struggle — a confrontation in which the West bears at least as much responsibility as Moscow."[1] As he remarks, "The West has insisted on provoking counter-productive confrontation with Moscow in trying to shoehorn NATO into Ukraine. Can you imagine an American reaction to a security treaty between Mexico and China that included stationing of Chinese weapons and troops on Mexican soil?"[2] Consequently, Fuller calls for "The restoration of rationality to US policies towards the Ukraine"[3] where, according to him, Washington has been playing a dangerous game of chicken with Russia in "virtually unilateral ideological efforts to rejuvenate the Cold War"[4] with that great country.

Discussing Russian–American relations in the broader context of global international developments, Fuller, who is an expert on these issues, rather differs from Tariq Ali. He underscores the relative decline of US power.

The US recorded a government debt that was up to 101.53% of the country's Gross Domestic Product in 2013[5] (102.98% in 2015), and in the 2014 international WIN Gallup Poll of 64 countries the United States was perceived as "the single greatest threat to world peace." [6]

According to Fuller, "the US...once reigning power [is] in a state of relative international decline"[7] caused by a number of "domestic reasons and reflecting the rise of new powers — China, India, Brazil and others — who along with Russia are able to reshape the global economic order."[8] However, Washington does not want to accept that and considers its empire as ageless

1 Graham Fuller, "Graham Fuller's Five Middle East Predictions for 2015," http://grahamefuller.com/340/, January 3, 2015.
2 Op. cit.
3 Graham Fuller, "150211 – Three Encouraging Disastrous Political Overreach," February, 11, 2015.
4 Op. cit.
5 "United States Government Debt to GDP in 1940-2015," http://www.tradingeconomics.com/united-states/government-debt-to-gdp
6 Graham Fuller, "Dangers of a Declining Global Power," http://grahamefuller.com/dangers-of-a-declining-global-power/, June 14, 2015.
7 Op. cit.
8 Op. cit.

and an absolute global good, attempting to continue its domination at the price of "great peril — including national financial ruin."[1] Although the last statement might be exaggerated, Fuller is rightly critical that Washington "still feels entitled to carry on its geopolitical struggle up to the very doorstep of the enemy." He correctly notes that "American warships in the 'Russian lake' of the Baltic Sea maneuvering right up to the borders of Russian waters are amazingly provocative in nature. Same for US military presence just off Chinese waters."[2] Consequently, he suggests, "It can be productive to look at things from the perspective of other players: how would Washington feel if Russian or Chinese warships were routinely cruising just outside US territorial waters, testing our electronic defenses, and building bases in Mexico, Cuba, or Venezuela?" He believes that in an increasingly multi-polar world, such provocative acts at the other major powers' borders might lead to a dangerous zero-sum game with all of its potential consequences.

In marked difference to the majority of American analysts, Fuller is willing and able to adopt a broader outlook on current events and show some understanding of the feelings and interests of the other sides. Because of the prevailing conformism in the West and the political pressures, such an insight is unfortunately infrequent, but it is still not completely absent.

The famous chess Grandmaster Lev Alburt was born in Odessa, and after a distinguished career in the Soviet Union, because of his political views, he emigrated to the US in 1979. He seems to be very concerned about the fate of his former country and American–Russian relations in general. In a 2015 article he expresses his astonishment that American elites are united in their disdain for Russia and their hatred for Russia's president, Vladimir Putin.[3] He sees this as a new and rather unusual phenomenon caused by the lack of accurate information and therefore a created misunderstanding of post-Soviet Russia's development and aspirations. In addition, he notes that it runs against the American tradition of critical discussion and pluralism.

In view of the present situation, when the media and politicians provide incomplete and thus highly misleading information, Lev Alburt, even as a former Soviet dissident of Jewish descent, does not hesitate to defend Vladimir Putin from the misrepresentations and hostilities prevalent in his adopted country.

Though Putin, who is a highly educated man, worked for a few years in the Soviet foreign intelligence service (KGB First Chief Directorate), in the early 1990s he entered the service of Anatoly Sobchak, who was an outspoken anti-communist and became Mayor of Leningrad (St. Petersburg). Sobchak

1 *Op. cit.*
2 *Op. cit.*
3 Lev Alburt, Grandmaster, "Vladimir Putin, America's Reluctant Foe," *Chess News*, June 22, 2015.

soon promoted Putin to the post of Leningrad's First Deputy Mayor, and the two seem to have held similar political orientations. In August 1991, they jointly opposed the pro-communist coup (August 19–21, 1991) and supported Boris Yeltsin, and on August 20, 1991, "Putin demonstratively resigned from the KGB Reserves."[1] Writing for American readers in order to oppose the dominant narrative and to dispel existing prejudices, Alburt intends to present the Russian leader at his best but without lies or flattery. He emphasizes Putin's loyalty to his old friends, even if they, like Sobchak himself, got into serious trouble, and he recalls that by commemorating the Armenian genocide, in the Spring of 2015, Putin did what he thought was right even at the price of drawing anger from the Turkish leaders with whom he had just signed several important agreements.

Writing on his political role, Alburt indicates that as president, Putin "brought some normalcy and hope to the embittered, long suffering nation"[2] and continued to promote the free-market economy, even introducing a 13% flat income tax. Alongside the high energy prices, his economic policy thus contributed to the growth of state revenue and the economic boom in the country.

During Putin's first decade in office, his foreign policy was intended to develop understanding and long-term partnership with the US based on a commonality of interests. the dismemberment of Yugoslavia was a shocking experience for most Russians and — because of the negatively perceived role played by American economic advisors and business people in the country during the Yeltsin period (which is not mentioned by Alburt), by 2000 the majority of Russians viewed America unfavorably. Putin himself wanted to change this attitude. He still believed in a Russo–American commonality of interests, and rightly or wrongly, he personally liked President George W. Bush.[3]

Unfortunately, all of his efforts and a number of serious political and military concessions, some of which might have even run against Russia's direct interests, did not bring the expected results.

Putin did not protest even when George W. Bush decided to take the US out of the ABM Treaty in order to undermine the relative parity of the Russian and US nuclear forces. At that time there was in the US, even in the US Senate, considerable resistance against the President's decision, but Putin declared that "While we prefer to keep the treaty, America's withdrawal from it is not a threat to Russia's security — America is our

---

1 *Op. cit.*
2 *Op. cit.*
3 *Op. cit.* This fact has been confirmed by a number of other sources and my own research in Moscow.

friend. No arms race, no counter actions."[1] At least partly because of that, American opposition to Bush melted away.[2] At that time Putin still believed that Russian and American interests were compatible and he counted on President Bush's appreciation.

A number of events soon demonstrated that Putin's optimism was simply misplaced. In fact, the 2002 US withdrawal from the ABM Treaty, which once was seen as a cornerstone of Russian–American parity, proved to be only a starting point. As the "Russo–American Drama" unfolded, Putin was put into the position of being "the spurned lover and persistent suitor."[3] NATO's eastward expansion and America's support for every country and every politician willing to present itself as hostile to Russia, or its would-be victim, gradually started to change the Russian leader's attitude. As Scott McConnell, a founding editor of the traditional American journal *The American Conservative*, observes, "Though it might sound surprising, the principal legacy for Obama would be not the opening of Iran, even if it were to fulfill all positive expectations, but the deepening Cold War, potentially even hot war with Russia."[4] Consequently, Alburt warns that "If further driven by American hostility, Russia at some point will reciprocate in kind, supporting American enemies, all over the world, an old Soviet practice."[5] He believes that until now Putin "resists the temptation, and urging of his aides, and of the vast majority of the population to go tit-for-tat."[6] Still, he thinks that "America should try to diffuse tensions and to reach an understanding with Russia before the current hatred becomes fixed and institutionalized as it was during Cold War I."[7]

Although I appreciate Lev Alburt's courage and his knowledge of Russia, I still believe that both he and a number of Russian politicians, including at times Putin himself, did not have a true grasp and understanding of the major differences between the American and Russian approaches to their bilateral relations. Dmitri Trenin, who understands this issue, has many times indicated that while Moscow expects equal treatment and a partnership based on compromise, Washington wants obedience and for a long time has not been willing to accept any other, even a Western nation, as an equal partner. This is a real bone of contention.

Not only in the US but in a number of other Western countries including the UK and Poland, hawkish opinions dominate the public discourse. In the

---

1 Lev Alburt, *Op. cit.*
2 *Op. cit.*
3 *Op. cit.*
4 Robert Scott McConnel, "Why is Washington Addicted to War?" *American Conservative*, July 15, 2015.
5 Lev Alburt, *Op. cit.*
6 *Op. cit.*
7 *Op. cit.*

US, the new National Military Strategy "specifically calls out Iran, Russia and North Korea as aggressive threats to global peace" alongside non-state groups — particularly the 'violent extremist organizations' (VEOs) such as the Islamic State and the Taliban."[1] Going even further, US Air Force General Paul J. Selva, whom President Obama wanted to promote to the post of Vice-Chairman of the Joint Chiefs of Staff, told the Senate Armed Services Committee on July 14, 2015, that he "would put the threat to this nation in the following order: Russia, China, Iran, North Korea, and all of the organizations that have grown around ideology that was articulated by al-Qaeda."[2] During the July 9, 2015, confirmation hearing of Marine Corps General Joseph Dunford, who was nominated by Obama as the next chairman of the US Joint Chiefs of Staff, he added one step more, saying openly that "Russia presents the greatest threat to our [American] national security."[3]

It would be easy to dismiss such statements as typical of generals looking for advancement in their careers, especially when the US State Department made a statement that "Kerry did not share the assessment, even though Russia's actions in Ukraine posed regional security challenges."[4] However Chatham House produced a report just that June that indeed focused on Russia as perhaps the greatest threat. "The Russian Challenge" was prepared by the Royal Institute of International Affairs, including two former British ambassadors to Moscow, Sir Roderic Lyne and Sir Andrew Wood, and the head of Chatham House Russia and Eurasia Programme, James Nixey.[5]

Mary Dejevsky, a columnist for *The Independent* and a member of Chatham House, noted that "the thrust of the report is hawkish"[6] and reflects the increasingly hard line towards Russia taken by the think-tank, following the EU summit at Vilnus and everything that happened afterwards.[7] In my reading the report is outwardly hostile without any serious analysis of Russia's historical background and the existential threats it currently faces. In some parts it even sounds overtly offensive, though perhaps less so than many statements by American journalists and politicians. Russia is presented as a rogue nation that does not want to adopt a semi-liberal system, which the West "naively" expected it to adopt. It wants to instead preserve its own geopolitical independence and does not intend to integrate

1 Aaron Mehta, "Pentagon Releases National Military Strategy," Defense News, July 2, 2015.
2 Paul M.L. Cleary, "More Pentagon Generals Line Up to Proclaim Russia's Existential Threat to US," *Foreign Policy*, July 15, 2015.
3 *Op. cit.*
4 "Kerry doesn't view Russia as existential threat: State Department," *Reuters*, July 10, 2015.
5 Chatham House Report, *The Russian Challenge*, June 5, 2015.
6 Mary Dejevsky, "On the Chatham House Russia Report," http://valdaiclub.com/russia_and_the_world/79160.html, July 8, 2015.
7 Chatham House Report, *Op. cit.*

into the Western-controlled political and economic multinational blocs and institutions.

According to the Report, "The war in Ukraine is, in part, the result of the West's laissez-faire approach to Russia."[1] Consequently, the West needs to "develop and implement a clear and coherent strategy towards this aggressive and renegade country and "overall Western cohesion is critical for success."[2] In order to further isolate Russia, Chatham House advises discussions with China and all former Soviet-dominated states which, according to it, "have reasons to be concerned about Russian policies, whether or not they admit it."[3] The British think-tank also suggests the use of more economic pressure on Russia and insists that "Western states need to invest in defensive strategic communication and media support in order to counter the Kremlin's false narratives."[4] This is, in fact, a call for increased anti-Russian propaganda, and a refusal to recognize the country's right to explain and defend itself. As Mary Dejevsky says, the reality "that Russia is acting for the most part defensively, from the position of weakness"[5] has been completely disregarded.

Fortunately, even in the UK, such hawkish views are not totally accepted and, with the exception of the US, almost everywhere else public opinion is divided. Mary Dejevsky stresses that "although the hawks may be more numerous, [they] are not alone on the skies over London."[6]

The same might be said of Poland, a country which for many centuries was a close neighbor of Kievan Rus and then Muscovia (later called Russia), Ukraine and Belarus. The history of those long relations was often been rocky and full of mutual tension and animosity which have never been completely forgotten; the past still weighs on current political perceptions. For more than three centuries the kings of Poland, in Cracow and then Warsaw, ruled over all Ukraine, Belarus and even some parts of present Russia, such as Smolensk. Between the 15th and 17th centuries, the Polish–Lithuanian Commonwealth (or Serenissime Res Publica Polonia) was the largest country in Europe and during Russia's Time of Troubles (1598–1613) Poles were able to occupy Moscow and to plunder the Kremlin. However, since the Ukrainian Cossack uprising which broke out in 1648, this great country (or probably, rather, empire) entered into decline; and Moscow, restored to its previous strength, started to expand, acquiring by the Treaty of Andrusovo in 1667, after the first Northern War, a large part of Ukraine, including Kiev.[7]

---

1 *Op. cit.*
2 *Op. cit.*
3 *Op. cit.*
4 *Op. cit.*
5 Mary Dejevsky, *Op. cit.*
6 *Op. cit.*
7 Robert Frost, *The Northern Wars. State and Society in Northeastern Europe (1558–1721)*, Longman, 2000, p. 13.

With the modernized and greatly strengthening reforms introduced by Peter the Great, the Russian Empire expanded even further and participated in the three following Partitions of Poland in 1772, 1793, and 1795, which for more than one century put an end to Polish national independence, until the establishment, after World War I, of the Second Polish Republic.

The post-World War II period of Soviet hegemony over Eastern and Central Europe and the imposition on Poland of the modified, though much milder version, of Soviet-style socialism, added new offences to the historical memories. The Solidarity Movement created in Poland in the 1980s and supported by the West, and in practice all the political parties descending from it, soon became not only anti-Soviet but hostile to Russia. Post-communist Poland was then admitted to NATO and the European Union and became one of the most zealous American allies in Europe. At the same time Polish media, schools and universities were transformed into tools of aggressive Russophobic propaganda which caused some criticism even in Western Europe, and elicited calls for some reserve from a number of Polish intellectuals including the late Pope John Paul II.

However, since 2013, Polish public opinion on the Ukrainian crisis has been visibly polarized. Not only a number of prominent Polish scholars on international relations and Russia, such as Professors Bronislaw Łagowski, Andrzej Romanowski, Stanislaw Bielen, Andrzej Walicki, Ryszard Ziemba and Anna Razny, but also many other people, have criticized the anti-Russian and exclusively pro-American Polish foreign policy for the past 20 years. There are many voices like that on the Polish internet and even in the print media, and perhaps the most thoughtful of them was the recent book by a law professor at Warsaw University, Witold Modzelewski.[1]

Alongside the relatively mild split of public opinion in Europe, and the highly complicated civil war in Ukraine, and without much of the practical impact, there are also some political divisions in Russia itself. Although precisely because of the Ukrainian conflict and Western anti-Russian pressures, Putin has achieved skyrocketing public support and his "approval rating is at record levels with 9 out of 10 Russian saying they have positive view of their President,"[2] there is also a minority made up of a modest number of quite wealthy and potentially politically influential people, who especially with Western support might represent a decisive challenge to the Russian leader and the values and orientations he represents.

The Russian elite is deeply divided and some Russian scholars consider that as the greatest challenge for the country. In spite of all Putin and his

---

1 Witold Modzelewski, *Polska-Russia. Co dalej?*, Waszarva, 2015.
2 Alberto Nardelli, Jennifer Rankin, and George Arnett, "Putin's approval rating at record level," http://www.theguardian.com/world/datablog/2015/jul/23/vladimir-putins-approval-rating-at-record-levels, July 23, 2015.

team's efforts, the desired socio-political consensus at the top has still not been achieved. In September 2014, the mostly pro-Western opposition organized an "All Russian March for Peace" which, especially in Moscow, drew from 5,000 to 26,000 participants.[1] For Moscow, with its more than 11 million inhabitants including hundreds of thousands of Ukrainians, that would not be an impressive number, and most likely very few ethnic Ukrainians living there showed any interest in the event. In fact it was rather an internal Russian confrontation at the level of the elites. One of the leading demonstrators was Professor Nina Belayeva, who teaches at the prestigious neo-liberal Moscow Higher School of Economics. She argued that "the whole reason for this crisis is that Russia has refused to recognize Ukraine's European choice,"[2] and she marched holding a sign reading, "Ukraine's European choice = An example for Russia."[3] She was soon confronted by the supporters of present Russian policy who recalled that the putsch which overthrew President Yanukovych in February 2014 was organized by the Western intelligence services.[4] Thus the march was quite small, but was in more than one way a symbolic incident.

The sometimes controversial and yet very intelligent and knowledgeable Israeli journalist Israel Shamir argues that to present the civil war in the Ukrainian southeast (and the whole Ukrainian crisis) as an ethnic conflict between Ukrainian and Russian nationalists, though not completely wrong, is still a great over-simplification.[5] During a number of his recent visits to Russia and Ukraine, he met many pro-Russian Ukrainians and quite a few pro-Kiev Russians in Moscow and St. Petersburg. The last are not only numerous but also often quite wealthy, "influential and prominently placed in Moscow, as opposed to numerous but disenfranchised pro-Russian Ukrainians in Kiev."[6] Consequently, he is inclined to think that "the civil war goes [on] in Ukraine and Russia, and it is not ethnic strife as both sides often pretend."[7] According to him and to some other observers who are by no means either pro-Communist or particularly radical-leftist, this is rather a further continuation of the internal struggle, typical for post-Soviet countries, started in 1985, "between a comprador bourgeoisie and its enemies: the industrialists, workers, military."[8]

---

1 Alec Luhn, "Thousands Protest in Moscow over Russia's involvement in Ukraine," http://www.theguardian.com/world/2014/sep/21/protest-moscow-russia-ukraine, September 21, 2014.
2 *Op. cit.*
3 *Op. cit.* and personal interviews.
4 *Op. cit.*
5 Israel Shamir, "Kiev: Chestnuts Blossom Again," *Unz Review, An Alternative Media Selection,* June 17, 2015.
6 *Op. cit.*
7 *Op. cit.*
8 *Op. cit.*

In 1991 the Western-supported compradors won. The Soviet Union disintegrated and its industry and armed forces were dismantled and its science and leading research institutes eliminated. Millions of people lost their employment and means of living, and the successor states to the Soviet superpower became subservient to the West.

As Putin correctly stated, it was an enormous tragedy for the majority but at the same time many other people enriched themselves. The whole new and powerful class of oligarchs (big business) arose by grasping large parts of what had been the state's property in the economy. Just as in Poland, Western companies bought up factories in order to dismantle existing or potential competitors. The local agriculture was destroyed and, like all post-Soviet nations, Russia and Ukraine were added to the global imperial economy.

In Ukraine, however, no serious effort to change the trend had ever been possible. In Russia, Vladimir Putin, supported by some oligarchs and by the Russian Foreign Intelligence Service, rose to power in 2000 and started to slowly introduce some limited reforms and to restore the Russian state, culture and society, but he was never able, or perhaps even never willing, to change the economic and socio-political structures inherited from Yeltsin's time. His effort, maybe even realistically conceived, was to play the role of mediator and arbitrator among the conflicting social groups and political forces existing in the country. However, as the Israeli journalist wrote, "He crossed the red line in his foreign policy while protecting Syria and securing [annexing] Crimea. He began to re-industrialize Russia, produce wheat, and buy Chinese goods, bypassing the dollar."[1] In addition, in order to achieve all this he had to limit the power of a number of influential but corrupt and fraudulent big business people (the oligarchs).

In spite of taking all those steps which caused intense anger in Washington and its allies, Putin, who considered these steps to be political necessities, had neither intended to make a break in the existing Russian–Western relations nor to challenge Russian business and intellectual elites, which since the Gorbachev–Yeltsin era has been both very pro-Western and highly influential in Moscow. Israel Shamir rightly said that during the more than 15 years of Putin's leadership, "the Reaganite compradors retained their position in Moscow. They control the most prestigious universities and the High School of Economics, they run the magazines and newspapers, they have the financial support of oligarchs, and foreign funds, they are represented in government, they have the mind of [I believe only a part of] the Russian intelligentsia."[2] It is perhaps even possible that Putin did not

---

1 *Op. cit.*

2 *Op. cit.* His description corresponds exactly to what I have noticed myself during my trips and longer stays in Moscow between 1997 and 2011.

anticipate such a strong and severely punitive Western reaction, in the same way that in the Fall of 2013 he apparently had not foreseen the forthcoming coup d'état in Kiev in February 2014.

While in Washington, and especially within the Beltway itself, there is no pro-Russian lobby, there are in Moscow numerous wealthy and influential men and women who not only embrace American views but serve American interests. Most common people in Russia have always been and still remain attached to their country and are willing to stand up for their motherland (rodina), but the post-Soviet elites are largely Americanized.[1] Consequently, it is true that "people identified as pro-Putin [Sovereignists] are a minority in the Moscow establishment."[2]

It should be stressed here that in Russia the support for the current leader, who might often otherwise be subject to criticism and even sarcastic comments, does not necessarily mean personal support. For most Russians, to support Putin means to support a sovereign Russian nation, with its traditions and aspirations. It also means a readiness to defend it against real or perceived external threats and dangers. Because of their different history and inherited value systems, the attitudes of many Russians might thus differ from those of Americans or even Europeans, and the ongoing Ukrainian crisis made that more acute and noticeable.

However, as the elites became largely Westernized and adopted an imitation of the Western life style and neoliberal worldviews, the unity and strength of the country has diminished. The Russian Federation is not the Soviet Union, and most of the economics and cultural life of the country are now run by the new bourgeoisie and are outside of state control. I think that this, in fact, has established a real "duality of the Russian power structure"[3] which might not only "influence Russian policy towards Ukraine"[4] but might also explain some of the reasons for the American elites and their allies' visible scorn and challenging attitude towards Russia. Western political and military leaders must be well aware that they have many friends to rely on in Moscow.

It is perhaps for that reason that most of Putin's concessions and peaceful gestures have remained disregarded or unreciprocated, and both he and his nation are frequently humiliated and insulted. Consequently, any better understanding of the crisis that includes Ukrainian developments but also involves both Russia and perhaps even Eurasia, cannot be separated from

---

1 Being present at the World Russian Forum on June 22, 2013 in Washington D.C., I had a chance to hear from Dr. Leonid Gozman, Deputy Director of Rosnano Corporation that even closely associated with Putin are dreaming about leaving Russia for the US. World Russia Forum 2013, http://www.russiahouse.org.

2 Israel Shamir, *Op. cit.*

3 *Op. cit.*

4 *Op. cit.*

Russian domestic socio-economic problems and the geopolitics of this nation.

According to many Russian scholars, Russia established itself on the Eurasian lowland on the rather artificial border between Europe and Asia, being for most of its history largely isolated from the major cultural centers of both Europe and Asia, and it created its own original Russian civilization independent of the Western and Asian civilizations.[1] Although this image is over-simplified, and various influences from the West and the South played major roles in Russian history, it remains true that this country has never been a part of the West as we know it. The recent post-Soviet effort to change that has proved to be a failure, and I do not think such a project can be put into practice in a way beneficial to both sides.

However, the cultural differences together with the geostrategic importance of the country and its rich natural resources contributed to the repeated wars and tensions between the Western nations and Moscow. During the Soviet period, Western hostility led by the US increased, but even after the end of the state-socialist experiment and the disintegration of the Soviet Union, it did not disappear. Hostility has now been directed against its successor state, the Russian Federation.

As discussed in earlier chapters, any prospect of the re-emergence of Russia as a great power center in Eurasia, and probably even more the possibility of its alliance with Germany and other European nations, still is viewed by Washington as the greatest potential challenge to its global domination. George Friedman argues that this fear was the reason for US participation in both World Wars and the ensuing Cold War.

It is also now the real main cause of the present Ukrainian crisis, the goal of which is not only to weaken, if not perhaps even divide and completely destroy, Russia, but to disrupt Moscow's close links with Berlin and some other major European capitals such as Paris and Rome, and, if necessary, to check the present build-up of the Chinese "Silk Road" and China's further economic expansion into Europe.

In addition to all these more or less practical goals, it is also possible that by provoking the Ukrainian crisis and getting involved in the "Battle for Russia," Washington intended to put into practice the long-cherished dream of solving the perennial "Russian Problem."

Russia's place in the global international system and the international status of the country has always been the subject of Western doubts and

---

1 This is particularly characteristic for the Eurasianists such as Pyoter Savitsky and Lev Gumilov, but, though in a different way also accepted by the Russia-island school of Vadim Cymborski, with the possible exception of pro-Western Atlanticists and some other scholars. N. Askenkampf, S. Pogorelskaya, "Politicheskaya mysl'v retrospective," *Geopolitika. Antologiya*, Moscow, 2006, pp. 23-28.

uncertainties. At the same time relations with the West have been the main source of concern and focus of attention for all Russian leaders. The West has made numerous attempts to weaken or even destroy this country, ranging from military invasions to milder, but often no less dangerous, political moves to foment internal upheavals in and around Russian borders. Such initiatives have often been seen as the best way to poke (if not to kill) the Russian "bear," and one of the best examples was the West's long support for Ukrainian nationalism by almost all, even otherwise mutually hostile Western powers, including both Imperial and Hitler's Germany, the Austro-Hungarian Habsburg Empire, Britain, and the United States. In the 19th century the idea of creating an "anti-Russia" out of people closely related to Russians, in Russia's neighborhood or its former territories, was nourished even by the great German statesman Chancellor Otto von Bismarck. Although he always stressed the need for good relations with St. Petersburg, he probably also wanted to see Russia weaker and thus easier to negotiate with.

After World War II, the US followed a similar but more aggressive policy. In his latest book,[1] Brzezinski suggested Western enlargement to the East under US leadership and control.[2] He also proposed creating a new consultative organ for that purpose and suggested it could be located in Kiev, the ancient capital of Kievan Rus, in order to symbolize "the West's renewed vitality and the enlarging scope."[3] Though Professor Brzezinski is now voicing different and more moderate opinions,[4] it is quite likely that similar or even more hawkish views have many other supporters among members of the American establishment.

However, I do not believe this would be realistic or even beneficial in its longer-term outcomes for Washington's prospects. Both the present political leadership and the majority of the Russian people would certainly resist that and cause a heavy price to be paid by the hegemonic power. It is

---

1 Zbigniew Brzezinski, *Strategic Vision: America and Crisis of Global Power*. Basic Books, 2012.

2 According to him, "a Russia left to its own devices and not deliberately drawn into a larger democratically transformative framework [in the same ways as defeated Germany and Japan] could again become a source of tension and occasionally even a security threat to some of its neighbors," and it "remains unable to define for itself a stable role that strikes a realistic balance between its ambitions and its actual potential." *Op. cit.*, pp. 144–145.

3 Zbigniew Brzezinski, "Balancing the East, Upgrading the West US Grand Strategy in an Age of Upheaval," *Foreign Affairs*, January/February 2012, pp. 99–100.

4 As Brzezinski told the Polish broadcaster TVN24, "We must guarantee to the Russians that free, democratic European Ukraine would not seek to join NATO, which Russia sees as a threat, but will act like Finland, which is a free, independent European country, but is not a member of NATO," *WashingtonBlog*, March 10, 2015.

also by no means certain that the US would have enough resources to impose its will on Eurasia, and "because of the country's unique history — at first separate from world power, then an overnight superpower — it has little experience of sharing power with others."[1] Finding solutions which would be agreeable to all parties involved would be very challenging. Consequently, it seems to me that it would be more practical and at least in the long term more beneficial for all parties, if the West, perhaps in accordance with Leslie H. Gelb's proposals, started to give more respect to the Russian nation and its long and complex heritage. The present hegemonic power and its allies might start to approach Russia in like they do China, Saudi Arabia and perhaps now also Iran: as a different civilization and at least a relatively independent power center.

Such recognition would preclude further soft power warfare against Russia and would allow it to develop according to its own traditions and at its own pace. The famous American diplomat and expert on Russia George F. Kennan strongly advocated such an alternative approach even toward the end of his life in his interview with the *New York Times* on May 2, 1998.[2] Just as in the case of China, Saudi Arabia, India or Pakistan, the US and its allies might, and even should, be able to look after their economic and security interests there, but they could let Russia go its own way and preserve its traditional allies and zone of special interests, including Ukraine as important particularly for security reasons. The Russian Problem for the West might thus not disappear but become accepted as one of many, frequently more important, challenges in our pluralistic and globalized world.

It is understandable that the Americans, due to their unique history and the still enormous power at their disposal, want to transform the rest of mankind into their "own image and proximity." However, as the American scholar and journalist Paul Klebnikov, who studied post-Soviet Russia in depth and paid for that with his own life,[3] mused, "The American model had

---

1 D.B. Kanin, S.E. Meyer, "America's Outmoded Security Strategy," *Current History*, January 2012, p.22.

2 http://www.nytimes.com/1998/05/02/opinion/foreign-affairs-now-a-word-from -x.html

3 Paul Klebnikov who had a PhD from the London School of Economics, was the first editor of the Russian edition of Forbes and gained a reputation for investigating post-Soviet business dealings and corruption. In his book, *Godfather of the Kremlin: Boris Berezovski and the Looting of Russia*, he describes the privatization process used by Yeltsin as "the robbery of the century" and consequently ran into numerous problems. According to a New York reviewer the book was "richly detailed" and "effectively angry." On July 9, 2004 Klebnikov was attacked and killed on a Moscow street by unknown assailants, whose identities have never been found. Authorities described the attack as a contract killing and the publisher of Forbes claimed that the murder was "definitively linked to his journalism." www.wikipedia.com, Paul Klebnikov, retrieved October 3, 2012. Although Wikipedia is not always a reliable source

political, economic and cultural components. Could it work in a country as large and as old as Russia?"[1] According to him, "The history of Boris Yeltsin's regime suggests that it could not."[2]

I think the same would be true in the case of Ukraine which, in addition, is a relatively new and multiethnic nation, without much common history but with often contradictory cultural traditions and economic interests. As the people living there are not immigrants and they want to preserve their different identities, it would be difficult, if possible at all, to change their historical memories and impose one single language and culture on them. The roots of Ukraine's internal crisis in the last few years are important in their impact on Russian–Western relations. However, following the results of my research, I do not think the present unitary form of state is sufficient to provide this beautiful but heterogeneous country with a chance of internal peace and harmonious development.

The federal state system, or at least the granting of local autonomy to its various regions, would correspond much better to the existing situation. In addition, although the Ukrainian state within its present borders was established mainly because of the Soviet Union's, and some other foreign powers', decisions and in their interests, it would be better for its future if any foreign involvement were limited or even completely eliminated. This country, which is so rich in history and natural resources, should stop being a chessboard for the Great, and even, as in the case of the US, quite remote, powers' games and confrontations. Only after that would Ukraine be able to find its own identity and its various ethnic groups enjoy more peace and security.

Unfortunately, there is not much chance of that now. As the respected Ukrainian-Canadian scholar and former Head of the Department of Public Administration under the President of Ukraine, Professor Mikhail Molchanov, indicates, "By this time, it should be obvious that the West does not want the conflict in Ukraine to be resolved any time soon."[3] According to him, if the West had a real interest in its solution, it would put pressure on Kiev and the separatists in Donbas.[4] Instead of that, all political, economic and recently even military pressures are directed towards Russia, which, though, as he writes, "admittedly is the separatists' best friend and supplier...has no

---

of information, I think this information is rather credible and corresponds to my personal knowledge of this period of Russian history.

1 P. Klebnikov, *Godfather of the Kremlin: The Decline of Russia in the Age of Gangster Capitalism*, Harcourt Inc., New York, 2000, p. 321.

2 *Op. cit.*

3 Mikhail Molchanov, "(Un)solving Ukraine's conflict," *Open Democracy*, July 16, 2015.

4 *Op. cit.*

direct stakes in the conflict at hand."[1] Putin only supports the separatists' demands for "an amnesty, local autonomy and full implementation of the Minsk agreements"[2] which "Kiev does not want to implement and therefore protracts the conflict."[3]

Particularly important here is the Ukrainian government's refusal to announce the promised amnesty to the separatists. In practice, Kiev demands their unconditional capitulation, and Professor Molchanov concludes that in this situation, "the choice facing the Donbas militia leaders seems to be simple: continue fighting or face imprisonment (or worse) at the hand of the Ukrainian authorities."[4]

It does not seem much more practical for the Kiev government and some Western nations to demand that Moscow must "seal the border and stop the influx of volunteers [and material supplies] into the conflict zone"[5] before any constitutional changes and the announcement of political amnesty in the country take place.

That is not only impractical for Putin, who up to a point staked his political reputation on supporting the ethnic Russians who were left outside their country's borders after the end of the Soviet Union, but I believe it is not politically possible for any elected Russian leader to now leave these people to the vengeance of the Ukrainian nationalists.

An ensuing stalemate is thus inevitable and I do not see any sign of a compromise in the offing. For Washington and at least some of its allies, including the present Canadian government, it is first of all a smart tactic for weakening the Russian Federation and probably can be seen as one more attempt to overthrow Putin. No less important, it is also a tool to isolate Moscow from Western Europe, especially France and Germany, and cut Russia off from Western technology and banking. I think that without a full-scale war no better way to destroy Russia could be found.

Until now, this American game has seemed to be largely successful,[6] and as of August 2015 the NATO Force Integration Units, proposed the year

---

1 *Op. cit.*

2 *Op. cit.*

3 *Op. cit.*

4 *Op. cit.* Officially, "Kiev promises an amnesty after the elections, and the law on the status of territories after Ukraine's full control over its eastern borders is restored." Molchanov is right to comment, "to many an observer, inside and outside, this must look like deceiving one's opponents and negotiating in bad faith."

5 *Op. cit.*

6 One of the most painful and difficult to control outcomes of that is the dramatic reversal of perhaps one of the best outcomes of Putin's period: the significant improvement in the last decade in Russia's demographic situation, with Russians living longer and having more children. However according to the Russian statistical service Rosstat, this trend has now been reversed. The death rate in the first quarter of 2015 was 5.2% higher than a year ago, while

before, were scheduled to be deployed in Eastern Europe, right on Russia's borders.[1] However, this does not necessarily mean that a full-scale war is just around the corner. According to a Stratfor analyst, "Each side is currently walking in some space between escalation and trying to keep some control over that escalation without launching a full war."[2]

He only seems to be concerned about a possible but, in my opinion, unlikely Russian military invasion. As he writes, "with meaningful progress in diplomatic negotiations so far sorely lacking, and with few positive signals from the West at the moment, Russia may be considering sending its own message in eastern Ukraine in the next few weeks."[3] Keeping in mind the overwhelming superiority of the Western side, and all Putin's policy on the Ukraine issue, this seems to me the least likely development. However, I agree that the situation looks neither peaceful nor stable.

I don't know how long such a situation is going to persist. Much will depend on the nature of American involvement and on what kind of political orientation prevails among American leaders.

---

the birth rate was 5.7% less. No less worrying might be the fact that for the first time in years the number of suicides and alcohol poisoning has increased. Russian Deputy Minister of Health Veronica Skvortsv has considered this "a big problem." All those negative developments might be seen as a sign of a new social crisis. Paul Robinson, "Three Headlines," https://irrussianality. wordpress.com/2015/08/05/three-headlines/, August 5, 2015.
1 "In Eastern Ukraine, Rumors of Escalating Conflict Abound," Geopolitical Diary, www.stratfor.com, August 4, 2015.
2 *Op. cit.*
3 *Op. cit.*

BIBLIOGRAPHY

Anon., "A New Quality of Relations – International Roundtable," *International Affairs*, vol. 57, 2011.

Anon., "Defense Spending as a Percent of World Expenditure" In: *The Military Balance*, International Institute for Strategic Studies London: Routledge, 2014 and 2015.

Anon., "Russia and France: A New Quality of Relations, "International Roundtable". *International Affairs*, vol. 57, 2011.

Allison, Graham and Dmitri K. Simes, "Russia and America: Stumbling to War," *The National Interest*, April 20, 2015.

Arbatov, Alexei, "Collapse of the World Order? The Emergence of a Polycentric World and Its Challenges," *Russia in Global Affairs*, September 23, 2014.

Baron, Samuel, "Plekhanov: Russian Comparativist." In John H. Kautsky (Ed.), *Karl Kautsky and the Social Science of Classical Marxism*, E. J. Brill, Leiden, 1989.

Blackwell, Robert D. and Dmitri K. Simes, "Dealing with Putin," *The National Interest*, November 16, 2014.

Brown, Archie, "Perestroika and the End of the Cold War", *Cold War History*. February 2007.

Brown, Archie, *The Gorbachev Factor*, Oxford University Press, 1996.

Brucan, Silviu, "Europe in the Global Strategic Game," In: Bjorn Hettne, *Europe: Dimension of Peace*, London: Zed Books, 1988 .

Brzezinski, Zbigniew, "Balancing the East, Upgrading the West US Grand Strategy in an Age of Upheaval," *Foreign Affairs*, January/February 2012.

Brzezinski, Zbigniew, *The Grand Chessboard: American Primacy and Its Geostrategic Imperatives*, New York: Basic Books, 1997.

Carden, James W., "Why Russians Still Don't Hate Communism," *The National Interest*, October 23, 2013.

Carl Osgood, and Rachel Douglas, "The US Moves Towards First Strike Capability," *Executive Intelligence Review*, March 15, 2013.

Cleary, Paul M. L., "More Pentagon Generals Line Up to Proclaim Russia's Existential Threat to US," *Foreign Policy*, July 15, 2015.

Cohen, Stephen F., "America's New Cold War with Russia: Obama Congress and the Media Continue Their Dangerous One Dimensional Approach," *The Nation*, February 2013.

Cohen, Stephen, *Failed Crusade: America and The Tragedy of Post-Communist Russia*, New York: Norton, 2000.

Cohen, Stephen, *Soviet Fates and Lost Alternatives*, New York: Columbia University Press, 2011.

Cross, Anthony, *Russia Under Western Eyes 1517–1825*, London: Elek Books, 1971.

Derlugyen, Gyorgy, "Was Russia Ever a Colonial Empire?" *International Affairs* (Moscow) March 1998.

Elliot, J. H., *Europe Divided, 1559–1598*. London: Collins, 1968.

Ellman, Michael, *Socialist Planning*, Cambridge: Cambridge University Press, 1989.

Ericson, Richard E., "The Classical Soviet-Type Economy: Nature of the System and Implications for Reform," *Journal of Economic Perspectives*, vol. 5, Autumn 1991.

Farley, Robert, "Three Ways China and the US Could Go to War in the South China Sea," *The National Interest*, June 6, 2015.

Franklin, Simon, *Writing, Society and Culture in Early Rus*, Cambridge University Press 2002.

Frost, Robert, *The Northern Wars. State and Society in Northeastern Europe, 1558–1721*, Harlow (U.K.): Longman, 2000.

Gates, Robert, *Duty: Memoirs of a Secretary of War*, New York: Alfred A. Knopf, 2014.

Gelb, Leslie H., "Russia and America: Toward a New Détente," *National Interest*, June 9, 2015.

Goldstein, Lyle J., "What Does China Really Think about the Ukraine Crisis?" *The National Interest*, September 4, 2014.

Gomart, T., "Dva Orientira dlya Rossii," *Rossiya v Globalnoi Politike*, 8/2010/ Nz6, November/December.

Gorbachev, Mikhail, *Perestroika: New Thinking for Our Country and the World.* New York: Harper & Row, 1987.

Gramsci, Antonio, "Lo Revoluzione contre il Capitale," *Avanti*, December 24, 1917.

Hunt, Edwin S. and James Murray, *A History of Business in Medieval Europe: 1200–1550*, Cambridge University Press, 1999.

Ikenberrry, G. John, "The Illusion of Geopolitics. The Enduring Power of the Liberal Order," *Foreign Affairs*, May/June 2014.

Jack A. Smith, "The Hegemonic Games: The US vs. PRC," *Global Research*, May 31, 2015.

James Garden, James, "Reckless: Obama Advisors Go Rogue On Ukraine," *The National Interest*, March 20, 2015.

Kanin, D. B. and S.E. Meyer, "America's Outmoded Security Strategy," *Current History*, January 2012.

Klebnikov, P., *Godfather of the Kremlin: The Decline of Russia in the Age of Gangster Capitalism*, New York: Harcourt, 2000.

Klein, Naomi, *The Shock Doctrine: The Rise of Disaster Capitalism*, New York: Metropolitan Books, 2007.

Kotz, David M. with Fred Weir, *Revolution from Above: The Demise of the Soviet System*, London and New York: Routledge, 1997.

Kramarenko, A. "Ideologiya Vneshnei Politiki Sovremennoi Rossii," *Mezhdunarodnaya Zhizn* 8/3, 2009.

Kreutz, Andrej, *Russia in the Middle East: Friend or Foe?* Westport: Praeger Security International, 2007.

Kreutz, Andrej, "The Rise and Fall of Soviet and Eastern European Communism. An Historical Perspective," *Studies in Political Economy* (Ottawa, Canada) 38:109-138, 1992.

Lane, David, *The Capitalist Transformation of State Socialism, The making and breaking of state socialist society and what followed.* London: Routledge, 2014.

Lane, David, *The Capitalist Transformation of State Socialism: The making and breaking of state socialist society and what followed.* London: Routledge, 2014.

Legvold, Robert " 'Protracted Conflict' How the Crisis in Ukraine Became the New Cold War," *Newsletter of the National Fellowship*, Woodrow Wilson Foundation, Fall 2014.

Leiber, Kier A. and Daryl G. Press, "The New Era of Nuclear Weapons, Deterrence and Conflict," *Strategic Studies Quarterly*, Spring 2013.

Leibin, Vitaly and Valeriy Fadeev, "My ich ne Brosin," *Expert*, N 24(909) 09 June 2014.

Longworth, Philip, "Muscovy and the Antemurale Christianitatis," In: Guya Svakfed (Ed.), *The Place of Russia in Europe*, Budapest, 1999.

Malia, Martin, *The Soviet Tragedy. A History of Socialism in Russia, 1917–1991* New York, Free Press, 1994.

Martin, Janet, *Medieval Rus: 980–1557*, Cambridge University Press, 2008.

Marx, Karl, *Secret Diplomatic History of the Eighteenth Century*, London: 1899.

McConnel, Robert Scott, "Why is Washington Addicted to War?" *American Conservative*, July 15, 2015.

Mearsheimer, John J., "China's Unpeaceful Rise," *Current History*, April 2006.

Mearsheimer, John, "Why the Ukraine Crisis is the West's Fault: The Liberal Delusions That Provoked Putin," *Foreign Affairs*, September/October 2014.

Menon, Rajan, "Avoiding a New 'Cuban Missile Crisis' in Ukraine: Unlike in 1962, Russia has geography and national will on its side in Ukraine," *The National Interest*, May 22, 2015.

Meyendorff, John, *Byzantium and the Rise of Russia*, New York: St. Vladimir's Seminary Press 1989.

Migranyan, Andranik, "Washington's Creation: A Russian–China Alliance?" *The National Interest*, July 10, 2014.

Mills, C. Wright, *The Causes of World War Three*, New York: Simon and Schuster, 1958,

Mills, C. Wright, *The Power Elite*, Oxford University Press, 1956.

Monaghan, Andrew, "A New Cold War? Abusing History, Misunderstanding Russia," Royal Institute of International Affairs, *Chatham House Research Paper*, March 2015.

Nikiforuk, Andrew, "What Really Killed the Soviet Union? Oil shock? Red Empire just run out of fuel, say growing number of experts," *The Tyee*, March 13, 2013.

Noonan, Thomas "The Khazar Qaganate and its impact on the early Rus state: the Translatio Imperii from Itil to Kiev," in Anatoly M., Khazanov and André Wink, *Nomads in the Sedentary World*, IIAS Asian Studies series, Routledge, 2001.

Noonan, Thomas, "European Russia c. 500–1050," in Timothy Reuter and Rosamond McKitterick, *The New Cambridge Medieval History*, Vol. 3. Cambridge University Press, 1999.

Nye, Jr., J. S., *The Paradox of American Power. Why the World's Only Superpower Can't Do It Alone*, Oxford University Press.

Panfilova, J., "Problemy Osmysleniya Mesta Rossii v Mire," *Kosmopolis*, 2007/2008.

Pfaff, William, *The Irony of Manifest of Destiny: The Tragedy of American Foreign Policy*, New York: Walker and Company, 2010.

Pick, Lisa, "EU-Russia energy relations: a critical analysis," *POLIS Journal*, vol. 7, Summer 2012.

Pillar, Paul, "Twist of History and Interests in Ukraine," *The National Interest*, April 20, 2014.

Poe, Marshall T, *The Russian Moment in World History*. Princeton: Princeton Povest' Vremennykh Let, *Biblioteka Literatury Drevney Rusi*, vol. 1, part 2. Moscow, 1997.

Rousset, Marc, *La nouvelle Europe. Paris-Berlin-Moscow. Le continent paneuropéen en face au choc des civilisations*, Paris: Godefray de Buillon, 2009.

Rybakov, Boris A., *Early Centuries of Russian History*, Progress Publishers (Germany), 1965

Sakwa, Richard, *Frontline Ukraine. Crisis in the Borderlands*, I.B. Taurus, 2015.

Sand, Shlomo, *The Invention of the Jewish People*, London, Verso, 2009.

Saratte, Mary Elise, "A Broken Promise? What the West Really Told Moscow about NATO Expansion," *Foreign Affairs*, 93: 5, September-October 2014.

Shleifer, A. and D. Treisman, "Why Moscow Says No: A Question of Russian Interest, Not Psychology," *Foreign Affairs*, January – February 2011.

Simes, Dmitri, "Losing Russia," Foreign Affairs 86: 6, November-December 2007.

Szabo, Stephen F., *The Diplomacy of German Unification*, New York: St. Martin Press, 1992.

Timasheff, N.S., *The Great Retreat: The Growth and Decline of Communism in Russia*, New York: E.P. Dutton and Company, 1946.

Todd, Emmanuel, *Après L'Empire: Essai sur la decomposition du système américain*, Paris: Gallimard, 2002.

Treisman D., "Inequity: The Russian Experience", *Current History*, October 2012.

Trenin, Dmitri "The West and Russia Now in Permanent Crisis," *Global Times (China)*, November 4, 2014.

Trenin, Dmitri, "Russia Reborn," *Foreign Affairs*, November/December 2009.

Trenin, Dmitri, "Russia vs. the West: End of the Round One," *Carnegie Moscow Center*, June 9, 2014.

Trenin, Dmitri, "The Snowden Case as the Mirror of US-Russia Contentions," *Carnegie Moscow Center*, August 2, 2013.

Trenin, Dmitri, "The Ukraine Crisis and the Resumption of Great-Power Rivalry," *Carnegie Moscow Center*, July 9, 2014,.

Trenin, Dmitri, "What Will Putin Do in Foreign Policy?", *Diplomaatia*, no. 105, Tallinn, May 2012.

Trenin, Dmitri, "Russia Leaves the West," *Foreign Affairs*, July/August 2006.

Vibikov, M.V., "Rus Bizentiynskoy Diplomatii, Dogovory Rusi c Grekami, XV," *Drevnyaya Rus Voprosy Medievistiki*, 2005.

Walker, Jacob, *The Rise of Democracy in Pre-Revolutionary Russia: political and social institutions under the last three Czars*, New York: Praeger, 1962.

Waltz, K., "Globalization and American Power," *The National Interest*, Spring 2000.

Waltz, Kenneth, "Globalization and American Power," *National Interest*, Spring 2000.

Warner, David A. (translator): *Ottoman Germany: The Chronicles of Thietmar of Merseburg*, Manchester, 2001.

Wegren, Stephen K. (Ed.), *Return to Putin's Russia. Past Imperfect, Future Uncertain.* Lanham, MD: Rowman Littlefield, 2013.

Wilson, Francesca, *Muscovy Russia Through Foreign Eyes 1553–1900*. New York: Praeger, 1970.

Winter, Edward, *Russland und des Papsttum*, Vol. 1, Berlin: Academie-Verlag, 1960.

Wren, Melvin C. and Taylor Stults, *The Course of Russian History*, Fifth Edition, Prospect Heights, IL: Waveland Press, 1994.

Zelikov, Philip and Condollezza Rice, *Germany Unified and Europe Transformed. A Study in Statecraft*, Cambridge Massachusetts: Harvard University Press.

Zimin, Aleksander A., *Pamyatniki Russkogo Prava*, vol. 1, Moscow 1952.

Printed in the United States
By Bookmasters